TENNYSON

Edited and Introduced by

REBECCA STOTT

LONGMAN
LONDON AND NEW YORK

Addison Wesley Longman Limited
Edinburgh Gate
Harlow, Essex CM20 2JE, United Kingdom
and associated Companies throughout the world.

*Published in the United States of America
by Addison Wesley Longman Inc., New York.*

First published 1996

ISBN 0 582 23713 0 CSD
ISBN 0 582 23712 2 PPR

British Library Cataloguing-in-Publication Data

A catalogue record of this book is
available from the British Library

Library of Congress Cataloging-in-Publication Data

Tennyson / edited and introduced by Rebecca Stott.
     p.   cm. — (Longman critical readers)
   ISBN 0–582–23712–2 (ppr) — ISBN 0–582–23713–0 (CSD)
    1. Tennyson, Alfred Tennyson, Baron, 1809–1892—Criticism and
interpretation. I. Stott, Rebecca. II. Series.
PR5588.T415 1996
821'.8—dc20

          96–1911
          CIP

Set by 20K in 9/11½ Palatino
Produced by Longman Singapore Publishers (Pte) Ltd.
Printed in Singapore

Contents

General Editors' Preface

The outlines of contemporary critical theory are now often taught as a standard feature of a degree in literary studies. The development of particular theories has seen a thorough transformation of literary criticism. For example, Marxist and Foucauldian theories have revolutionised Shakespeare studies, and 'deconstruction' has led to a complete reassessment of Romantic poetry. Feminist criticism has left scarcely any period of literature unaffected by its searching critiques. Teachers of literary studies can no longer fall back on a standardised, received, methodology.

Lecturers and teachers are now urgently looking for guidance in a rapidly changing critical environment. They need help in understanding the latest revisions in literary theory, and especially in grasping the practical effects of the new theories in the form of theoretically sensitised new readings. A number of volumes in the series anthologise important essays on particular theories. However, in order to grasp the full implications and possible uses of particular theories it is essential to see them put to work. This series provides substantial volumes of new readings, presented in an accessible form and with a significant amount of editorial guidance.

Each volume includes a substantial introduction which explores the theoretical issues and conflicts embodied in the essays selected and locates areas of disagreement between positions. The pluralism of theories has to be put on the agenda of literary studies. We can no longer pretend that we all tacitly accept the same practices in literary studies. Neither is a *laissez-faire* attitude any longer tenable. Literature departments need to go beyond the mere toleration of theoretical differences: it is not enough merely to agree to differ; they need actually to 'stage' the differences openly. The volumes in this series all attempt to dramatise the differences, not necessarily with a view to resolving them but in order to foreground the choices presented by different theories or to argue for a particular route through the impasses the differences present.

The theory 'revolution' has had real effects. It has loosened the grip of traditional empiricist and romantic assumptions about language and literature. It is not always clear what is being proposed as the

vi

new agenda for literary studies, and indeed the very notion of 'literature' is questioned by the post-structuralist strain in theory. However, the uncertainties and obscurities of contemporary theories appear much less worrying when we see what the best critics have been able to do with them in practice. This series aims to disseminate the best of recent criticism and to show that it is possible to re-read the canonical texts of literature in new and challenging ways.

RAMAN SELDEN AND STAN SMITH

The Publishers and fellow Series Editor regret to record that Raman Selden died after a short illness in May 1991 at the age of fifty-three. Ray Selden was a fine scholar and a lovely man. All those he has worked with will remember him with much affection and respect.

Acknowledgements

We are grateful to the following for permission to reproduce copyright material:

Columbia University Press for an extract from *Between Men: English Literature and Male Homosocial Desire* by Eve Kosofsky Sedgwick. © 1985 Columbia University Press; the author, Professor Terry Eagleton his essay from *1848: The Sociology of Literature* ed. Francis Barker et. al. published by the University of Essex; Johns Hopkins University Press and the authors, for articles by Jeff Nunokawa in *E.L.H.* vol. 58 (1991) and Alan Sinfield in *E.L.H.* vol. 57 (Spring 1990); Indiana University for the article 'Women Red in Tooth and Claw: Nature and the Feminine in Tennyson and Darwin' by James Eli Adams in *Victorian Studies* vol. 33, No. 1. (Autumn, 1989); the author, Dr. Elaine Jordan for her essay '1857–1867: Divorce, Democracy and Thermodynamics: Getting Heated'; Routledge and the author, Dr. Isobel Armstrong for an extract from her *Victorian Poetry: Poetry Poetics and Politics* (1993); University of Texas Press and the author, Joseph Bristow for his article Nation Class and Gender: Tennyson's Maud and War' in *Genders* vol. 9 (1990) pp 93–111; The Editor, *Victorian Newsletter* for the article 'Victorian Weaving: The Alienation of Work into Text in "The Lady of Shalott" ' by Gerhard Joseph in *Victorian Newsletter* vol. 71 (1987) pp. 7–10; The Editor, *Victorian Poetry* for the essay 'The Ideological Moment of Tennyson's "Ulysses" ' by Matthew Rowlinson in *Victorian Poetry* vol. 30 (1992) and 'Patriarchy, Dead Men, and Tennyson's *Idylls of the King*' by Linda Shires, first printed in *Victorian Poetry*, vol. 30 (1990).

Introduction

Lord Alfred Tennyson came of age, with Darwin and Gladstone, in 1830, the year he published his first collection of poetry, *Poems, Chiefly Lyrical*. He died in 1892, only nine years before Queen Victoria. His writing spanned sixty-two years, years in which he became Lord Alfred Tennyson, Poet Laureate, comforter of the widowed Queen (Queen Victoria told Tennyson 'Next to the Bible *In Memoriam* is my comfort') and voice of an empire. William Thackeray once wrote of him: 'he reads all sorts of things, swallows and digests them like a great poetical boa-constrictor' and it seems at times as if Tennyson has swallowed what we have come to call the Victorian Age, or that his poetry is a fossil which enables us to observe with twentieth-century critical apparatus all the complex sinews and musculature of that age. Just as the DNA of the dinosaur can be reconstructed from the fossilised remains of a single mosquito in *Jurassic Park*, so it seems the Victorian Age can be reconstructed from the delicate and exquisitely detailed poetry of Tennyson. Except that just as each new advance in palaeontology brings us new dinosaurs, new fossils, the development of twentieth-century criticism brings us new Victorian Ages, indeed new Tennysons.

Tennyson's close affiliation with the Victorian Age has often been damaging to his reception. For many modernist writers Tennyson came to represent moral discursiveness, empty rhetoric, verbosity – the suffocating weight of literary inheritance. Virginia Woolf's comic heroine Orlando, waking up in the Victorian Age, discovers that damp 'gets into the inkpot as it gets into the woodwork – sentences swelled, adjectives multiplied, lyrics became epics'[1] and she finds that her own writing suffers as the tides of her blood run sluggishly. Pound called the Victorian Age 'a rather, blurry messy sort of a period, a rather sentimentalistic, mannerish sort of a period' and hence Tennyson's poetry came to embody the 'convoluted tushery'[2] he saw. Contemporary critics such as Carol Christ have argued that the modernists misread Victorian poetry, that they constructed a simplified version of Victorianism to suit their own ends and that they identified within it the failures which would defeat their own enterprise.[3] T. S. Eliot is the exception of his generation, perhaps.

Eliot's influential essay of 1936 on *In Memoriam* described Tennyson's poetry as riven by tensions between surface and depth, faith and doubt, poetry which registered the diverse and sometimes contradictory impulses of modern poetry.

Tennyson's last years of writing coincided with those years in which Matthew Arnold was calling for literature to fill the void left by the collapse of religion, in which Literature was being constructed as a discipline in itself with a civilizing mission. The history of the development of English studies is therefore very closely related to the history of Tennyson criticism. If in the 1890s literature was to be endowed by some with a civilizing mission, then the poetry of Tennyson, reaching into the furthest corners of the Empire, would civilize the young and nationalize and cultivate the newly colonized by endorsing the values and beliefs of the dominant culture. To be used as a means of ideological control and indoctrination within the early years of English studies, Tennyson's poetry needed to be constructed and shaped in certain ways.

Tennyson's poetry has therefore often been taken to be emblematic of certain beliefs and values which have been believed to be fundamental and universal truths about humanity and common to all peoples. Criticism of this kind, presenting essentialist humanist values as eternal absolutes, seems to be implicit in much criticism of Tennyson until the 1960s. Such criticism, Alan Sinfield argues, seems harmless enough 'but it rules out effective consideration of the historical conditions which govern the activities of writing and reading . . . By removing from visibility the power structures and ideologies, the institutions and practices, which determine the conditions of actual lives, it inhibits political awareness and change.'[4] As Tennyson's poetry came to stand for all that was believed to be good and true about British culture and British values, then inevitably certain problems or political contradictions within the poetry were glossed over and certain deviant or problematic poems fell from the canon. Simultaneously until the 1960s it was generally taken for granted that 'great' poets did not involve themselves in the petty political issues of their day but spoke of higher transcendent truths, and it was towards these truths that readers were directed to turn their eyes.

Of course there is no pure unadulterated Tennyson to be discovered. Poetry has so often been the battleground for debate, and the poetry of so national a poet is perhaps bound to be used as the site for numerous such debates: in the 1830s the reviews of Tennyson's first collection of poetry, *Poems, Chiefly Lyrical*, focused upon potential new directions for poetry and the ways in which the condition of poetry might be seen to mirror the condition of England. With the publication of *In Memoriam*, Tennyson's poetry became a focus for questions of faith and doubt and evolutionary theory. The texts we read yield only answers to the questions we ask of them. Stanley Fish argued in 1980 that it is meaningless to talk of texts as objects since 'text-objects' are the product of individual 'interpretive strategies';[5] in other words Tennyson's poetry at any time will be shaped by the reading strategies applied to it. Just as the modernists made Tennyson into the bogeyman as a means of identifying what they believed they were not, so did the Victorians themselves construct a Tennyson in his own lifetime as the purveyor of values which we can now see he was at best strongly sceptical about. Tennyson's poetry has changed as criticism has changed, as reading strategies have changed, as politics (and particularly sexual politics) have changed.

Gerhard Joseph's essay on the reception of Tennyson's 'Lady of Shalott' reads the poem as an allegory of recent literary history, showing how the poem has metamorphosed as different interpretive strategies have been applied to it, from New Criticism through post-structuralism to Marxism and thence to Joseph's own reading of the poem. He returns to the New Critical arguments (that the poem is about the making of poetry), but tries to politicize this reading by arguing that the poem is about the estrangement of literary labour or in other words the estrangement of the text from the author or producer, thus combining a Marxist and New Critical reading. The New Critics, he argues, still believed in the concept of an author but by rejecting the concept of intention (that the only meanings to be found in a poem are those 'intended' by the author) they could cut off the text from that author. Many contemporary critics have gone further, rejecting the notion of a unified author in or above the text as a kind of author-God, as they reject the notion of a unified self as a Western humanist construction. Thereby contemporary criticism minimizes the importance of the author, stressing instead the importance of the reader in the making of the text's meaning. For Joseph such diminishment of the importance or relevance of the author increases the alienation of literary labour.

This entire process is mirrored for Joseph in the movement of the poem itself; the yearning of the text thus comes to express his own yearning for the days when authors were authors and not concepts. Elsewhere Joseph has lamented 'the polysemic, anti-essentialist notion of authorial self and world' which has invaded recent Tennyson studies with its 'linguistic turn'. Thus 'The Lady of Shalott' comes to speak poignantly to a critic whose own work, with its distinctive blend of feminist, deconstructionist and psychoanalytical methodologies, seems estranged and full of yearning for unfashionable critical notions. Such romantic yearning and nostalgia

3

for the days when it was possible to talk about a unified authorial self can be detected, he argues in the introduction to his recent book, *Tennyson and the Text: The Weaver's Shuttle* (1992), not only in his own work but in the works of eminent contemporary theorists such as Jacques Derrida and Paul de Man. He seems to imply, therefore, that such a yearning is part of the human condition and thus that Tennyson's poem speaks of that condition. For the Victorians that characteristic Tennysonian yearning spoke of the absence of God, the void left by the withdrawal of religious certainties. For a post-structuralist critic such as Joseph writing in 1987, Tennyson's yearning speaks of an absence brought about by contemporary ideas concerning the fractured self. T. S. Eliot once called Tennyson the 'saddest poet in the English language'; this may not now be conceived as a universal *essentialist* sadness, but nonetheless it has to be acknowledged as a sadness so acute as to be able to express the diverse longings and desires of both Victorian agnostic and post-structuralist critic alike.

In the Centenary Edition of *Victorian Poetry* Gerhard Joseph, who edits the volume, summons the shade of the now hundred-year dead Tennyson who, emerging from a cloud of tobacco smoke, complains about the nature of the critical essays which have been assembled to commemorate him:

> All this relentless gender-mongering and speculation about whether I did or did not sleep with Arthur Hallam or yearn for my mother's breast? All this talk about 'repression', 'sexual confusion', 'patriarchal functions', 'cultural formation of masculinities', 'Heideggerean temporalities', 'deconstruction' of one binary opposition or another, ideological moments and disruption – not to mention attributing to *me* the thought of snakes masturbating at the sight of buffaloes?[6]

Despite the grumblings of this Tennyson spirit, there have been no shortage of critics who have pointed out that so many of the tropes and metaphors used in current contemporary critical theory are to be found in Tennyson's own poetry. Post-structuralist criticism makes much of punning and playing with 'text' (which comes from 'textere' – to weave) and with reaping. Both metaphors are abundant in Tennyson's poetry, particularly 'The Lady of Shalott', and Joseph weaves such tropes in and out of *Tennyson and the Text: The Weaver's Shuttle*. Just as contemporary critics make much of the instability of the text and the way in which the text can be seen to be the site for a struggle for meaning and interpretation, Tennyson also famously said that 'Poetry is like shot-silk with many glancing colours. Every reader must find his own interpretation according to his ability, and according to his sympathy with the poet';[7] and elsewhere: 'I hate to be tied down to say "*This* means *that*", because the thought within the image is much more than any one interpretation'.[8] Alan Sinfield's remark about the open nature of all texts curiously echoes Tennyson's words: 'There can be no security in textuality: no scriptor can control the reading of his or her text'.[9]

The greatest re-evaluation of Tennyson's poetry has taken place since 1960, and more particularly within the last decade, coinciding as always with the continuing development of English studies. Perhaps the two most influential areas of contemporary criticism which have re-animated and politicized Tennyson scholarship have been cultural studies (in its broadest sense including New Historicism and cultural materialism) and feminist theory. This volume attests to the vitality of the outcome. Other notable areas of Tennyson scholarship have been influenced by gay theory, deconstruction, Marxist analysis and, to some extent, by psychoanalytic criticism. Tennyson's poetry has consequently become the battleground for debates about masculinity, sexual politics, androgyny, empire, nationalism and the changing and problematic role of the Victorian poet.

Tennyson: of politics, ideology and the contradictory text

With the abandonment of the concept of the unified human subject and with the advent of cultural studies, earlier critical strategies have given way to more subtle and complex readings of the ways in which texts engage with the dominant ideologies of their time. Cultural materialism is a term used by the Marxist critic Raymond Williams, and is related to, but distinct from, New Historicism. Alan Sinfield is one of the main practitioners of cultural materialism in Britain and in 1986 he published a small but radically influential book called simply *Alfred Tennyson* in the Blackwell Rereading Literature series edited by Terry Eagleton. It drew on what would become later defined as a cultural materialist programme.[10] Behind this method of reading and analysis is an express 'committment' to the 'transformation of a social order which exploits people on grounds of race, gender and class'.[11]

Cultural materialism is influenced by Raymond Williams's proposition that the project of ideology is to present power relations as harmonious and coherent. The task of the cultural materialist is to draw attention to and expose this process. Instead of presenting dominant ideology and power relations as all-pervasive and unbreakable, Raymond Williams argued for the presence of subordinate, residual, emergent, alternative and oppositional cultural forces alongside the dominant in varying states of resistance. For the cultural materialist this means understanding any given text as a 'cultural intervention': what view of reality does it promote or serve within specific historical conditions? By revealing the values stated or implied within a text, they can therefore be revealed not as eternal, unchanging values (the essential humanist tendency of New Criticism) but as 'questionable constructions made by other people in other circumstances'.[12] For Sinfield and other cultural materialists the text does not promise a final definitive meaning but is, and will continue to be, the site for a struggle over meaning which is always political.

Sinfield argues that canonical texts will always be resistant to such new readings because decades of conservative criticism have promoted certain values and explained away any awkwardness within them. To 're-read' Tennyson after decades of such essentialist humanist readings is inevitably to be a difficult and controversial task. In his book Sinfield draws out a Tennyson engaged in struggle with the dominant thinking of his time, increasingly marginalized as poetry itself was marginalized in an age dominated by materialist and utilitarian interests, and provoking in his poetry uncomfortable questions about ideology, sexuality and language. He is shown to be a poet who, far from being the standard bearer of his age's dominant values, can be seen as often ambiguously and painfully at odds with them.

In his 1990 essay chosen for this collection, 'Tennyson and the Cultural Politics of Prophesy', Sinfield begins by arguing that stories are central to all cultural production, for it is through stories that we understand and live in the world. Stories make the world *plausible* and the criteria of plausibility are political for the story seeks to persuade us that the way things are are the way things *have to be*. Tennyson, however, writing as an unheeded outsider in an increasingly materialist world, seeks to validate the *implausible* utterances of his alienated and unheeded prophetic figures. His poetry demands alternative criteria of plausibility; he did not seek to argue that the way things were were the way things had to be. But he was also made Poet Laureate and became a best-selling author. Why was this so? Sinfield argues that Tennyson's writing, in endorsing a poetic, spiritual alternative to a materialist world, was in fact only fitting into the binary formations of classic capitalism in which poetry, literature, the spirit are imagined as repudiations of a mechanized urban world and the 'conscience of capitalism'.

If Tennyson endorses an alternative understanding of the world, it may seem as if he is standing out against his culture or moving beyond the scope of customary discourse. In fact, Sinfield argues, Tennyson is merely telling another of culture's prominent stories by reminding us that some stories and some tellers are more powerful than others. Tennyson's stories, then, are not subversive but they are political. In another text, 'Tiresias', the alternative truth that this unheeded outsider wishes us to accept is troubling, calling as it does for expiation and scapegoating. Nonetheless Tennyson's poem seems to ratify this wisdom and as critics, Sinfield argues, we must acknowledge that such a 'truth' needs to be challenged. Instead of assuming, as the formalist critics tended to do, that good literary writing will always induce and cultivate 'good' attitudes, Sinfield argues that 'magic does not guarantee wisdom'. For Sinfield 'the tricks are excellent, but we need to read the fine print'.

In returning to an assessment of his own critical enterprise, Sinfield argues that too many modern critical strategies seek to uncover the ambiguities, slippages and paradoxes within a text, thus allowing the sagacious author and text to transcend politics and history through the implied completeness and complexity of their vision. Turning to the appearance in 1987 of Christopher Ricks's *The Poems of Tennyson* (replacing the earlier 'definitive' edition of 1969), Sinfield offers it as an excellent instance of the way in which Tennyson is constructed within the institution of literature. In seeking to establish the authentic text through detailed scholarly study, this edition and others like it only serve to undermine the stability of the text, an inevitable fact. The attempt to stabilize the text is itself always culturally significant. The definitive, 'indispensable' Ricks edition of the poems is not transcendent as we might have supposed, a magically pure, sagacious, and seamless given, but instead, like Tennyson's poetry, is put together by people in a cultural politics. In finishing with Ricks himself, the 'sage' of Tennyson studies, Sinfield completes his project which was to 'relate a prominent Tennysonian motif to assumptions that still permeate literary studies generally'.

Isobel Armstrong is a critic who has taken issue with the critical strategies of Sinfield, particularly in her recent book *Victorian Poetry: Poetry, Poetics and Politics* (1993). This book is an important re-evaluation of Victorian poetry and Armstrong sees this task as restoring 'the questions of politics, not least sexual politics, and the epistemology and language which belongs to it'. Such a task may at first seem to be complementary to that identified by Sinfield in his cultural materialist agenda, but it is evident that Armstrong is one of those critics whom Sinfield takes issue with in his 1990 essay as being too concerned with teasing out the *ambiguities* of any given text rather than identifying (and where necessary challenging) its reactionary or conservative values. In her turn Armstrong confronts Sinfield:

> First, in order to pin Tennyson to political and religious positions, Sinfield has to eliminate the possibility of ambiguity in poetic language. Or when confronted with two contending meanings he has to opt for one as being 'really' the intended meaning. Similarly, in order to argue Tennyson's political bad faith he has to argue that Tennyson's 'real' interests as a sympathiser with the landed gentry and as a supporter of nationalism and imperialist interests must give a poem a particular historical meaning even when it appears to be struggling against it . . . He excludes the element of struggle with the element of ambiguity.[13]

Armstrong offers her own critical strategy in response to Sinfield's as one which seeks to offer 'a more generous understanding of the text as struggle' without, however, constructing the text as 'merely' complex and ambiguous (this, she asserts is typical of certain aspects of deconstruction which tend to concentrate on a text's ludic energies rather than its conflicts). Few texts, she argues, are at ease with their own internal difficulties and are instead the sites of active struggle for meaning.

In *Victorian Poetry* Armstrong suggests that there is 'a doubleness at the centre of Victorian poetry' in which it is sometimes possible to perceive 'two concurrent poems in the same words'. Such evidence of struggle within texts should be seen as a *responsive* rather than a *symptomatic* discourse, struggling within the logic of their own contradictions, threatened by internal collapse. The New Hegelian reading, she claims, avoids symptomatic interpretations and avoids the endless ludic contradictions which sometimes emerge from deconstruction:

> This post-Hegelian reading recognises the antagonistic struggle of dialectic rather than its resolutions or its free play. It assumes that an active ideological creativity is constitutively at work in the poem's structure and language and is thus necessarily a political and cultural way of reading.[14]

The extract from *Victorian Poetry* reprinted in this volume enacts just such a reading. Armstrong looks at Tennyson's reworkings of a group of poems first published in 1832 and republished in 1842 which includes 'The Palace of Art', 'The Lady of Shalott' and 'The Lotos-Eaters'. Hallam died in the year after the publication of the 1832

Poems and the slow modification and adaptation of the poems reveals, in Armstrong's hands, a gradual critique of Hallam's aesthetic positions. On the one hand, then, Tennyson's adaptations show a critique of the poetry of sensation (as defined by Hallam) and on the other an increasing concern with labour, exploitation and power, and with forms in which culture perpetrates violence. There was to be a search for a new politics and a new aesthetics for Tennyson.

Armstrong begins with the revisions to 'The Palace of Art' as a 'double poem of a highly conscious kind', arguing that the poem offers a direct critique of Hallam's pure art as a self-enclosed system. By the 1842 version the poem's landscapes depict human exploitation of the land and human labour showing them out of harmony with nature, thus destroying the basis of Romantic assumptions about the relations between man and landscape. The figure of the Soul is shown to be isolated, indifferent to a suffering history and contemptuous of the people. Finally the poem also exhibits, according to Armstrong, the poet's understanding of the real condition of women within contemporary culture by imagining the Soul, and thus art, as feminine, and its collapse as the inevitable demise of poetry in an arid society suffering impossible demands. Armstrong offers two dialectical readings of the poem's ending working against each other to endorse further its portrait of an 'empty and pathologised' culture.

In her analysis of 'The Lady of Shalott', Armstrong rejects New Critical readings of the poem as oversimplified, instead reading the poem as another double poem, one in which two readings are simultaneously at work. In the first conservative and deterministic reading the Lady is locked into a world dominated by rigid oppositions, condemned to passivity and death. Alternatively the second reading, she argues, shows us a poem which dissolves and interrogates the fixed positions of this world, showing us a Tennyson who is aware of the coercive power of myth and myths of labour in particular by his alignment of agrarian workers and women as exploited and alienated workers. In 1842, Armstrong argues, this was 'Tennyson's most intense critique of oppression'. Armstrong suggests that these contradictions are latent within the 1832 poems whilst the 1842 revisions force these contradictions into the open, thus forming a critique. Similarly 'The Lotos-Eaters' can be read as an impossible struggle with the ideology of consciousness, labour and consumption in which, once again, two oppositional readings are at work: one in which the passivity of the Lotos-Eaters is caused by eating the Lotos, and in the second in which passivity is caused by exhaustion from labour. The second reading offers a critique of exploitation and mindless labour (opium and alcohol often allayed the horrors of industrial work). The exploration of the poem is close to Marx's understanding of the ways in which estranged labour converts all energy expended outside work into dehumanized experience. Tennyson thus reveals the psychological state created by the new industrial conditions of labour. In all, then, Armstrong argues that the revisions of 1842 are 'an extraordinary response to the worsening social conditions of the 1840s and turn the poem of 1832 virtually into a new text as the brutalising suffering of the 1840s finds a place in it'.

Terry Eagleton, Marxist critic and recently appointed Warton Professor of English Literature at Oxford, is another critic who is committed to political change. Like Sinfield he believes that political change will be coupled with 'a fierce conflict over signs and meanings' as one group 'strives to wrest the most cherished symbols from the grip of its rivals and redefine them in its own image'.[15] In the conclusion to his widely read book *Literary Theory: An Introduction* (1983) he outlines a way out of the crisis in English studies, not in terms of producing a new method of analysis, but by changing the *goals* of textual examination, examining instead the ways in which discourses of all kinds are used for particular ends. This, he argues, although a radical strategy, is little more than a return to a more traditional form of study, that of the study of rhetoric: the study of linguistic devices as a means of persuading, inciting or pleading. He is thus far close to the critical strategies of Sinfield. Political criticism is to be the way forward for the subject, a practice which is to unite cultural practice and political practice. Unlike the practice of the liberal humanist critic this project involves the enriching and deepening of our lives not through the transformation of the *individual* (civilized through contact with literature – the humanist enterprise) but through the transformation of a society divided by class, gender and race. Such criticism would involve the study not only of canonical literary texts but of cultural artefacts of all kinds.

We can see Eagleton's project at work in his 1978 essay on Tennyson's *The Princess* and *In Memoriam*. Eagleton draws on both psychoanalytic and Marxist strategies and outlines a set of ideological contradictions within the mid-Victorian bourgeois state. The ideological project of *The Princess* he reads as an imaginary resolution of these contradictions, through a refashioning of the Lacanian 'symbolic order'. For Eagleton the bourgeois state had problems reaching its 'manhood' due to a transitional crisis in the nature of state power occasioned by the sharpening of class struggle in the 1840s and the spectre of revolution in Europe. The hegemony of such state power sought acceptability by deferring to the civilizing values of moral nobility characterized as feminine. The poem provides, for

Eagleton, 'a psychoanalysis of the bourgeois state' by curtailing the disruptiveness of desire and reconsolidating the symbolic order in 'a suitably refurbished form'. The poem cannot close down all contradictions, however, and Eagleton outlines the disturbances which are deeply scored upon the surface of the text. *In Memoriam*, however, is finally able to grow into manhood by a transcendence of 'feminine' grief and a recognition of the necessity of the absent phallus (Hallam as the transcendental signifier of all losses) enacting a triumphant reaffirmation of bourgeois sexual reproduction. This, for Eagleton, is made possible by 1848 and the threat of revolutionary upheaval which forces the transcendence of private, 'feminine' melancholy.

Sinfield, in the introduction to his book on Tennyson, argues that Eagleton's concept of hegemony is oversimplified. Eagleton had argued that the confusion of gender categories in *The Princess* is finally and necessarily closed down in order to reaffirm the symbolic order. Sinfield disagrees:

> Overall, I see the confusion of gender categories as more difficult, then and now, for bourgeois hegemony to handle than Eagleton does. Although Tennyson may try eventually to close down the challenge, he is playing a risky game, one which is likely to leave uncomfortable residues.[16]

Furthermore Sinfield's reading of *In Memoriam* in his book on Tennyson argues that 'its blurring of gender divisions offers to the modern reader a challenge which later writers could hardly envisage, let alone sustain'.[17] For Sinfield the blurring of gender roles is part of a dissident strategy; for Eagleton it is a means to restabilize such roles and thereby affirm the dominant order. What we have here is one of the fundamental debates within political criticism and cultural studies: a debate about whether dissidence and dissident discourse are both allowed and finally reappropriated by the dominant ideology, or whether the social order is itself riven through with 'faultlines' produced by the contradictions within dominant ideology.

The woman's cause is man's?: Tennyson, sexuality and sexual politics

Earlier I argued that the two most significant advances in Tennyson scholarship have been that of cultural studies (which we might also call political studies) and feminist studies. The study of gender, sexuality and sexual politics in Tennyson's poetry is by no means solely a twentieth-century phenomenon. Tennyson reviews have been scored through with questions of 'femininity' and 'masculinity' since he began writing. The Victorians established early a long-lasting association between sexuality and poetry. The role allotted to poetry within bourgeois culture was to be a feminine one in opposition to 'masculine' commerce and industry. As the national poet, Tennyson was persistently associated with all that was considered feminine: Alfred Austin for instance, Victorian reviewer, complained about 'the feminine, narrow, domesticated, timorous Poetry of the Period' and furthermore that Tennyson was 'of his age almost wholly and solely' in this matter. Tennyson, for Austin, lacks manliness, his poetry has no 'dust, and clang, and hot blood in it'.[18]

Sexual politics have become integral to a wider discussion of the politics of Tennyson's poetry. Tennyson, worrying away at binaries, at the rigid gender distinctions set in place by Victorian culture, writes about androgyny and the duality of gender in many poems but particularly *The Princess*, of course, and John Killham has shown how ideas about androgyny within the poem relate to early socialism and campaigns for women's rights. For Elaine Jordan, Tennyson's ideas about androgyny 'have a bearing . . . upon all Tennyson's work, and the ways in which it has been received'.[19] Issues of sexuality and gender can never be isolated; they are always embedded in other discourses. Literary theorists of all kinds have come to realize that to leave such questions 'to the feminists' is to diminish their own critical enterprise. For Eagleton, for example, the effect of social disruption in the 1840s becomes rapidly integrated into the social formation through gender binaries. What is constructed as marginal (and thus feminine) at any one time depends upon ideological positionings, so to look at what is constructed as feminine (such as a marginalized poetry at mid-century for instance) or masculine will tell us about the shape of the binaries within dominant ideologies (what is 'inside' and what is 'outside'). Whilst Kate Millett in 1969 might have called Tennyson's *The Princess* 'a case history of the poet's own problems of sexual identity'.[20] current feminist analysis, working with more complex models of power relations, is more likely to begin with a concept of the text as the site of different and competing discourses or ideologies in conflict.

In 'Women Red in Tooth and Claw: Nature and the Feminine in Tennyson and Darwin', James Eli Adams argues that in the mid-nineteenth century age-old personifications of Nature as feminine were disturbed as new evolutionary ideas came into circulation but, more importantly, such disturbances of Nature conceived as Mother were, in their turn, to unsettle a traditional and comforting archetype of womanhood. Tennyson's poetry reveals these close relations between science and gender throughout early Victorian discourse. Once again Adams is interested in ideology and discourse, concerned to reveal how Tennyson's poetry works to challenge or smooth over Victorian ideological problems. It became increasingly difficult to maintain the analogy of nature as vigilant, long-sighted and sagacious mother as evolutionary science showed the perpetual struggle to survive within the natural world. Darwin strived to maintain the analogy for as long as he could in an attempt to soften the impact of his ideas by presenting nature as a feminine agency which is attentive to the individual not just the type, but eventually even he could not hold it in place.

Ten years *before* the publication of Darwin's *Origin of Species* Tennyson had imagined a sinister Nature, neglectful of her offspring, and finally characterized as a woman in demonic form in sections LV and LVI of *In Memoriam*. This monstrous (yet still maternal) femininity which defies male desire forces the reader to question the nature of female desire: what do women want? Tennyson imagines the new world presented by Victorian science as the work of a feminine Nature which had betrayed its maternal role in *In Memoriam*. In *The Princess*, written during the composition of *In Memoriam*, the same identification is established in the opposite direction: Tennyson associates Ida's resistance of male desire and her rejection of motherhood with the mechanisms of evolution. Nature in *The Princess* is reconstituted in the figure of Ida in that she is more concerned with her grand designs than she is with the Prince as an individual. However, whilst the two poems might take different directions they seem to converge in their resolutions 'as the disruptions of loss are repaired in a renewed continuum of being that is confirmed by an emblematic marriage'. For Adams, Tennyson articulates a conservative attitude toward the advancement of women in the closing stanzas of *The Princess* but thereby also shows how important the construction of a notion of 'woman' is to that conservative ideology. Ideals of femininity were held up as forces of continuity and vigilance in a moment of crisis and punctuated by revolution. The Victorians were haunted by the spectre of revolution, stressing urgently instead the benefits of gradual (evolutionary) progress. An ideal of femininity as maternal agency was thus crucial to the maintenance of that ideology. Whilst Victorian typologies of the feminine might have been disturbed by the new scientific ideas, yet the same speculation thereby prompts a new recognition of the significance of the feminine, 'not only as a biological category but as an organizing principle of Victorian discourse'.

'In any period there is a web of symbolic cross-reference, in which one set of events may become a metaphor for another' and Elaine Jordan in her essay, omitted from her 1988 book *Alfred Tennyson*, deftly uncovers such entangled webs using interdisciplinary methodologies which draw on a wide variety of textual and visual material produced between 1857 and 1867. The title, 'Tennyson, 1857–67: Divorce, Democracy and Thermodynamics' indicates the scope of its investigation. Interdisciplinary or anti-disciplinary work has become more and more sophisticated over recent decades, partly in response to the growth of cultural studies and partly brought about by the arguments of feminist and post-Foucauldian scholars that the nineteenth century produced a 'multiplicity of discourses' about sexuality and that these discourses operate in a similar multiplicity of different contexts (political, religious, medical, philosophical, economic and scientific).

Like Adams, Jordan shows how discourses of sexuality and fears of working-class revolution are related to new scientific thinking, thus that divorce, democracy and thermodynamics can be interrelated at a particular historical moment. Like Eagleton, Jordan chooses to limit her investigation to a mid-century decade. She treats Tennyson's poetry alongside other cultural artefacts not just as a window to observe the ideological dynamics of the period but rather as a cultural *intervention*, a means by which sense is made of the moment of mid-century crisis. Like Adams, too, she is concerned with the figuration of a fictional female type, the adulterous wife, and in three texts – the opening of Tennyson's *Idylls* entitled 'The False and the True' (1857), Augustus Egg's triptych of paintings which came to be known as 'Past and Present' (exhibited 1858) and Mary Braddon's 1862 sensation novel, *Lady Audley's Secret* – she shows how female adultery comes to be blamed for national evils.

Jordan locates these texts within a range of overlapping mid-century legislative changes: divorce reform brought in via the Matrimonial Causes Act of 1857, legislation controlling the sale of poisons, and the Obscene Publications Act of the same year. Female sexuality and particularly adultery became associated with contagion and poison. Later by 1868 and Tennyson's 'Lucretius', female sexuality and social degeneration are conjoined through a vision of a teeming fecundity threatening revolt and invasion. Jordan locates this text within two other mid-century contexts: the riots around Hyde Park in July 1866 as the Reform League campaigned for an extension of the franchise to all men rather than only property holders, and the Morant Bay Rebellion in Jamaica in 1865 in which Governor Eyre imposed iron force on the rebels, executing hundreds of people. Jordan puts all these events together and points out that all concern a threat or appeal to masculine authority and anxieties

about deciding the limits of protest and authority. Perhaps the most compelling interaction of discourses, however, is identified in 'Lucretius' where the newly discovered entropic laws of thermodynamics provide a metaphor for fears of social degeneration and vice versa.

If such overlapping sexual, political and scientific discourses provide the framework for a mid-century moral panic, Tennyson's 'medievalizing, classicizing poems', claims Jordan, 'make a local panic into something timeless' and she suggests in both poems that women's desires are poisonous and destroy male authority, representing 'a masculinity which in erecting a fearful dignity projects onto female figures and "red ruin" what it wants to disavow, and control'.

Tennyson, masculinity, manhood and empire

If Adams and Jordan examine mid-century figurations of femininity as a means to show the close and complex relations between science, sexuality and politics, two other essays in this collection by Joseph Bristow and Linda Shires turn their attention to models of masculinity and patriarchy constructed in Tennyson's poetry and within the Victorian period. Historical and political contexts remain central to all these studies attesting to the influence of cultural studies and to the increasing sophistication and intricacy of gendered readings. Joseph Bristow's essay 'Nation, Class and Gender: Tennyson's *Maud* and War' takes as its subject the testing climate of the Crimean War and examines the 'textual and cultural contradictions that place extraordinary pressures on ideas about Victorian manhood and, just as importantly, poethood in a poem strategically placed to speak on behalf of the nation at a key turning point in nineteenth-century British history'. Bristow explores Victorian tensions between being a poet and being a man in an age when poetry was becoming feminized and when the expression of emotion in poetry was seen to be increasingly at odds with Victorian masculinities. He shows that by the 1860s Tennyson 'could stand as a *model* for poetic strength and sensitivity of mind . . . *and* as a man *effeminized* in his vocation'. *Maud* has two purposes: to demonstrate how women can heal the emotional suffering of men, and to reveal how a monodrama can prove that poetry is ideally suited to men because it enables full expression of the maddening emotions which constitute 'proper' masculinity. Bristow sees the text as a 'representative document of the conservative masculinism of its age' (in its reproduction of a Ruskinian conception of the angel-wife) but also as giving a 'unique inflection to this prevailing ideology of gender' by betraying 'the precariousness of the noble masculinity it attempts to vindicate'.

Once again we are in the terrain of the cultural materialist in which dissident discourse can be discovered 'warrening' (Stuart Hall's phrase) within dominant conservative ideologies. The text 'betrays' the values it seeks to endorse by revealing the cracks. But such a cultural materialist approach has been appropriated by critics such as Bristow to provide a gendered reading. Bristow finally argues that pushed to its logical extremes the poem finally resolves the problem of how to unify masculinity with poethood by arguing that men must go mad in order to prove they are men – the finest men are those who are able to demonstrate not only physical but psychical violence.

The poem enacts a conflict between antagonistic types of Victorian manhood: effeminate radicals (money-making pacifists using economic arguments to oppose the Crimean War) and manly conservatives (soldierly gentlemen standing for freedom and honour under the banner of nationalism). Emotional response comes to be a sign of the fine masculinity of the manly conservatives (responding with nationalistic fervour) and cool-headed rationalism a sign of the effeminacy of the pacifist radicals. In making this sleight of hand Tennyson must make women, and in particular the figure of Maud, come to embrace both the military and maternal identities of Britain itself. Conflicts with the conservative model of the gender hierarchy are thus seen within representations of both men and women. The poem's hero must become 'more than a woman' (maddened) to save himself from becoming less than a man (effeminate).

Bristow calls for new work to be undertaken to study the cultural history of Victorian masculinities in relation to class and political identity. He argues that we need more understanding of the ways in which emotionality between men was sublimated into forms of nationalistic heroism: 'To trace the history of Victorian masculinity may well reveal more about the material conditions in which modern hegemonic masculinities, so often based in violence, have emerged during the past hundred and fifty years'. Once again cultural activity is to be coupled with political activity for Bristow as it is for many contemporary critics and theorists who have replaced some of the more apolitical and ahistorical reading practices of deconstructionists and structuralists: 'to learn more of the genealogy of military manhood is perhaps to enable late twentieth-century men in the West to find a new vocabulary with which to change the – perhaps not so unusual – fury to be located in Tennyson's poem'.

The previous four essays by Eagleton, Adams, Jordan and Bristow have all focused on Tennyson's mid-century poems, using them as a means to read and explore the competing ideologies at work in this period of political and social upheaval. Although the reading practices of the four critics are distinctly different, they nonetheless all begin from the premise that the text is produced by and is in dialogue with the distinctive ideologies of its moment of production. Matthew Rowlinson's 1992 essay 'The Ideological Moment of Tennyson's "Ulysses" ' does not share this premise. Tennyson's poem has come to be seen as a poem which supports an imperial ideology and Rowlinson draws on reception theory to show us that, written in 1833, it was largely ignored by reviewers and absent from anthologies until the late nineteenth and early twentieth centuries when the poem suddenly started to appear in anthologies produced as early classroom texts. This would suggest that its entry into the canon of literature was due to it being seen as a vehicle for the propagation of imperialist ideas in a late-Victorian drive to establish the English language as a world language. If 'Ulysses' is now highly visible in the canon this is due to the establishment of English literature as an academic discipline and as a system of values which could be reproduced throughout the Empire. Its popularity, then, is due to historical developments that considerably *postdate* its writing and publication.

In the Britain of the 1830s the concepts of empire 'had yet to find verbal form'. The word imperialism is not used in relation to British policy abroad until 1868 and it is not until the second half of the nineteenth century that we see the construction of an imperial ideology. Rowlinson argues, then, that if we ask about the imperialism in 'Ulysses' we are asking about the *prehistory* or *preconditions* of a fully articulated imperialist discourse. Rowlinson then turns to a more formalist examination of the text itself, showing how it enacts an interchange of early and late, beginnings and endings, margins and centres. The appearance of the text as at once early and belated with respect to the ideology of imperialism recapitulates the structure of the text itself. Louis Althusser's essay 'Ideology and Ideological State Apparatuses' is finally used as a means to show that the 'time of textuality' of this text is not the moment of its production – 1833 – but instead the point at which 'Ulysses' and the discourse of a colonialist pedagogy intersect.

Linda Shires, like Bristow, is concerned in her essay 'Patriarchy, Dead Men and Tennyson's *Idylls of the King*' with models of masculinity. She takes issue with traditional American gender studies (exemplified by writers such as Showalter and Gilbert and Gubar) for straitjacketing the literary text, closing down its more radical meanings particularly by the overuse of the term 'patriarchy' as a

monolithic entity. For Shires and other more recent feminist critics
the works of patriarchy, like the works of ideology, are rich and
complex. The way forward, she argues, is to draw on the work of
gender critics, particularly gay theorists (Alan Sinfield, Jonathan
Dollimore, Richard Dellamora, Joseph Bristow, Christopher Craft,
D. A. Miller, Eve Sedgwick *et al.*), which has tended to gather around
the literature of the 1890s and to extend our study *backwards* to the
mid and early Victorian period.

Shires sets out to understand the oscillations of gender and models
of masculinity in the nineteenth century by an examination of the
various stages of Tennyson's *Idylls of the King* which took several
decades to reach its final version. Taking as her focal point
Tennyson's persistent fascination with the lifeless (dead or dying)
male body, Shires argues that if at the beginning of his career as a poet
Tennyson supports a myth of the paternal manly male, by the end of
his career he is less certain about the value of such a standard.
Gradually his poetry reveals that patriarchal masculinity is little more
than a role men play. Moreover, Tennyson does not restrict himself
to heterosexual models of masculinity but plays with homosocial and
asexual models. Her goal, she says, is to show how his poems
'participate in the Victorian invention of, exposure of, and death of
the figure of the patriarch' showing along the way how patriarchy
is in constant flux as an ideal.

Shires again uses a model of critical analysis influenced by Williams
and the British Marxist school of criticism in discussing the various
residual, dominant, and emergent gender ideologies at work in
Tennyson's unfolding poem and in the Victorian period itself. Sinfield
and others argue that Tennyson's poetry might be working in the
service of conservative values yet nonetheless a cultural materialist
reading will show how the text 'betrays' or reveals the cracks in the
value system it seeks to endorse. Shires's Tennyson is a more
conscious Tennyson. There is a place in Shires's reading strategy for
biographical details as she suggests that Tennyson's own family
background and his aggressive father made him suspicious of
patriarchal authority. This Tennyson comes to 'recognize' the dangers
of certain kinds of models of masculinity and a world grounded in
rigid gender difference.

For Eve Kosofsky Sedgwick, however, Tennyson's poetry was
potentially subversive to a degree that, and in a way that, 'Tennyson
himself was the last to perceive'. Sedgwick's 1985 book *Between Men:
English Literature and Male Homosocial Desire* was received as a
landmark in literary studies and has been extremely influential in
gender studies since. In her substantial introduction she argues for
a model of gender relations which is based on a careful charting of

the ways in which male relationships between men are cemented
by the traffic in women as exchangeable objects or counters of value
(the works of Luce Irigaray and Claude Levi-Strauss on the exchange
of women within kinship systems can be seen as influences here):

> concommitant changes in the structure of male 'homosocial
> desire' were tightly, often causally bound up with the other
> more visible changes; that the emerging pattern of male
> friendship, mentorship, entitlement, rivalry, and hetero- and
> homosexuality was in an intimate and shifting relation to class;
> and that no element of that pattern can be understood outside
> of its relation to women and the gender system as a whole.[21]

Her aim, she argues, is 'to explore the ways in which the shapes of
sexuality, and what *counts* as sexuality, both depend upon and affect
historical power relationships'.[22]

In her chapter on Tennyson's *The Princess*, entitled 'Tennyson's
Princess: One Bride for Seven Brothers', Sedgwick argues that,
although Tennyson may be blind to the potentially subversive nature
of his narratives, it is in his *formal* struggles with structural and
stylistic problems that we are able to see the 'enabling incoherences
of his society's account of itself'. Hence the struggle in *The Princess*
between inside frame (the romance story told by the seven narrators)
and outside frame (the circumstances and place in which the story
is told in the present). The substance of the poem concerns the
enforcement of women's expulsion within the framework of male
homosocial exchange. The Prince's position in the narrative, though
favourably presented against the misogynistic views of the Prince's
father, nonetheless serves to ratify the male traffic in women. By
endorsing a medieval chivalric code by which women are exchanged
between men as part of a familial and social structure, it obscures the
contemporary situation of its middle-class audience. It legitimates,
dehistoricizes, and glamorizes the bourgeois family by tracing its
roots back to aristocratic origins in feudal society. Why and how
does Tennyson endorse such contemporary familial and social
arrangements and to what ends?

Sedgwick traces the formal tensions between the poem's inner and
outer frames showing how they dramatize issues of class and
gender. Seven male narrators share the narrator position as they joke
about using their sisters as gifts between them, as they share the
role of the Prince, thereby ensuring that women, words and a
collective identification with an aristocratic Prince become the bonds
that hold the men together. The poem sets out to embody and hold

together the contradictions of male homosocial and heterosexual desire in a given society.

The significance of the final essay in this collection, Jeff Nunokawa's 1991 essay '*In Memoriam* and the Extinction of the Homosexual', is its succinct and iconoclastic confrontation with the most vexed issue of Tennyson scholarship: the issue of Tennyson's sexuality as it is expressed and constructed in the most tricky of all Tennyson's poems, *In Memoriam*. Some critics have sidestepped this issue by arguing that expressions of same-sex love must be situated historically. In other words that Tennyson's expressions of love to Hallam in this poem do not necessarily prove the existence of 'perversion' (Gordon Haight's term). But, as Ricks has argued, even the Victorians themselves found this poem disturbing.[23]

Nunokawa argues against Christopher Craft's Foucauldian reading[24] that as the heterosexual is defined against the homosexual, then the heterosexual absorbs the homosexual thereafter always containing it within the structure of heterosexuality. Instead, Nunokawa argues that *In Memoriam* proposes a *developmental* model of male sexuality whereby homoeroticism is presented as an early phase of the formation of the heterosexual husband and father. The establishment of homosexuality as a phase to be grown out of in the individual psychosexual and evolutionary movement towards heterosexual patriarchy is endemic in Victorian and post-Victorian ideology, sited in the English public school.

This evolutionary and hierarchical model is used in the poem to figure the differences between Hallam and Tennyson in social and economic terms as well as the differences between them sexually (Hallam has ascended to the higher species of heterosexuality). It thus promotes a conception of *potential* equality between terms situated at different stages of development, for although they are at different stages those behind will inevitably reach equality with those in front. When, Nunokawa suggests, Tennyson alludes to Shakespearean desire it would be clearly understood by the Victorians as an allusion to Hellenism. But Tennyson, in associating his desire for Hallam with Shakespearean homoeroticism, revises Shakespearean homoeroticism in order to make it fit the Victorian (evolutionary) model. For Shakespeare in Sonnet 116 devotion is marriage; for Tennyson devotion is distinctly *not* marriage because, in the Victorian evolutionary model, it *precedes* marriage which is a higher stage. In revising Sonnet 116 *In Memoriam* converts Shakespeare's claim for the deathlessness of his desire into an announcement of its mortality.

In a more complex section of his argument Nunokawa shows how Shakespeare had connected the permanence of his love with the permanence of his text. Tennyson alludes to Shakespeare's lines: 'If this be error and upon me proved / I never writ nor no man ever loved'. When he recasts the Shakespearean love as temporary rather than permanent (by adjusting it to the Victorian model) he thereby cancels the condition upon which Shakespeare's text depends. Thus the homoerotic disappears within the trajectory of male desire. Its cancellation ensures that matured male love leaves behind no trace. Nunokawa finishes his essay with a brilliant identification of *contemporary cultural rewriting* of Tennyson's model of the cancelled or extinguished homosexual:

> The funeral that Tennyson hosts for his own puerile homoerotic desire in *In Memoriam* has its afterlife in the glamorous rumour of preordained doom that bathes the image of live-fast-die-young gay boys such as Dorian Grey, Montgomery Clift, James Dean, Joe Orton . . . and helps explain why the dominant media inaccurately identifies AIDS with, even *as*, the early death of gay men.

Herbert Tucker, in his introduction to the most recent (and fine) collection of critical essays published in 1992,[25] assesses the state of contemporary critical scholarship on Tennyson and notes, as I have done, the prevalence of cultural studies in the last decade. He applauds the fact that it is revitalizing the study of Tennyson and has resituated that study in important historical and political contexts, but he also worries that contemporary criticism of this kind no longer attends to textual detail in the way that is necessary in fully engaging with Tennyson: 'The synoptic ambition of cultural studies risks losing touch, in other words, with the particularity of given poems, which tends to escape notice in proportion to the breadth of compass such studies attempt'.[26] There are, however, notable exceptions where such cultural studies adopt a deconstructive focus on language and textuality. He suggests that the way forward for Tennyson criticism is a kind of 'cultural neoformalism' in which formalist close reading strategies are combined with the wider cultural and political agendas of cultural studies, both locally alert and historically circumspect. My sense in surveying the plethora of Tennyson criticism written since Tucker's collection is that such a change is taking place.

If Tennyson's poetry is like shot-silk with many glancing colours, perhaps the essays in this collection have altered our perception of the texture of that material. Melville once said of his monumental book *Moby Dick*, another textual dinosaur: 'It is not a piece of fine feminine Spitalfields silk – but it is of the horrible texture of a fabric that should be woven of ships's cables and hausers. A Polar wind blows through it, & birds of prey hover over it'.[27] As a writer consistently and ironically conscious of the precariousness of gender identity, Melville cannot resist, of course, the allusion to the *manliness* of his text in his opposition of silk and a fabric made up of rough ship's cables. But if it is possible first to cancel the implied gendered emphasis, I would like to suggest that Tennyson's silky surfaces have, under the critical microscopes of these critics, something of the horrible, ropey, knotty texture of Melville's.

Roland Barthes in 1968 (another year of revolutions) wrote an essay which announced the death of the author and the birth of the reader. No longer was the biography of the author to be the key which would unlock all texts as if the author were some kind of God, but instead the text was to be conceived of as 'a multidimensional space in which a variety of writings, none of them original, blend and clash. The text is a tissue of quotations drawn from the innumerable centres of culture.' In the 'multiplicity of writing', Barthes argues, 'everything is to be *disentangled*, nothing *deciphered*; the structure can be followed, "run" (like the thread of a stocking) at every point and every level, but there is nothing beneath' . . . For Barthes this refusal of final central meanings is a revolutionary activity, for in the end it is also 'a refusal of God and his hypostases – reason, science, law'.[28]

The critics of this collection have ranged over the fabric of Tennyson's poetry following those threads which run across its multitudinous and multidimensional spaces. Disentangling these texts using late twentieth-century critical reading strategies is to recognize the complex ways by which they are also entangled in the dominant ideologies of their time, is to realize that there are no clean edges to such pieces of fabric, but that they are shot through with historically and politically specific discourses and inseparable too from the critical essays through which we see them:

> From his mighty bulk the whale affords a most congenial theme whereon to enlarge, amplify, and generally expatiate . . . only think of the gigantic involutions of his intestines, where they lie in him like great cables and hausers coiled away in the subterranean orlop-deck of a line-of-battle-ship.[29]

Notes

1. Virginia Woolf, *Orlando* (Harmondsworth: Penguin Books, 1963), p. 162.
2. See Carol Christ, *Victorian and Modern Poetics* (Chicago and London: Chicago University Press, 1984).

3. Ibid.
4. ALAN SINFIELD, *Alfred Tennyson*, Rereading Literature Series (Oxford: Basil Blackwell, 1986), pp. 3–4.
5. STANLEY FISH, 'Interpreting the *Variorum*', in *Modern Criticism and Theory: A Reader*, ed. David Lodge (London and New York: Longman, 1988), pp. 325–9.
6. GERHARD JOSEPH, Introduction to the Centenary Edition of *Victorian Poetry*, 30, 3–4 (Autumn 1992), p. 193.
7. Alfred Tennyson to Boyd Carpenter in CHRISTOPHER RICKS, *Tennyson* (Basingstoke: Macmillan, 1989), p. 127.
8. HALLAM TENNYSON, *Alfred Lord Tennyson: A Memoir by His Son* (London: Macmillan, 1897), I, p. 524.
9. ALAN SINFIELD, *Faultlines: Cultural Materialism and the Politics of Dissident Reading* (Oxford: Clarendon Press, 1992), p. 48.
10. For an outline of this programme and an analysis of its genesis see SINFIELD, *Faultlines*.
11. ALAN SINFIELD and JONATHAN DOLLIMORE (eds), Foreword to *Political Shakespeare* (Manchester: Manchester University Press, 1985).
12. SINFIELD, *Faultlines*, p. 22.
13. ISOBEL ARMSTRONG, *Victorian Poetry: Poetry, Poetics and Politics* (London and New York: Routledge, 1993), p. 9.
14. Ibid., p. 21.
15. TERRY EAGLETON, *The Rape of Clarissa* (Oxford: Blackwell, 1982), p. 2.
16. SINFIELD, *Alfred Tennyson*, p. 136.
17. Ibid., p. 153.
18. ALFRED AUSTIN, 'The Poetry of the Period', 1870, in *The Victorian Poet: Poetics and Persona* (London: Croom Helm, 1987), pp. 117–26.
19. ELAINE JORDAN, *Alfred Tennyson* (Cambridge: Cambridge University Press, 1988), p. 12.
20. KATE MILLETT, *Sexual Politics* (London: Virago, 1977), pp. 76–7.
21. EVE KOSOFSKY SEDGWICK, *Between Men: English Literature and Male Homosocial Desire* (New York: Columbia University Press, 1985), p. 1.
22. Ibid., p. 2.
23 RICKS, *Tennyson*, p. 219.
24. CHRISTOPHER CRAFT, ' "Descend and Touch and Enter": Tennyson's Strange Manner of Address', *Genders*, 1 (1988), pp. 83–101.
25. HERBERT F. TUCKER, Introduction in *Critical Essays on Alfred Lord Tennyson*, ed. Herbert F. Tucker (New York: G. K. Hall and Co., 1993).
26. Ibid., p. 7.
27. HERMAN MELVILLE in a letter of 1851 quoted by Harold Beaver in 'On the Composition of *Moby-Dick*' introduction to *Moby Dick*, ed. Harold Beaver (Harmondsworth: Penguin Books, 1986), p. 18.
28. ROLAND BARTHES, 'The Death of the Author', in *Modern Criticism and Theory: A Reader*, ed. David Lodge (London and New York: Longman, 1988), pp. 170–1.
29. MELVILLE, *Moby Dick*, p. 566.

1 Victorian Weaving: The Alienation of Work into Text in 'The Lady of Shalott'*

GERHARD JOSEPH

Gerhard Joseph looks at Tennyson's 'The Lady of Shalott' as *the* Victorian poem which has 'lent itself most readily to the insinuation of theory into American commentary on Victorian poetry'. Pre- and post-New Critical readings showed a shift, he argues, from ontological to aesthetic emphases. Subsequent post-structuralist readings (by Herbert Tucker, Timothy Pelaton, Harold Bloom and Geoffrey Hartman) have read the poem as an allegory describing the drift of the signifier, as an expression of a desire for 'reality-mastery', as an example of the 'parabolic drift' of the reading process itself. Working in dialogue with a Marxist reading of the poem by Isobel Armstrong (a later version of which is included in this collection) and with the work of Marxist intellectuals such as Lukacs and Adorno, Joseph offers his own reading: that the poem is about the estrangement of literary labour. Contemporary post-structuralist theory accepts the notion that there is no authorial presence behind the drift of signifiers. For Joseph, Tennyson's Lady, cut off from her work, depersonalized into a drifting signature, is a parable of the processes of critical evolution from New Criticism to post-structuralism.

> One must find the Weaver, the proto-worker of space, the prosopopeia of topology and nodes, the Weaver who works locally to join two worlds that are separated according to the autochoton's myth by a sudden stoppage, the metastrophic caesura massing deaths and shipwrecks: the catastrophe . . .
>
> (Serres, 52)

While our collective critical gaze must of necessity limit itself to the fixed canon of a dead poet's work, it constantly seeks out fresh views, rescuing this poem from a stale response, relegating that one to the category of the thoroughly investigated – until a shift of intellectual fashion generates a new hierarchy of emphasis. Thus, as

---

*Reprinted from *Victorian Newsletter* 71 (1987), pp. 7–10.

Jerome Buckley has remarked in a survey of Tennyson criticism, 'among Tennyson's shorter poems, "Ulysses" has received the most extensive reinterpretation in our time' (3). Buckley is surely right about 'our time' in the widest sense, but I would suggest that the short Tennyson work that has recently come in for the most interesting – and fashionable – re-valuation is 'The Lady of Shalott'. Indeed, if one is looking for a single manageable example, it may well be the *Victorian* poem that has most readily lent itself to the insinuation of theory – especially Derridean and Lacanian theory – into American commentary upon Victorian poetry. And I do stress 'American', for the impact I wish to describe is thus limited. Perhaps because of the anti-structuralist militancy in England of so authoritative a Tennysonian as Christopher Ricks, as well as a variety of larger reasons, theory, especially French theory, has on the whole been met with greater reserve in English Tennyson studies than in the United States.

While it was from the first one of Tennyson's most popular poems, 'The Lady of Shalott' generated a good deal of controversy after its initial publication and became a touchstone for an estimate of the youthful poet's qualities. J. W. Croker's notorious review of the 1832 *Poems* in the *Quarterly Review* lavished a heavy-handed irony upon what Croker felt to be a vaporousness of mood for the poem in general and of motivation for the Lady's behaviour in particular (81–96). Conversely, Edgar Allen Poe saw the poem's 'suggestive indefiniteness of meaning, with a view of bringing about a definiteness of vague and therefore spiritual *effect*' as the very source of the poem's – and Tennyson's – greatness (14:28). Subsequent nineteenth-century readers tended to divide themselves into ones who prized its amorphousness ('It was never intended to have any special meaning', averred Stopford Brooke in 1894 [127]) and those who tried to spell out apparent allegorical implications.

Tennyson's own desires in the matter were constantly being canvassed with respect to this poem, among others, and he was clearly of two minds in responding. In general and to the extent that he was willing to speak at all, he would insist upon a hermeneutic openness, upon what he called the 'parabolic drift' of narratives like 'The Lady of Shalott' that only seemed to develop one-to-one allegorical correspondences. 'I hate to be tied down to say "*This* means *that*" because the thought within the image is more than any one interpretation', he told Boyd Carpenter. 'Poetry is like shot-silk with many glancing colours. Every reader must find his own interpretation according to his ability, and according to his sympathy with the poet' (qtd in Tennyson 2:127). Norman Holland or the early Stanley Fish couldn't have been more insistent upon the reader's interpretive prerogatives. But in other moods Tennyson derogated even minimal indeterminacy in favour of univocal meanings spelled out by the author. As to the Lady's motivation, he told Canon Ainger, 'The new-born love for something, for some one in the wide world from which she has been excluded, takes her out of the region of shadows into that of realities'. When early twentieth-century readers were not content with impressionistic evocations of the poem's fairy-tale atmospherics, its 'pure magic', they used that opposition recorded in Hallam Tennyson's *Memoirs* (1:117) of his father as a cue for ontological allegory of either a Platonic or Aristotelian persuasion – at least up to the time of the New Criticism.

While the rehabilitation of Tennyson's reputation has gone on apace during the past forty years, he did not benefit directly from the New Criticism's championing of a complexity that demanded close explication. A chapter in Cleanth Brooks's *The Well Wrought Urn* singles out 'Tears, Idle Tears' as the exception to the rule that Tennyson's work does not display the subtleties of paradox and ambiguity (136–44), while F. R. Leavis excluded Tennyson from *Revaluation* on the ground that he offered little opportunity for local analysis (5). To the extent that Tennyson did draw positive attention, it was in the light of the New Criticism's tendency to see most poetry as more or less obliquely about aesthetics, about the poet's self-referential forging of well-wrought urns. Within that emphasis, the ontological oppositions of 'The Lady of Shalott' generated by Tennyson's cue in the *Memoir* gave way to aesthetic ones for critics who, armed with Wimsatt-Beardsley strictures against the intentional fallacy, trusted Tennyson's tale rather than his *post-hoc* explanations. The poem thus came during the 1950s to be read as a parable concerning the problematics of mimesis in Tennyson's early art, presumably as a reflection of his ambivalence about the artist's removal from the world. The earliest of such readings, which appeared in G. Robert Stange's unpublished Harvard dissertation of 1949, eventually found its way into Walter Houghton and Stange's highly successful anthology of 1956, *Victorian Poetry and Poetics*. 'The poem suggested', their notes to 'The Lady of Shalott' read, 'that the artist must remain in aloof detachment, observing life only in the mirror of the imagination, not mixing in it directly. Once the artist attempts to lead the life of ordinary men his poetic gift, it would seem, dies' (16).

If there was indeed such a shift from what I have called ontological to aesthetic emphases, pre- and post-New Critical readings nevertheless tended to share an uncomplicated view of mimesis. That is, in the poem's parable the Lady, whether an artist figure or not, is trapped within a clear-cut dualism, wherein the mind confronts not

26

the 'real' world but rather its imitation – a 'shadow' or 'mirror' of
the real. What neither the ontological nor the aesthetic reading
questions is that a primary 'substance' exists as a base of the
secondary 'shadow', a 'reality' of which the Lady's tapestry is a copy
via the reflective mediation of the mirror.

But of course the essential thrust of current representation theory
is to undermine such a Metaphysics of Presence, to fragment the
High Mimetic mode implicit in the opposition of 'shadow' or 'mirror'
and 'substance'. What we have today instead is the infinite regress
of post-structuralist thought where we are invited to follow, in Jacques
Derrida's words, 'a book in the book, an origin in the origin, a center
in the center' (296) beyond the inmost bound of human thought. It
thus seems particularly timely that recent approaches to 'The Lady of
Shalott' have made a good deal of a perspectivist detail which, from
what I can tell, was never even noticed by our interpretive
community – much less stressed – before a two-page note by David
Martin in a 1973 issue of *Victorian Poetry* called attention to it:
namely, that Lancelot's image flashes into the Lady's crystal mirror
'From the bank and from the river' (255–56). That is, in her reaction
to the sight of Lancelot the Lady has to contend not only with a
mirror image but also with a reflection of that same river's reflection
of him, not only with a second but also with a third-order reflection –
what Herbert Tucker in an unpublished study of Tennyson has
playfully called 'at least a three bank cushion shot'. In the inner
cosmic play of frames implied by her optical situation, the Lady is
caught within a perceptual maze, a Derridean *mise en abyme*, in which
the putative original image of Lancelot bounces endlessly and
without grounding between river and glass, 'multiplying variety in a
wilderness of mirrors' ('Gerontion'), teasing the Lady (or at any rate
some recent commentators upon her plight) out of thought.

'The Lady of Shalott' has thus taken on a paradigmatic force today
that extends well beyond the poem's exemplification of the early
Tennyson's aesthetics. This is especially the case for such talented
younger Yale-trained Tennysonians as Tucker and Timothy Peltason
– not to mention their teachers Harold Bloom and Geoffrey Hartman:
for giving the poem a Lacanian twist, Hartman has read the Lady's
passion for direct, unmediated contact with the world, her
unwillingness to rest content with ungrounded representation, as
the best poetic expression of a Western 'desire for reality-mastery
as aggressive and fatal as Freud's death instinct':

> 'I am half sick of shadows,' says the Lady of Shalott, and turns
> from her mirror to the reality of advent. She did not know that by
> her avertedness, by staying within representation, she had

postponed death. The most art can do, as a mirror of language, is to burn through, in its cold way, the desire for self-definition, fullness of grace, presence; simply to expose the desire to own one's name, to inhabit it numinously in the form of 'proper' noun, words, or the signatory act each poem aspires to be. (8)[1]

Thus, when the knights and burghers of Camelot gather around the barge which has floated her body down to Camelot, they can know her only as a signatory act, the words 'The Lady of Shalott' by which she inscribes herself upon the prow of her barge. The Lady thus becomes in death what she was, unbeknownst to herself in life: a poetic text in microcosm, a 'floating signifier' in Hartman's inspired punning application of Lévi-Strauss. Tennyson's poem thus serves Hartman precisely as 'The Purloined Letter' did Lacan in his now famous seminar on Poe's story – as an allegory describing the signifier's drift through the abyss, isolated from the signified, its audience, and the intention of its sender. For as Tennyson's poem has drifted free (certainly in such a reading as the present one) of his stated 'intention' in the *Memoir*, so the Lady's proper name has in its Lacanian strangeness drifted free of hers – and is therefore a parable of the 'parabolic drift' itself, what Paul de Man called an 'allegory of reading'.

A certain amount of the above has been said before – indeed, some of it by myself on another occasion (403–12) – but the radical depersonalization of the sign (implicit in Heidegger's influential remark that we do not speak the language but it speaks itself through us) brings me to a different theoretical turn, in this case a Marxist one. Isobel Armstrong has examined the ideology of 'The Lady of Shalott' in the context of two forms of exploitation in the 1830s: the displacement of rural workers and the enforced passivity of women. She thus sees why the peasant reapers of the poem's opening along with the Lady are set against the aristocracy and the entrepreneurial powers, the 'knights and burghers' of Camelot, at the poem's close. The dominant mythology which forces the agricultural labourer to become his own grim reaper, the cotton worker of the 1830s to weave his own destruction (since their very success assures that they are being displaced by machines that will do their good work faster), converges with the ancient myth of the woman as weaver. For Armstrong the beauty of the poem is thus 'the inconspicuous ease with which it defamiliarizes [the reapers] and cotton weavers and [their] exploitation by making the lady a proxy who carries the meaning of estranged labor'.[2]

While such a reading strikes me as most suggestive, my own emphasis concerns what the poem says about the estrangement of *literary* labour. It is certainly true that the interpretations generated by the New Criticism that I referred to earlier saw the work as a detachable artifact free from biographical encumbrance. But while such readings tended to deny a privileged relevancy to an author's apparent intention except from internal evidence within the poem, New Critics did not go so far as to deny the existence of an author altogether. More recent readers, however, who emphasize 'The Lady of Shalott' status as 'text', a 'sign system', or a 'signatory act', accept the notion popularized by Roland Barthes, Foucault, and others that we can get at nothing behind the semiotic system itself (certainly not a full-blown Tennysonian consciousness), nothing behind the drift of signifiers. The Lady (and by extension the poet 'behind' her), that is, do not make a 'work' that expresses the personality of a worker who produced it with reference to a palpable world. Rather, both Lady and poet are themselves the media through which, in the current parlance, a warp and woof weaving of a 'text' happens – and the serendipitous fact that the word 'text' comes from the Latin 'texere', 'to weave', has been a conceptual/etymological pun which the likes of Barthes, Derrida, Michel Serre, and especially J. Hillis Miller, the master of our weaving guild for the year, have pursued down some fanciful avenues.

Such a theoretical movement from the poem as a 'work', the output of a poet as craftsman, to an authorless 'text' resulting from the impersonal play of signifiers along the intersection of *langue* and *parole*, exemplifies an increasing alienation or reification, in the Marxist sense of those linked concepts. The classical definition of reification appears in 'Reification and the Consciousness of the Proletariat' (87–92), a long, densely argued, and difficult essay in Georg Lukács's *History and Class Conciousness*, in which Lukács applies to the realm of idealist German philosophy the techniques Marx used to analyse class economics in *Capital* (see Marx: 645). But we need not get bogged down in Lukács, Hegelian obscurities nor even take account of the romantic base of Marxist reification theory to extract from his work a brief sense of the term that will be useful for the present occasion. As a result of the commodification of labour in the modern world, a piece of work becomes 'cursed' into a 'mysterious thing', a mystification that is conveyed in a terminology of the numinous that is otherwise rigorously abstract and analytical. A worker's labour thus becomes something objective and independent of him, something that takes on a life of its own and whose function in his life he cannot fathom. But not only does he face an alien world of 'cursed', reified objects, his own activity becomes a commodity which, subject to non-human detachment from the natural laws of society, must go its own way independent of his will.

Reification for Marx and Lukács thus has a double aspect – an alienated world of objects *and* an alienated consciousness divorced from that world which it can only contemplate across a puzzling abyss. In the posture of the scientist for whom, in the words of Marx's first thesis on Feuerbach, 'reality, what we apprehend through our senses, is understood only in the form of the object of contemplation, but not as sensuous human activity', reification takes on a material form. The idealist's opposition to such empiricism, however, does not overcome reification but only reveals more pointedly what has been repressed by it – 'sensuous human activity'. Thus, both the neutral scientific observer and the transcendent philosophic seer of nineteenth-century thought occupy the same detached, contemplative stance, unable to enter into life. They are unable to 'see' and 'be' at the same time, as Carolyn Porter, following Emerson, has put it in her book on the plight of her participant-observer in American literature, to which my own formulation is crucially indebted (esp Chapter 2, 'Reification and American Literature'). Further, the more intense the struggle of the modern mind to overcome the contemplative condition, the tighter the hold it has upon the bureaucrat, technologist, and scientist. And, I would add, the literary critic.

For, applying Lukács's theory to the contemporary critic as worker, I would suggest that the New Critical insistence upon the 'work' as a discrete object cut off from authorly intention, and subject to a detached critical analysis modelled upon scientific 'objectivity', is already an advanced stage of alienated consciousness. But the more recent theoretical posture whereby all we have is a 'text' whose producer is a fiction of the theoretically naive and whose reference to anything besides other texts is highly questionable – such a cognitive endgame carries reification to a further extreme, to the 'prison-house of language' within which many of us have now resigned ourselves to live. From my own cell within that dwelling, I would thus read 'The Lady of Shalott', despite its feudal and fairy-tale trappings, as a figure of that change, a parable of recent literary history charting the movement from a New Critical analysis of authored 'works' to a post-structuralist reading of unauthored 'texts'. For within her poem the Lady, a proto-worker of space transforming aesthetic categories, has moved from weaving a work to becoming a text. That the tapestry she weaves is quite specifically a 'work' is accentuated by a detail that is easy to miss, the craft function of her mirror: since tapestry is woven from the reverse side, the Lady needs a mirror to see the design that she weaves. But that craft function is woven inextricably into its epistemological one: if the Lady needs the mirror to fashion her own design, the stimulus from the outside, a *mis en abyme* flash of textuality that intensifies the mirror properties, makes it difficult for her to see her own production aright. Indeed, that fracturing of image makes it impossible for her to work at all. As a result of that difficulty, the work, of which she is the indubitable creator, becomes cursed – as she does herself – into a disembodied text, the reified signifier of her name on the boat which Hartman and others have stressed and that is open to the misprisonings of knights and burghers in and out of Camelot, in and out of the poem. For it is the depersonalization of herself into a drifting signature, into her 'proper' name in the Derridean sense, that makes for the poem's most relevant 'parabolic drift' at this theoretical moment.

I can, in conclusion, imagine a strong counter-argument – a Barthesian or Derridean reading which would see the movement from the controlled pleasure generated by the work to the free *jouissance* generated by the text[3] as the *release* from New Critical reification. But, doubling back, that possibility – and the cognitive indeterminacy it privileges – strikes me as merely the latest triumph of the reified. For as Adorno has cheerfully defined our cultural dilemma,

> The more total society becomes, the greater the reification of the mind and the more paradoxical its effort to escape reification on its own. Even the more extreme consciousness of doom threatens to degenerate into idle chatter. Cultural criticism finds itself faced with the final stage of the dialectic of culture and barbarism. To write poetry after Auschwitz is barbaric. And this corrodes even the knowledge of why it has become impossible to write poetry today. Absolute reification, which presupposed intellectual progress as one of its elements, is now preparing to absorb the mind entirely . . . (19–34)

Notes

1. See also PELTASON for a comparable treatment of the poem as a parable of advent, and COLLEY for an additional Lacanian reading.
2. I would like to thank ISOBEL ARMSTRONG for allowing me access to and permission to quote from her manuscript.
3. BARTHES has celebrated the movement from 'work' to 'text'. For a careful discussion of the work's survival, see GOODMAN and ELGIN.

Works cited

ADORNO, THEODORE, 'Cultural Criticism and Society', *Prisms*, Cambridge: Harvard UP, 1981.

ARMSTRONG, ISOBEL, ' "The Lady of Shalott". Victorian Mythography and the Politics of Narcisism', in *The Sun is God*, ed. Barrie Bullen, Oxford: Oxford UP, 1988.

BARTHES, ROLAND, 'From Work to Text', in *Textual Strategies: Perspectives in Post-Structuralist Criticism*, ed. Josué V. Harari, Ithaca: Cornell UP, 1979.

BROOKE, STOPFORD, *Tennyson: His Art and Relation to Modern Life*, London, Isbister, 1894.

BROOKS, CLEANTH, 'The Motivation of Tennyson's Weeper', *The Well Wrought Urn*, New York: Reynal, 1947.

BUCKLEY, JEROME, 'The Persistence of Tennyson', in *The Victorian Experience: The Poets*, ed. Richard Levine, Athens: Ohio UP, 1982.

COLLEY, ANN C., 'The Quest for the "Nameless" in Tennyson's "The Lady of Shalott" ', *Victorian Poetry* 23 (1985): 369–78.

CROKER, J. W., Unsigned Review, *Quarterly Review*, 49 (April 1833): 81–96. In John D. Jump, *Tennyson: The Critical Heritage*, London: Routledge & Kegan Paul, 1967: 66–83.

DERRIDA, JAQUES, 'Ellipsis', *Writing and Difference*, trans. Alan Bass, Chicago: U of Chicago P, 1978.

GOODMAN, NELSON and CATHERINE Z. ELGIN, 'Interpretation and Identity: Can the Work Survive the World?', *Critical Inquiry* 12 (1986): 564–75.

HARTMAN, GEOFFREY, 'Psychoanalysis: The French Connection', *Psychoanalysis and the Question of Text*, ed. Geoffrey Hartman, Baltimore: Johns Hopkins UP, 1978. Rpt. *Saving the Text: Literature/Derrida/Philosophy*, Baltimore: Johns Hopkins UP, 1981.

HOUGHTON, WALTER and G. ROBERT STANGE, *Victorian Poetry and Poetics*, Cambridge: Riverside Press, 1956.

JOSEPH, GERHARD, 'The Echo and the Mirror *en abyme* in Victorian Poetry', *Victorian Poetry* 23 (1985): 403–12.

LEAVIS, F. R., *Revaluation*, London: Chatto & Windus, 1959.

LUKÁCS, GEORG, 'Reification and the Consciousness of the Proletariat', *History and Class Consciousness*, trans. Rodney Livingston, Cambridge MA: MIT Press, 1971: 87–92.

MARTIN, DAVID, 'Romantic Perspectives in Tennyson's "The Lady of Shalott" ', *Victorian Poetry* 11 (1973): 255–6.

MARX, KARL and FREDRICH ENGELS, *The German Ideology*, trans. Salo Ryanaskaya, London: Lawrence & Wishart, 1965.

PELTASON, TIMOTHY, 'Tennyson's Fables of Emergence', *Bucknell Review* 29 (1985): 143–70.

POE, EDGAR ALLEN, *The Complete Works of Edgar Allen Poe*, ed. James H. Harrison, 17 vols, 1902, New York: AMS Press, 1965.

PORTER, CAROLYN, *Seeing and Being: The Plight of the Participant Observer in Emerson, Adams, James, and Faulkner*, Middletown, CT: Wesleyan UP, 1981.

SERRES, MICHEL, *Hermes: Literature, Science, and Philosophy*, ed. Josué V. Harari and David F. Bell, Baltimore: John Hopkins UP, 1982.

TENNYSON, HALLAM, *Alfred Lord Tennyson: A Memoir*, 2 vols, London: Macmillan, 1897.

2 Tennyson and the Cultural Politics of Prophesy*

ALAN SINFIELD

For Sinfield Tennyson 'is not a given to be discovered, but a concept, or bundle of concepts, that we have produced' (see below).
His controversial and influential book *Alfred Tennyson*, commissioned in 1986 for the Rereading Literature series edited by
Terry Eagleton, has altered the course of Tennyson studies. It is an
example of what would come to be called Cultural Materialism,
influenced by the work of the British Marxist, Raymond Williams,
which seeks to understand texts as 'cultural interventions'. Stories
seek to persuade us of their versions of the world, seek to make
the world plausible. The cultural materialist's task is to show how
ideology works through texts to present power relations as harmonious and coherent. In the essay reprinted here of 1990 Sinfield
shows how Tennyson offers us *alternative* criteria of plausibility
through the prophetic figures of his poetry who are always
unheeded, marginalized figures. This, Sinfield argues, does not
move us beyond the scope of customary discourse, but instead
corresponds to the binary formations of Western capitalism in
which poetry is constructed as capitalism's marginalized 'other'.
Finally Sinfield shows, through an attack on the sage of Tennyson
studies, Christopher Ricks, how this prominent Tennysonian motif
of prophetic sagacity still permeates literary studies generally.

The plausibility of prophecy

It is generally agreed that Tennyson's subjective, lyric poetry is pre-
eminent of its kind; the quarrel, often, is about how much of his
other work engages us to the same degree. Yet even among the poems
commonly recognized as personal, it is striking how many are
involved in narrative. The dramatic monologist is characteristically
telling his or her story – Oenone, the Lotos-Eaters, Tithonus, Tiresias;

---

*Reprinted from *English Literature History* **57**, 1 (Spring 1990), pp. 175–95.

other recognizably lyric figures are presented through a narrative
structure – Mariana, the Lady of Shalott, the king in 'Morte d'Arthur';
In Memoriam and *Maud* extend the first-person, lyric mode, in effect,
to form narrative. This feature is entirely self-conscious in the writing:
it is foregrounded through framing passages setting up the story,
allusions to pre-existing stories in which the present characters
figure, and the telling of stories by Tennyson's speakers.

In a way, the link between lyric subjectivity and narrative is
obvious. Speakers explore and define their states of mind by telling
their stories; they are both formed and expressed by the experiences
they relate; it is, we may say, a poetry of experience. I don't wish to
dispute that, but to add that story tends to invoke explicit standards
of plausibility: it asks us to agree that things might indeed happen
thus and thus. Actually, all communication supposes criteria of
plausibility, including a lyric like this from *In Memoriam*:

> Now fades the last long streak of snow,
>> Now burgeons every maze of quick
>> About the flowering squares, and thick
> By ashen roots the violets blow.[1]

If we found the natural effects described here incredible (if, for
instance, they violated our sense of seasonal consistency), or, more
subtly, if we found the mood that is suggested incoherent, then the
poem would stumble for lack of plausibility. These are the customary
demands that underwrite all communication, and Tennyson's
attention to physical detail shows that he understood as much. But
in such a lyric the appeal to credibility is inconspicuous – we would
probably notice it only if it were violated. In lyric, the common-sense,
empiricist convention is that an individual says how she or he feels,
and it seems absurd or impertinent for us to deny that the poet indeed
feels as the poem says. Indeed, a certain originality, even eccentricity
of mood is expected. So plausibility seems not to arise, and criticism
has tended to concern itself with the quality of the feeling and of its
expression. Once you have a story, on the other hand – characters not
the author, and extension in time – plausibility seems more directly
at issue.

As a general principle, lyric claims to derive meaning from the
speaker's consciousness, whereas stories invite us to check meaning
against the world. The distinction is of the greatest importance. Lyric
is allowed to transform the world, to describe it through the eyes
of feeling – Tennyson is the master at this. But story reminds us that
meaning, communication, language, work only because they are
shared, that making yourself understood is interactive, a social affair.

There is no point in making up your own language, for no one else will understand you; if you persist, you will be thought mad.

That plausibility depends on the acquiescence of others is apparent when we observe how people in other cultures than our own make good sense of their world in ways that seem strange to us: their outlook is supported by their social context. As Colin Sumner remarks, 'all understandings, ideas and perceptions are obviously perfectly sensible and necessary in specific social situations'.[2] The criteria of plausibility are structured into the social order, and therefore they are political. The reason why societies normally keep on functioning normally is that most people believe that is the way things have to be. Anything else is implausible.

Browning's monologists usually have someone to convince; their purpose is to present their story so that it carries conviction, and when they fail they are presumed immoral, deranged or both. Thus those poems proclaim that credibility is interactive. However, in Tennyson's writing story often seems to repudiate its social dimension. Many of the most important stories, in Tennyson's view, are precisely those that violate customary standards of plausibility. King Arthur asks Sir Bedivere what he saw at the lake:

> 'I heard the ripple washing in the reeds,
> And the wild water lapping on the crag.'
>
> (Ricks, 2:9, 70–1)

This seems likely enough, but that is why the king knows that Sir Bedivere has not thrown Excalibur into the lake: the extraordinary has not happened. Two criteria of plausibility are in play: Sir Bedivere's common-sense notion of how the world goes, and the king's expectation that his passing will be accompanied by magical signs. Tennyson makes the latter win, for when the sword is thrown in the lake the extraordinary happens.

In a different instance, St Simeon Stylites's claims of heavenly favour for his life of self-punishment, Tennyson supplies no magical sign to endorse the prophet's vision, and readers generally conclude that the self-styled saint is deluded. This is Tennyson's most Browningesque monologue. Usually, though, Tennyson is on the side of the visionary who seems to challenge the norms of language and society in holding to her or his improbable story. And although the prophet figures are mostly not believed within the poems, they are credited by the reader. This is partly because of the magical power of their language. Oenone calls upon Ida:

> Hear me, for I will speak, and build up all
> My sorrow with my song, as yonder walls
> Rose slowly to a music slowly breathed,
> A cloud that gathered shape.
>
> (Ricks, 1:422–3, 38–41)

Oenone wants her utterance to gain substance in the world not
through conventional plausibility but through its incantatory magic
– in the same way that Troy was built by the music of Apollo. So she
tells her story of Paris and the three goddesses, improbable as it
might seem. And although she cannot know the implications of her
song, the reader recognizes her concluding words as true prophecy:

> What this may be I know not, but I know
> That, wheresoe'er I am by night and day,
> All earth and air seem only burning fire.
>
> (Ricks, 1:433, 262–4)

Readers should know that the outcome of the abduction of Helen
was the burning of Troy, so Oenone's story is confirmed for us. By
this strategy, as well as the power of the language Oenone is given
to speak, Tennyson ratifies the prophetic insight for the reader, against
the everyday, sensible assumptions of Oenone's contemporaries.
Oenone appeals to Cassandra, who was (notoriously) right but not
believed (line 259): that is the typical situation of the Tennysonian
sage.

Tennyson's prophet figures redefine the authority of story and
extend the authority of lyric. Customarily, story is ratified by its
plausibility in the world, lyric by the author's personal experience
and tentative generalizations from it. Tennyson's prophets demand
the best of both worlds: they tell stories, but in (apparent) violation
of mundane criteria of plausibility; they claim instead an interior, lyric
kind of authority, but don't limit their pretensions to the personal. It
is a distinctive and provocative poetic, one that aspires to validate
implausible utterances.

Of course, we should not necessarily take the strategy of the
disbelieved but ultimately ratified prophet at face value. The fact
that readers do acknowledge Tennyson's intuitive visionaries as
endorsed by the language and allusive framework of his poems
indicates that, actually, their visions are not – were not – finally
implausible. Tennyson and much of the subsequent poetic tradition
understand themselves as lonely, beleaguered figures committed to
spiritual values in an overwhelmingly materialist world, and we

read the poems in the light of that tradition. It underwrites the poet's thought in *In Memoriam*:

> But in my spirit will I dwell,
>   And dream my dream, and hold it true;
>   For though my lips may breathe adieu,
> I cannot think the thing farewell.
>
> (Ricks, 2:443, CXXIII, 9–12)

The poet's lips follow the customary rituals, he says, but his spirit insists on a different story. Tennyson demands an alternative criterion of plausibility, and poetry lovers have granted it. He dreamed his dream, held it true, and was not thought an isolated madman. He was made Poet Laureate, celebrated nationally and internationally, and became a best-selling author.

Tennyson's prophecy was credible after all because it fitted well with one half of a binary formation constituted in classic capitalism. Poetry, literature, the spirit, nature, personal religion, personal and family relations and the arts are imagined as repudiations of mechanical, urban, industrial and commercial organization, working counter to those features of the modern world. But, actually, the two are correlatives: the *whole framework* belongs together and each part supposes the other. Poetry and the rest are constituted within the field of, in terms supplied by, capitalism. This binary formation, which is imagined, roughly, as 'human' values versus a dehumanizing 'modern condition', seems to denote a necessary distinction, so caught are we in its world-view. But while we persist with those terms we will never rescue the 'human', because it is set up as the necessary and weaker term in the binary – it is the other of political economy that enables it to know itself, the resort of middle-class dissidents, the conscience of capitalism. The 'human' cannot triumph, because it affirms the binary through its very construction. And this is as true of recent attempts in Britain to discomfort Thatcherism by pointing to the underfunding of the arts as it was of the protest of Tennyson, the Oxford movement, the Pre-Raphaelites and the aesthetic movement.[3]

Maud is fascinating partly because it puts some customary Tennysonian motifs to the test – that is why it was unpopular. Taking Tennyson's hard-won modes of negotiating his culture's requirements of the poet and poetic language, it pushes them to a point of such *excess* that their validity begins to come into question. In particular, the lyric mode, wherein the poet's perception is allowed to incorporate the landscape, is deployed by a speaker of doubtful sanity. This undermines the distinctive authority claim of the lyric-prophetic insight. Are we to understand that the implausible vision that subordinates the physical world to personal intuition is not privileged, but akin to that of the lunatic? I've tried to argue this through elsewhere, suggesting that I may manifest Tennyson's impatience at his success with a readership he partly despised.[4] Correspondingly, there is special attention in *Maud* to the social criteria of plausibility. The speaker's weakened hold on reality and lack of social support make him unable to read other people in the usual way. He is in continual doubt about whether he is interpreting Maud correctly – 'What if' she looked kind because her brother wanted her to win support in the election, or because of 'her pitying womanhood'? 'If Maud were all that she seemed . . .' (Ricks, 2:535–7, I, 229–45, 252–6, 281). Does he correctly remember a conversation of Maud's and his father, or is it a displaced fiction?

> Is it an echo of something
>   Read with a boy's delight,
> Viziers nodding together
>   In some Arabian night?
>
> (Ricks, 2:538, I, 293–6)

Fairy tale and recollection cannot be distinguished, reality is uncheckable. He doesn't know how far to trust Maud's account of her brother, and resolves the point with a manifest shrug of the shoulders:

> Well, rough but kind; why let it be so:
> For shall not Maud have her will?
>
> (Ricks, 2:559, I, 766–7)

The speaker abandons the attempt to read the signals given out by Maud's brother, and accepts her story because he likes her. Yet he still lacks confidence in his ability to interpret Maud herself – just before the meeting in the garden he acknowledges uncertainty – 'If I read her sweet will right' (Ricks, 2:562, I, 846). In *Maud* Tennyson put his whole poetic under pressure.

Cultural production and the persuasiveness of Tiresias

It is through stories and the conditions of plausibility that we understand and live in the world. The criteria of plausibility delimit what we normally take to be possible. And they are important in relation to literature because that institution, in one aspect, is a reservoir of prestigious stories; it poses a distinctive authority claim.

As Nigel Harris points out, even the question 'What is a chair?' makes sense only within a system of meanings; otherwise a chair might be a bundle of sticks for making a fire or beating an enemy about the head.[5] Stephen Greenblatt approaches the issue by comparing two alternative attitudes to reality: on the one hand is a unitary, totalizing vision which claims an explanation for everything prior to particular experience (he instances psychoanalysis, or one version of it); on the other is the supposed uniqueness of each moment, leading to a stance of relativism, of neutrality (as for instance in existentialism). Roughly speaking, this dichotomy corresponds to that represented repeatedly by Tennyson, between a world informed by a spiritual principle, and a sceptical hedonism. But such an opposition only appears to include all the possibilities. I argue instead, in Greenblatt's phrasing, that we inhabit 'a network of lived and narrated stories, practices, strategies, representations, fantasies, negotiations, and exchanges that, along with the surviving aural, tactile, and visual traces, fashion our experiences of the past, of others, and of ourselves'.[6]

There are stories everywhere, in speech and behaviour as well as formal narrative. In the media, they are not just in the articles and programmes labelled 'fiction' and 'drama', but in those on current affairs, sports, party politics, science, religion, the arts, and those specified as education and for children. They are in the advertisements. At work, the definitions of tasks to be undertaken depend upon them, and the relations between the people involved – some face to face, some very distant. And in our intimate relations there are stories telling us who we are as individuals, who other individuals are and how we relate to them. In the expanded sense that I am now using, lyric poetry, as well as narrative, embodies story. The distinction I drew earlier, between the two, defines alternative strategies of story – with lyric, as I argued, tending to efface the social ratification of story, while narrative draws attention to it.

I have used the idea of story partly for its accessibility; a more substantial phrase is *cultural production*. Societies need to produce, materially, to continue – they need food, shelter, warmth, goods to exchange with other societies, a transport and information infrastructure to carry those processes. Also, they have to produce *culturally*. They need knowledges to keep material production going – diverse technical skills and wisdoms in agriculture, industry, science, medicine, economics, law, geography, languages, politics. And they need understanding, intuitive and explicit, of a system of social relationships through which the whole process can take place more or less evenly. The term 'cultural production' recognizes the crucial role these processes perform in the development and continuance of social systems. It draws attention to the fact that culture does not just appear out of people's minds as a good idea: it is implicated in the social order.

I would stress that stories are *lived*. They are not outside ourselves, something we hear or read about. They make sense for us – of us – because we have been and are in them. They are already proceeding when we arrive in the world, and we come to consciousness in their terms. Our language is the language that fits the stories; there is no other. As the world shapes itself around and through us, certain interpretations of experience strike us as plausible because they fit with what we have experienced already. They become common sense, we say they go without saying. Colin Sumner writes of the 'circle of social reality': 'understanding produces its own social reality at the same time as social reality produces its own understanding' (Sumner, 288). Since any given culture is organized *in terms of* certain stories, as we live in it we find that those stories *work*. Further, we try to understand unexpected events through the familiar stories. As Stuart Hall puts it, 'New, problematic or troubling events, which breach our expectancies and run counter to our "common-sense constructs", to our "taken-for-granted" knowledge of social structures, must be assigned to their discursive domains before they can be said to "make sense" '.[7]

Tennyson, I have suggested, takes another tack. He presents true wisdom as a lyric-prophetic understanding, constituted in the intuition of the visionary individual, often quite beyond the normative circle of social reality. Although he uses story, he disqualifies its implication that plausibility is a social affair. The issue arises in *In Memoriam*, in respect of the credibility of a putative vision of the deceased Arthur:

> If any vision should reveal
>   Thy likeness, I might count it vain
>   As but the canker of the brain;
> Yea, though it spake and made appeal
>
> To chance where our lots were cast
>   Together in the days behind,
>   I might but say, I hear a wind
> Of memory murmuring the past.
>
> (Ricks, 2:409, XCII, 1–8)

The experienced Tennyson reader knows that Tennyson would not in fact press such common-sense reservations; like Hamlet, he would take the ghost's word for a thousand pound. And in section XCV he accepts and tries to render plausible a ghostly experience of Hallam's spirit or the deity (Ricks, 2:411–3). As before, we may have the impression that Tennyson, in repudiating the 'sensible' explanation, is standing out against his culture. Actually, he is telling another of its prominent stories – that afforded by the western mystical tradition; and we can see this from the allusions in section XCV to Isaiah, Plato and Dante.[8] Tennyson is not moving outside the scope of customary discourse, but choosing and validating one strand against another.

Such strategic choice among discourses reminds us that some stories, some tellers, are far more powerful than others. Isaiah, Plato and Dante are invoked because their stories add authority to Tennyson's. Social and political conflict may be considered as a competition between stories: change occurs when a partly new story prevails. Most societies retain more or less their current shape not because subversives are infiltrated, penalized or neutralized, though they are, but because most people believe that things have to be more or less the way they are in the prevailing stories – that they cannot be improved upon, at least through the methods to hand. That is why one recognizes a dominant ideology: were there not such a powerful discourse, people would not acquiesce in the injustice and humiliation that they experience. The power to make your story stick is therefore very important – then you can win elections, or persuade people to buy your product, or accept conscription, or sexism, or unemployment.

We observe the power of story in *Maud*, where the speaker is unconvinced by the quaker who came 'To preach our poor little army down'; instead, he is impressed by 'The chivalrous battle-song' that Maud 'warbled alone in her joy' (Ricks, 2:542–3, I, 366–88). The quaker's story was unconvincing, but Maud's cheerful bloodthirstiness has power: we may suppose that it helps to produce the speaker's eventual commitment to warfare. Maud is influential here because the speaker is in love with her, but generally such power is not incidental, it is structured into the social order. Indeed, Maud's authority perhaps derives in part from her class position – the quaker, conversely, is despised because his 'ear is crammed with his cotton, and rings/Even in dreams to the chink of his pence' (Ricks, 2:542–3, I, 371–2).

There is an excellent illustration of the relative power of rival stories at the end of 'The Lady of Shalott'. The version published in 1832 ends with the 'Wellfed wits of Camelot' (the usual worldly people with common-sense criteria of plausibility) musing over the parchment that lies on the lady's breast – it reads:

> 'The web was woven curiously
> The charm is broken utterly,
> Draw near and fear not – this is I,
>   The Lady of Shalott.'

(Ricks, 1:395n)

Like other prophet figures, the Lady has her vision and proclaims her identity, though they are hardly appreciated. But in the 1842 version Lancelot, the powerful knight, has the last word:

> But Lancelot mused a little space;
> He said, 'She has a lovely face;
> God in his mercy lend her grace,
>   The Lady of Shalott.'

(Ricks, 1:395, 168–71)

A woman may have her own vision, the change tells us, but she will be patronized and trivialized by some stupid, important man.

The presentation of most of the prophetic figures I have discussed is effective because although their stories do not prevail in the immediate context, they are ratified for the reader through the power of language and the allusive framework in which they are set. One poem where the prophet's story is directly influential is 'Tiresias', and it demonstrates frighteningly the power of story. Tiresias tells of how his yearning 'For larger glimpses of that more than man' (Ricks, 1:624, 20) was satisfied, but at the expense of blindness and understanding beyond what people will credit. Now he has the prophetic power to 'speak the truth that no man may believe' (Ricks, 1:625, 49). But consider what 'truth':

> I spake of famine, plague,
> Shrine-shattering earthquake, fire, flood, thunderbolt,
> And angers of the Gods for evil done
> And expiation lacked . . .

(Ricks, 1:626, 59–62)

To one reader at least, myself, Tiresias's 'truth' seems most unsatisfactory – superstitious, reactionary, and dangerous. His fellow-citizens did well to find him implausible (they 'heard/And heard not': lines 58–9). The disasters he speaks of result, in my view, from natural causes or the injustice and inefficiency of the social order. The demand for 'expiation' suggests the scapegoating and retributive sacrificing of individuals or groups. It is an ominous message – calling to mind, now, the fulminations of right-wing clerics and the gutter press on AIDS. One might hope that Tennyson wanted readers to distrust this prophet, but Tiresias's mythic credentials and the way he invokes the standard Tennysonian social evil – the people (Ricks, 1:626, 63–75) – suggests that he is meant as a figure of genuine wisdom.

We are not told initially to whom Tiresias is speaking. When the young hearer is named Menœceus, the classically-informed realize that there is a scapegoat present. Menœceus is to be the sacrifice, and the purpose of the story is to persuade him to accept this. Tiresias explains that the great God Arês demands the death of one of the descendants of Cadmus by his own hand, in order to avert the destruction of the city in war. This notion surely fulfils the requirement of prophetic discourse – that it should be implausible to ordinary understanding. And instead of trying to reconcile the hostile parties (that would be too sensible), Tiresias persuades Menœceus to kill himself. Furthermore, so taken is he with the coercive power of stories, that the main inducement Tiresias offers Menœceus is the authority that his name will exercise after his death:

> No sound is breathed so potent to coerce,
> And to conciliate, as their names who dare
> For that sweet mother land which gave them birth
> Nobly to do, nobly to die. Their names,
> Graven on memorial columns, are a song
> Heard in the future; few, but more than wall
> And rampart, their examples reach a hand
> Far through all years, and everywhere they meet
> And kindle generous purpose, and the strength
> To mould it into action pure as theirs.
>
> (Ricks, 1:627–8, 116–25)

Not only is Menœceus to die, his name is to constitute a story so powerful that it will cause others to die in the future. In this, it will be helped by the surviving establishment, who do not go to war or sacrifice themselves, but arrange for the setting up and engraving of 'memorial columns' to encourage the others.

The prophet, meanwhile, looks forward to his own death and rest among the gods, for there his stories will be generally appreciated:

                              – the wise man's word,
        Here trampled by the populace underfoot,
        There crowned with worship.

(Ricks, 1:629,165–7)

Tiresias is able to die happy, because in this one culminating instance
he was believed. We are left to ponder the power of story, and the
desirability of such wisdom gaining plausibility.

Where has all the magic gone?

Literature is part of the process of storymaking, of cultural
production. Its writers make fictions that embody notions about the
world, and because it is a prestigious discourse, in certain quarters
at least, those stories are influential. That is why it is important, not
just to admire the structure and verbal virtuosity of 'Tiresias', not just
to be charmed by its 'magic'. Otherwise we subscribe to what Gerald
Graff calls the 'limited liability' model of literary meaning, whereby
the author is absolved from responsibility for his or her utterances.[9]
I think we show 'Tiresias' more respect if we try to engage seriously
with its attitudes. Tennyson wanted to add to their plausibility, so
that they would become more powerful in the world. If you share
parts of his political formation, you may elucidate those attitudes
respectfully. If not, you may prefer to challenge them, and analyse
their rhetorical strategies and their authority claims. Political change,
Terry Eagleton observes, will he coupled with 'a fierce conflict over
signs and meanings', as one group 'strives to wrest the most
cherished symbols from the grip of its rivals and redefine them in its
own image'.[10] Literature and criticism are places where such contest
occurs, and we need not shrink from it, any more than Tennyson did.
    That literature may influence us powerfully through its stories is
not, of course, a new thought – formalism has only ever been
established partially and temporarily in Britain and North America.
In *Reading and Discrimination*, an introductory book for students
along Leavisite lines, 'completely rewritten' in 1979, Denys Thompson
and Stephen Tunnicliffe declare:

> The oldest, and still the most widespread and popular form of
> entertainment is the telling of a story . . . Inevitably the novelist
> has his own sense of values, his own idea of what matters, what
> is interesting in life, what makes it worth living; and his stories
> cannot fail to express these ideas. Unwittingly we modify from

fiction our ideas of what human beings are and how they are
likely to behave, and develop our attitudes – of admiration or
disapproval – of the way they conduct themselves . . . This
applies as well to poetry and drama . . . If the writing is good, it
increases our awareness of other human beings, adds to our
knowledge of them, develops our sympathy, and extends our
insight into the way the world is going.[11]

The principal, but apparently scandalous modification that I propose,
is not to assume that all the texts called 'literary', or where 'the
writing is good', will tend, taken as a whole, to induce 'good'
attitudes. Magic does not guarantee wisdom.

The magic of Tennyson's poems is not separable from their political
stance: it informs totally their claim to lyric-prophetic authority.
Magic is what prophets have, and it enables them to assert 'truths'
that violate credibility from a purportedly outsider position. The
magic of Tennyson's poetry – its verbal power and its strategic use
of story – facilitates a claim of sagacity. The prophets' mystical powers
are the direct analogue of Tennyson's verbal magic. The tricks are
excellent, but we need to read the fine print.

As I have pointed out, Tennyson's attitude was actually neither
unique nor without credibility. It was one discourse in a debate
which is still flourishing. The idea of the writer as beleaguered
prophet, doomed to oppose the frivolity and self-interest of the
modern world but not to be believed, and yet specially gifted such
that his or her message may not be seriously challenged, is still
widely accepted. It is attractive metaphysically because it imagines a
source of wisdom somewhere beyond the customary interactive
processes through which meaning is produced in society. And it is
attractive politically because it claims to mark out a superior
discourse, one that can justifiably override other people's needs and
preoccupations. Those who believe in the magic of their culture invoke
a mystique that repudiates the plausibility of other discourses.

Tennyson saw himself in the prophet because he felt he was in a
similar relationship with his society – a wise but unregarded voice,
holding out alone against a wicked world. The disbelieved prophet
is an ideal posture for the conservative who distrusts the prevailing,
or developing, criteria of plausibility – who fears, perhaps, like the
speaker in 'Locksley Hall', 'a hungry people':

Slowly comes a hungry people, as a lion creeping nigher,
Glares at one that nods and winks behind a slowly-dying fire.
(Ricks, 2:127, 135–6)

The 'people' threaten to invoke a majority criterion of plausibility, at odds with the interests of an elite. In 'Merlin and the Gleam' those who are hostile to Tennyson's magic merge with the people generally:

> Once at the croak of a Raven who crost it,
> A barbarous people,
> Blind to the magic,
> And deaf to the melody,
> Snarled at and cursed me.

(Ricks, 3:207–8, 24–8)

However, he followed 'The Gleam' and worked at the magic.

Of course, sophisticated readers of poetry nowadays do not attribute to it prophetic power in the manner implied by Tennyson. Now, the literary text must be discovered to manifest ambiguity, irony, paradox, multivalency, polyphony, slippage. No doubt some will say that I should have done that with 'Tiresias', and I am confident that criticism could indeed work on that poem to discover its not-said, its silences. Even so, through the veil of indirection required in such modern critical strategies, the author and text glimmer through as magical and sagacious – as uniquely in command of language, and as transcending politics and history through the completeness of their vision and their engagement with human values. Moreover, the elaborate criticism of the professionals yields to more traditional simplicities 'lower down the educational ladder' (part of the rage against New Accents, Re-Reading Literature and *Political Shakespeare* is that they aim to make new thinking available to students – like Luther writing in German). There, old-fashioned sagacity is still assumed. In Brodie's Notes (a British high-school crib) on selected poems by Tennyson, a convenient index of what the examination system is liable to produce in schools, we learn that Tennyson

> seldom allowed himself to forget that, primarily, he was a God-gifted poet, and . . . his work always bore the stamp of his individual genius and was generally conceived from genuine inspiration. He loved England and her people, and could evoke in his poetry the glorious pageantry of her history.[12]

Such a sage, it seems, has to be right. So 'Of Old Sat Freedom on the Heights', another poem featuring a prophetic figure, is complacently glossed as taking

> a conservative stand on freedom. Though the poet wishes to see it spread through all classes of society, he eschews the 'falsehood

of extremes,' Right or Left. Where freedom is concerned,
Tennyson appears to come down staunchly on the side of the
Establishment, setting great store by the lessons of history. (71)

This reproduces not only Tennyson's conservatism but his
contradictions – freedom is to be 'spread' but class privilege is to
be maintained. The opportunity to comment on this, in the 'Revision
Questions' at the end of the booklet, seems to occur in the question:
'In what ways is Tennyson not merely lyrical but intellectual?' (92).
Love of the magic of poetry should not have to be in opposition to
clear and sensible thinking.

The implications of Tennyson's selection of the prophetic register,
and its involvement in contest in specific discursive conditions, may
be observed in 'The Ancient Sage'. In this late poem (1885), Tennyson
does not bother to put much distance between the sage and himself –
there is no evident historical or mythic referent. The sage takes as his
project the answering of a sceptical materialist, and his key move is
a story whose power lies precisely in the fact that it cannot be checked
against mundane standards of plausibility:

> And more, my son! for more than once when I
> Sat all alone, revolving in myself
> The word that is the symbol of myself,
> The mortal limit of the Self was loosed,
> And past into the Nameless, as a cloud
> Melts into Heaven.
>
> (Ricks, 3:145, 229–34)

Tennyson said: 'This is also a personal experience which I have had
more than once', and the *Memoir* by his son prints a letter recording
– in very similar terms – 'a kind of waking trance'.[13] The transposition
of his experience into 'The Ancient Sage' shows the kind of authority
that Tennyson wanted it to have. Not content with the status that
Western culture ascribes to first-person autobiography in simple
language, he sought directly the magical power of a sage speaking in
poetic language. Such was his commitment to the superior reality
of the visionary insight and its coincidence with the role of the poet.
He believed he was more himself, we might say, when he was in the
guise of an ancient sage.[14]

The implications of this choice of spokesman may be foregrounded
by observing the different kinds of plausibility that are supposed in
other discursive contexts. The prose account of Tennyson's trances
occurs in a letter written to Benjamin Paul Blood in 1874, in response
to a query about 'revelations through anaesthetics'.[15] Here the context

47

is rational enquiry into physical symptoms of drug use: it makes it harder for Tennyson to assert sagacious authority, and his tone is informal and anecdotal. He is not on his own ground. A scientifically-informed context is brought into play also by John Tyndall's recollection, provoked by reading 'The Ancient Sage' in 1893, of a conversation on similar lines with Tennyson in 1858, with Tyndall in the role of the sceptical young man. Tyndall, who became president of the British Association for the Advancement of Science, opposed aggressively Tennyson's attempt to reconstitute a religious world-view out of personal intuition – he warned against 'those expounders of the ways of God to men, who offer us intellectual peace at the modest costs of intellectual life'.[16] However, in 'The Ancient Sage' Tennyson declines this rationalist opponent.

We often assume that it was mainly scientific rationalism that produced a crisis of faith and doubt for people like Tennyson, but the young man clasps a scroll not of scientific data, but of verse. Tennyson's anxiety at this date was not science, but the scope of the sage and the authority of literature. The challenge to the vision of the sage comes from *lyric poetry*:

> O rosetree planted in my grief,
>   And growing, on her tomb,
> Her dust is greening in your leaf,
>   Her blood is in your bloom.
> O slender lily waving there,
>   And laughing back the light,
> In vain you tell me 'Earth is fair'
>   When all is dark as night.

(Ricks, 3:143, 163–170)

Of course, the sage is presented in poetry as well, but he speaks blank verse – the mode of Shakespearean dialogue and of the weighty speculations of Milton and Wordsworth. So the fiction is that his words are in direct, philosophical speech, and the sceptical lyric of the young man appears frivolous and contained by the sage's deliberations. The lyric manifests customary features – personal inspiration and evocative language – but it is outranked by the privileged speech of the sage. The prophet, once a figure for the poet, now has even more validity than the poet. It is a moment of defeat. After fifty years of trying to make lyric the basis of prophecy, Tennyson finds that he can establish prophecy only by repudiating lyric.

Authority and the text

The prophetic properties with which our culture has endowed poetry depend on the idea of *the text*. Sagacity is undercut if you aren't sure you have the true words of the prophet; you need the true icon to work the magic. Hence the efforts of editors. But there is no final point of stasis, and hence authority: for scholarship, criticism and biography also, it is now clear, are culturally productive. They make the categories and readings that they have purported, traditionally, to discover; they make the very concept literature and the very idea of the author.[17]

They intervene, for instance, in our understanding of Tennyson's trances, reorienting the topic through diverse frameworks. In Hallam Tennyson's *Memoir* to his father, the letter to Blood is printed in a section summarizing the poet's thoughts on 'his longing for the divine' (1:319–20). This is the context neither of Blood's enquiry about anaesthetics nor of the poems' contest for poetic authority – the *Memoir* lacks bite precisely because it assumes the sagacity that poems fight for. Then again, Robert Bernard Martin, in his biography of 1980, wants to uncover the anxious and hypochondriac Tennyson. He discusses the Blood letter in relation to Tennyson's fear of madness and epilepsy, pointing out that epileptic trances were associated, at the time, with masturbation.[18] Perhaps this is partly why the opposition to the prophet figure is so often characterized by sexual debauchery – Tiresias says it is because Menœceus has 'never known the embrace of love' that he can offer his 'maiden life' (Ricks, 1:629, 158–9). So another, different Tennyson emerges. He is not a given to be discovered, but a concept, or bundle of concepts, that we have produced.

These issues are focused by the appearance in 1987 of the second edition of Christopher Ricks's *The Poems of Tennyson* (first published in the Longman Annotated English Poets series in 1969). It affords an excellent instance of how Tennyson is organized within the institution of literature. The 1969 edition has structured a generation of critical and scholarly attention, transforming Tennyson, his manuscripts, and the manner of their composition and publication into a major scholarly and critical preoccupation. It has led us to feel that a certain range of materials constitute the proper context for study (you find critics quoting secondary materials from Ricks even when the fuller source is quite accessible). Now the second edition divides the poems among three volumes, tending to reconstitute once more our sense of what goes with what. Readers of *In Memoriam* will borrow from the library Volume 2, and as they browse around will find a context that includes 'Morte d'Arthur', 'Oh! that 'twere

possible', 'Break, break, break', 'In the Valley of Cauteretz' and *Maud*
– but not 'The Two Voices', 'On a Mourner' or 'Ulysses' (in Volume
1), or 'In the Garden at Swainston' and the eight discarded sections
of *In Memoriam* (in Volume 3).

It is customary to ponder whether we want all the equipment Ricks
provides. This question is part of the delusory pattern whereby
literary–academic culture imagines that it really prefers to read just
the poet's true words on the page, while somehow, mysteriously,
always postponing that goal. The new dust jacket quotes John Dixon
Hunt's opinion: 'the apparatus is itself constantly enthralling with
its impressions of the poet's public, publishing, creative and private
lives, from which one returns with renewed attention to the poems
themselves'. The insistence that one 'returns' to 'the poems
themselves' is characteristic of the way literary criticism has
imagined its relation to 'the text'. Brodie's Notes begin by cautioning
the student: *'The Notes are in no way intended as a substitute* for a
thorough knowledge of the poetry' (Hutchings: 4). Well, of course
not, it would be implausible to propose the contrary. Actually, poems
are never unmediated; even the sparsest text is an organization, as
should be immediately obvious when we consider the alternative
of facsimile reproduction of the author's manuscripts. And after
immersion in the Ricks apparatus, 'the poems' are not the same, one
cannot 'return' even to the point before that immersion.

Reading in an edition like this, the poem jostle with other of
Tennyson's writings, as well as a medley of commentary of diverse
kinds, and the authority of the text starts to slither. It cannot even be
kept separate. Unpublished fragments, after all, would seem to merit
as much respect as whole poems that were written but not published,
or published but then withdrawn; also, they have an interest of their
own – they may reveal attitudes that were weakened in printed
poems. It makes clear the political stakes to know that Tennyson jotted
down a fragment that begins: 'Wake middle classes, why so cold?'
(Ricks, 3:626). It is fascinating that he once wrote of his fear that the
heavenly Hallam would 'See with clear sight my secret shame', and
then obliterated that implication of a particular personal vice, writing
instead: 'See with clear eye some hidden shame' (Ricks, 2:368n, *In
Memoriam* LI, 7). The potential scope of gender and sexual relations in
his mid-century thought is indicated when we see that he wrote in a
draft of *The Princess*:

> if there be
> Men-women, let them wed with women-men
> And make a proper marriage.

(Ricks, 2:290n)

For the present discussion, it is interesting to note that in what we now call section LIV of *In Memoriam* Tennyson once declined to acknowledge the Christian revelation:

> For hope at awful distance set
>   Oft whispers of a kindlier plan
>   Though never prophet came to man
> Of such a revelation yet.

(Ricks, 2:370n)

It was to deal with this failure of spiritual authority that Tennyson proposed the lyric-prophetic authority of the poet.

It is not just that we glance up and down the page, from poem to notes. Editorial principles have been applied, inevitably, to the poems (modernization and regularization of punctuation and accidentals), and as a consequence the manuscript readings below are actually *more authentic*, since they preserve aspects of Tennyson's writing practice that the main text has tidied away. The apparatus – in my view necessarily and properly – undermines the main text. It reminds us, continually, of the choices Ricks has made, and of their inevitably unsatisfactory nature.

Further, Ricks prints the poems in order of composition, but in the text of Tennyson's latest version. These are two perfectly reasonable criteria, but they derive from two divergent notions of authenticity – what Tennyson thought first, at the moment of (presumed) intense creative conception; and what he thought last, at the moment of (presumed) ultimate aesthetic judgement. The issue reaches the point of contradiction with 'Morte d'Arthur' and 'Tiresias' and their framing poems, written at different times; and in the initial and published versions of 'The Lotos-Eaters', 'Early Spring' and 'Tithon'/ 'Tithonus'. At what stage in the sequence do such poems belong, and when does a draft become a poem? As with the new Oxford Shakespeare and its two states of *King Lear*, there comes a point where the editor decides that we have two distinct works. In some of the instances I've mentioned Ricks says Yes, in others No. Fine, he is the expert (we might say, the sage). But we are looking at editorial decisions, not 'the' poems.

We often hear that Tennyson tinkered with many of 'his poems' throughout his life. But they were not, at different points, *the same poems*. Sections of *Maud* ('Oh! that 'twere possible'; 'See what a lovely shell'; 'Go not happy day') were written long before *Maud* was envisaged. Ricks prints one of them separately, the others only within *Maud*. The point is not that he should have done something different, but that it is very difficult to say when Tennyson was writing *Maud* and when he was not; when a poem was finished; when a sequence of lines should be allowed to ascend from the footnotes to the full status of 'the poems themselves'. The main text is an unstable construct, and the reasons for believing so are to be found in precisely that textual apparatus that aspires to establish a privileged text.

It is not that Ricks should have done otherwise; rather, I meant to bring into focus the inevitable instability of writing and the fact that the attempt at stabilization is always culturally significant. Our culture has preferred to think of the Ricks *Tennyson* and its proliferation of material as merely a resource in the service of a transcendent principle of literary authority – as enhancing the plausibility of the sagacious author. There is indeed authority, but it is not transcendent. Professor Ricks has a sagacity of his own, and the institutions of literature combine to endorse it. However, the Ricks edition also makes space for contest. It allows us to see that literary authority, like other authority, is not magically pure, seamless and secure, but *put together* by people in a cultural politics. For despite the pretensions of the sage, plausibility is both interactive and political. The project of this article has been to relate a prominent Tennysonian motif to assumptions that still permeate literary studies generally. I have tried to make my story credible; at least, I claim, there is nothing up my sleeve.

Notes

1. *In Memoriam*, CXV, 1–4; quoted from CHRISTOPHER RICKS, ed., *The Poems of Tennyson*, 2nd ed., 3 vols. (London: Longman, 1987), 2:435. Hereafter quotations from this edition are cited in this article as 'Ricks', followed by volume, page and line numbers; in case of *In Memoriam* and *Maud* I supply volume, page, (part in roman) and line numbers.
2. COLIN SUMNER, *Reading Ideologies* (London, New York and San Francisco: Academic Press, 1979), 287. Further references appear in the text.
3. See ALAN SINFIELD, *Literature, Politics and Culture in Postwar Britain* (Oxford: Blackwell, 1989 and Berkeley: Univ. of California Press, 1989), chapter 13. The theoretical position presented in this article is elaborated in chapter 3.
4. ALAN SINFIELD, *Alfred Tennyson* (Oxford: Blackwell, 1986), 166–74. On poetry as one half of a binary construction, see 11–21, 54–6.
5. NIGEL HARRIS, *Beliefs in Society* (Harmondsworth: Penguin, 1968), 36–7.
6. STEPHEN GREENBLATT, 'Psychoanalysis and Renaissance Culture', in PATRICIA PARKER and DAVID QUINT, eds., *Literary Theory/Renaissance Texts* (Baltimore and London: Johns Hopkins Univ. Press, 1986), 218.
7. STUART HALL, DOROTHY HOBSON, ANDREW LOWE and PAUL WILLIS, eds., *Culture, Media, Language* (London: Hutchinson, 1986), 134.

8. See ALAN SINFIELD, 'That Which Is: the Platonic Indicative in *In Memoriam* 95', *Victorian Poetry* 14 (1976): 247–52.

9. GERALD GRAFF, *Professing Literature* (Chicago and London: Univ. of Chicago Press, 1987), 151–2, 229–30.

10. TERRY EAGLETON, *The Rape of Clarissa* (Oxford: Blackwell, 1982), 2.

11. DENYS THOMPSON and STEPHEN TUNNICLIFFE, *Reading and Discrimination*, new ed. (London: Chatto, 1979), 18–20.

12. RICHARD J. HUTCHINGS, *Tennyson: Selected Poetry* (Brodie's Notes; London and Sidney: Pan, 1979), 9. Further references will appear in the text.

13. HALLAM LORD TENNYSON, ed., *Alfred Lord Tennyson: A Memoir*, 2 vols (London: Macmillan, 1897), 1:320. Further references will appear in the text.

14. However, the autobiographical prose, as much as the 'poetic' rendering, is organized within available discourses, as we see from the echoes in it of Plotinus and Porphyry, and the fact that Tennyson goes on at once to compare the writing of St. Paul (*Memoir*, 1:320; see also 2:473–4).

15. See A. DWIGHT CULLER, *The Poetry of Tennyson* (New Haven: Yale Univ. Press, 1977), 255; and 1–8.

16. JOHN TYNDALL, *Fragments of Science for Unscientific People* (1871), quoted by WALTER E. HOUGHTON, *The Victorian Frame of Mind 1830–1870* (New Haven: Yale Univ. Press, 1957), 97. See SINFIELD, *Alfred Tennyson*, 179–81.

17. See RAYMOND WILLIAMS, *Marxism and Literature* (Oxford: Oxford Univ. Press, 1977), 45–54; MICHEL FOUCAULT, 'What Is an Author', in Foucault, *Language, Counter-memory, Practice* (Oxford: Blackwell, 1977), 113–38; STEPHEN ORGEL, 'The Authentic Shakespeare', *Representations* 21 (1988): 1–26.

18. ROBERT BERNARD MARTIN, *The Unquiet Heart* (Oxford: Oxford Univ. Press and London: Faber, 1980), 27–9; also 83–5, 238, 278–80.

3 1832: Tennyson and the critique of the poetry of sensation*

ISOBEL ARMSTRONG

Armstrong's seminal work of 1993, *Victorian Poetry: Poetry, Poetics and Politics*, offers a restoration of political questions to the study of Victorian poetry. Although she, too, is concerned with the politics of Tennyson's poetry, her critical strategy differs from Sinfield's in that she is more concerned with uncovering the text's ideological ambiguities and contradictions rather than identifying and confronting the text's reactionary or conservative values. Her book argues that there is a 'doubleness' at the centre of Victorian poetry, and thus an antagonistic struggle of dialectic within the poems. In this extract from the book Armstrong looks at a group of poems (including 'The Lotos-Eaters' and 'The Lady of Shalott') which were originally published in 1832 and rewritten for republication in 1842. She argues that Tennyson's rewriting during this period draws out the contradictions already latent in the 1832 version of the poems, converting contradictions into social critique. As the revisions settle, Tennyson can be seen responding to the social conditions of the 1840s and gradually producing a critique of the dehumanization and exploitation caused by industrial labour.

Poems (1832) sustains the almost breathtaking originality of *Poems, Chiefly Lyrical*. But it also begins to offer a critique of Hallam's positions. Less than a year after it was published, Hallam died. Some of the exuberance disappeared from Hallam and Tennyson's former group of friends – 'the Apostles' – who were increasingly dispersed in the subsequent decade. However, letters indicate how Tennyson's aesthetic evolved. The poetry of a number of friends – R. Monckton Milnes, R. C. Trench and the more distant John Sterling, friend of F. D. Maurice – indicates the pressures to which he responded. The movement to *Poems* (1842) is a movement of slow modification and adaptation. Some of the poems most heavily revised from 1832 to 1842 suggest in what direction Tennyson's work was moving. The poems are increasingly concerned with labour, appropriation and

---

*Reprinted from Isobel Armstrong, *Victorian Poetry: Poetry, Poetics and Politics* (London and New York: Routledge, 1993) pp. 77–94.

power, and with the forms in which culture perpetrates violence. Where volition and change, the themes of 1830, come into play they are defined in a cultural context. The movement is from an analysis in terms of individual psychology in 1832 to a firmer cultural analysis in 1842, even though, sometimes, it takes a cruder moral form.

The poems of 1832 are enigmatic in the same way as those of 1830, not declaring their meaning, refusing immediate interpretation, requiring that 'exertion' which Hallam required to dissolve the 'fortresses of opinion'. 'The Palace of Art', 'The Lotos-Eaters' and 'The Lady of Shalott', were all much altered in 1842, and in particular 'The Palace of Art'. All these are double poems of a highly self-conscious kind, but they presage the destruction or decadence of the poetry of sensation and search both for another politics and a new aesthetic. It is proper to say that by 1842 subversive conservatism was in a quandary.

Written in answer to Trench's reproach. 'Tennyson, we cannot live in Art', 'The Palace of Art' is too easily read as the journey of the solipsist soul from the aesthetic to the moral life.[1] It is described as 'a sort of allegory' in the dedication to Trench, but remembering the deceptive, indirect allegory of Tractarian aesthetics, akin to the aesthetics of Hallam in some ways, it would be best not to assume that it is immediately explicable. The Soul, a female figure whose feminine status will be examined shortly, 'shuts out Love', according to the dedicatory poem, and aestheticizes both 'Knowledge' and 'Good'. The poem itself gives some content to these abstractions, exploring the way in which desire mutates into cold, libidinal power (more emphatic in 1842), just as it bodies out Tennyson's unhelpful comment – 'the Godlike life is with man and for man'.[2] Though that is certainly an unorthodox comment, one interpretation suggests that the 'God-like' is a creation of the human imagination.

It is immediately apparent that the poem is not written in terms of the poetry of 'sensation', but in a more measured and abstract rhetorical, perhaps 'Ciceronian', manner. The Soul's 'pleasure-house' and its appurtenances at first sight resemble the 'pleasure-dome' of Coleridge's 'Kubla Khan', a poem much debated by the Apostles.[3] Yet even in 1832 'The Palace of Art' is not committed to the sensuous symbolism of that poem. It is colder, more ordered and distant, as the stanzaic form fragments the observations into discrete, objectified moments. The 'I' of the poem is a detached, self-conscious observer, always external to the allegorical 'Soul', granting it a long lease of the pleasure house constructed for it. The lack of 'sensation' may arise because not only isolation but stability is desired for the Soul. 'Reign thou apart, . . . Still as, while Saturn whirls' (14, 15):

Saturn's ring, Whewell says, was regarded as evidence for the stability of the universe, emerging from vapour detached from the sun and cooled into permanent form.[4] In 1842 stanzas on the *fixity* of the Soul's narcissism became the second section of the poem (stanzas XXIX–XXXVI in 1832). Displaying the voluptuary Keatsian elements, there is a consummate conflation of the *powerful* fountain of 'Kubla Khan' in the 'Spouted fountain-floods' (28) of Tennyson's poem and the rainbow torrent of the Arve in Shelley's 'Mont Blanc'. The 'torrent-bow' (36) of the waterfall suggests the refracted light of the rainbow torrent of the Arve. Both things suggested the energy and creativity of mind to the earlier poets – the capacity to make new combinations, as in refracted light. The Soul, however, turns away from these and burns incense to herself in self-worship, while the excluded world responds to this mystification. In 1832 the excluded world is introduced directly – 'Twas wonderful to look upon' (41). In 1842 this was sharpened to an ironical understanding of the blinding nature of myth: 'who shall gaze . . . with unblinded eyes . . .?' (41, 42).

The alienated Soul passes through a series of discrete, enclosed rooms which are a museum, or, rather, mausoleum to the whole culture and knowledge of the civilized world, occidental and oriental. Her environment is at once fragmented and overdetermined – not one picture but many, not one religion, but many – so that no myth is privileged above another: 'every legend fair' (125). Christianity, the 'maid-mother by a crucifix' (93) (followed by Venus in 1832 (XV)), is condensed into the emblems of the incarnation and the passion in a brief phrase. Arthurian legend (Faber's interpretation of the Arthurian legend in terms of the rites of the *mystae* was, we have seen, known to Tennyson), the origins of Roman polity, India, home of Sanskrit (which the early mythographers, known to Tennyson, Sir William Jones and Herder, believed to have been the origin of the human race), and Greece, which Hallam thought of as a culture of the feelings in comparison with the rationality of Rome, all coexist.[5] These legends of the Caucasian or Indo-European mind are jumbled together, just as portraits of the great philosophers and poets are hung in no historical order – Milton, Shakespeare, Dante, Homer. All is contemporary, simultaneous, available, and thus all is estranged. A ludic experiment with estranged forms is one result of this simultaneous existence of all cultures and myths: they have also become pure aesthetic artefacts and thus 'pure' commodities, available for use as representations – for the art of the Palace consists of representations of representations – in an aesthetic economy which plunders indiscriminately in spite of its purity. Since each representation is simply the equivalent of another they exist in a self-enclosed system. Hallam's 'pure' art thus becomes drained of meaning and history, a 'pure' luxury commodity.

The brilliant stroke in this analysis of a historicized culture which must be fragmented is the induction of the Soul through landscape painting, which suggests that the poem addresses not only Hallam but also Wilson. Wilson had ended his review of the 1830 poems with the praise of landscape description as the proper subject of the poet:

> long withdrawing vales, where midway between the flowery foreground, and in the distance of blue mountain ranges, some great city lifts up its dim-seen spires through the misty smoke . . . the breast of old ocean . . . or as if an earthquake shook the pillars of the caverned depths, tumbling the foam of his breakers, mast-high, if mast be there, till the canvas ceases to be silent.[6]

There is a palimpsestic revision of the pictorial section from 1832 to 1842 and the elements of Wilson's description are restlessly reconfigured – fitting, perhaps, in a poem which is about a palimpsestic culture. In 1832 the city and the flowery foreground appears – 'Some showed far-off thick woods mounted with towers . . . long walks and lawns and beds and bowers', to be replaced in 1842 (69–72) with a seascape of 'bellowing caves' (71). The lonely, isolated figure in a surreal landscape is supplemented in 1842 with stanzas depicting human exploitation of the land in the grazing of cattle, and in reaping, in 'sultry toil' (77), a double exploitation of land and human labour. Human beings, and more so in 1842, are *not* in harmonious relationship with nature. There is an irony in the 1842 phrase, 'but every landscape fair, / As fit for every mood of mind' (89–90). At a stroke Wilson's programme for descriptive poetry, and the Romantic account of the unity of mind and world, subject and object (which includes Hallam's account of Tennyson as a poet capable of creating moods which seem to evolve a 'natural correspondence' in the external world), are exposed as a fallacy. If the world is 'fit' for every mood of mind, as it is 'fitted' in Wordsworth's *Excursion*, that is because the mind does violence to landscape by appropriating a correspondence which it makes itself.[7] It exploits landscape in imagination and literally by exploiting people's labour on it. The landscapes preface the poem in 1832 because they destroy the basis of Romantic epistemology and its confident assumptions about the unifying power of mind. This pre-eminently modern substitute for religion, a relation with a landscape, is undermined from the start.

In 1832 the element of hubristic possession and appropriation is emphasized because the famous line 'I take possession of men's minds and deeds' was placed earlier.

> I take possession of men's minds and deeds.
>   I live in all things great and small.
> I dwell apart, holding no forms of creeds,
>   But contemplating all.
>
> (Note to line 128, 1842)

An indiscriminate self-projection to which consciousness always remains external leads, not to the 'complex' (19) states of being the Soul believes in, but to repetition. She 'multiplied' (3) all that she saw, inhabiting discrepant mythologies – 'Madonna, Ganymede, / Or Asiatic dame' (7–8) – while remaining detached. The whole of history and consciousness is available as a means to power – 'Lord over Nature, Lord of the visible earth, / Lord of the senses five' (179–80). It is power out of control. In 1832 the Soul is not only a historian or rather a historicist but, as a footnote adding extra stanzas indicates, a chemist, physicist, astronomer and a senuous Epicurean. Ricks notes some deleted manuscript stanzas which include philosophical thought 'from Plato to the German' (note to line 186, 1842). Indeed, it looks as though Tennyson had trouble in controlling and selecting the forms of thought over which the Soul exercises its power; the fields of knowledge are arbitrary, very much as they become for the Soul of the poem. In 1842 it is the Soul's isolation and indifference to a suffering history which is emphasized in stanzas inserted into section V (141–64). She 'trod' (157) over 'cycles of the human tale' (146). 'I sit apart, holding no forms of creeds' (211) is strongly defined in relation to political and social irresponsibility in 1842. Slavery and revolution are alike irrelevant to the Soul.

> The people here, a beast of burden, slow,
>   Toiled onward, pricked with goads and stings;
> Here played, a tiger, rolling to and fro
>   The heads and crowns of kings.
>
> (149–52)

The Soul's contempt for the people as 'swine' (199) was added even later in 1851 in a tasteless attempt to castigate her 'God-like isolation' (197) further. Tennyson's increasing emphasis on the Soul's isolation is in some ways a misprision of the earlier poem and suggests if nothing else how unstable and uneasy is the text we call 'The Palace of Art', just like Hallam's discontinuous phases of being. In 1832 the aesthetic principle appears to include within itself all human history and forms of thought, however helpless in its pluralism. In 1842, on the other hand, the aesthetic principle appears to have become a principle of exclusion set up in opposition to 'life' and society. Hence the passages on the Soul's unscrupulous empathies disappear, for empathy is at least an inclusive project, even though the Soul's empathies are misused in the pursuit of power. The move is from a 'Romantic' to a 'Victorian' conception of art. In 1832 everything is appropriated by a hubristic imagination. In 1842 the poem becomes an analysis of mistaken categories in which art is defined falsely as that which is not 'mixed up' (in Hallam's phrase) with life: but once the opposition has been established the attempt to heal it simply endorses the fracture. Hallam's political strategy, which enables the poet to dissolve orthodoxies, becomes acutely vulnerable.

Another mark of the 1842 revisions is the increasing helplessness of the feminine Soul. Hallam's essay 'On sympathy' conceives of the Soul as autonomous and feminine, just as in 'The Palace of Art'. The Soul is gendered as feminine because of Hallam's belief in the capacity of women to transgress fixed forms, though in Tennyson's poem it is sometimes androgynous, 'Lord' of the five senses. Hallam argues that the capacity for empathy is not a function of *narcissistic* power. Consciousness itself is not an undivided unity but a series of 'forms of self' and 'successive states', existing 'piece-meal, and in the continual flux of a stream'.[8] Thus the act of empathy, or sympathy, can never be an appropriation of the other by a total self, for the divided self will always recognize difference. 'Impetuous desire' to 'blend emotions and desires with those apparent in the kindred spirit' produces an identification of the 'perceived being with herself' which is conditioned by her understanding of it as other, a not-self.[9] The narcissistic rush of spirit and its *check* is the basis of morality and altruism. In 'The Palace of Art' of 1832, Tennyson explores a condition of narcissistic empathy in which the ego remains self-interested. It is a series of experimental, detached, power-seeking identifications for the sake of self-aggrandizement and thus the self is always 'outside' experience. It is a condition, as Tennyson says, without 'Love'. Hallam's God of love is a God of passion, libido and sexuality, derived from Plato, but peculiarly his own. The paradigm of divine love is the 'intense' experience of the erotic – 'I mean direct, immediate, absorbing affection for one object, on the ground of similarity perceived, and with a view to more complete [i.e. sexual] union'.[10] Moreover, such love cannot be complete unless it has understood incompletion, 'collision with opposing principles', or evil.[11] This God has nothing to do with theories of moral training or innate ethical sense subscribed to by natural theologians.

Effectively in 1842 the Soul is denied the sexuality which is in fact, for Hallam, constitutive of identity and relationships. Because Tennyson deleted the passages concerning the Soul's capacity for empathy, which were there in 1832, the Soul's world becomes increasingly passionless, unsexual and abstract. In 1842 she can 'prate' of the 'moral instinct' (205), the natural theologian's innate virtue consolidated by habit. All knowledge becomes a 'form' (211) of creed without content. The atrophied passions convert knowledge into a form of power which fails to create living relationships. The trauma is the more violent when she understands this incompleteness. The feminized Soul is crushed under the weight of a fragmented culture and cannot reconstruct it. Her crisis is much more like the crisis of Dorothea in Rome in George Eliot's *Middlemarch* forty years later than the hubris attributed to Tennyson by Trench. That the Soul is imaged as feminine suggests that the collapse of feminized art is an index of the poet's understanding of the real condition of women in contemporary culture. Certainly the collapse of feminized art issues in madness. It cannot maintain itself in an abstract and instrumental world which is always assimilating art to its own model, always replicating in art the alienating conditions of its own culture. Feminized art cannot be invoked to supplement an arid society but will simply reproduce its pathology and derangement, as in the deranged landscapes contemplated by the Soul. In a poem of 1829, 'Lines written at Malvern', Hallam writes that all knowledge springs from 'Our senses five'.[12] The Soul's lordship over the five senses in Tennyson's poem is precisely to subordinate and crush their possibilities. In a beautiful poem addressed to Tennyson, Hallam writes of a mad girl seen in an asylum, 'the mansion of the mad.' The girl is locked into a palace of art and solipsist pleasure to which 'nought external seemed akin'.[13] Hence the dissociation and alienation of madness. But Hallam explicitly refuses a 'penal' judgement. It is a world without a strong sense of the other, a world of deranged libido where the disabled mind makes no correlations through the passions. At the end of 'The Palace of Art' the landscapes at the beginning of the poem reappear in fragments as a nightmarish psychological *paysage intérieur*. They must logically become these enclosed and reflexive mental representations because the Soul has found no principle of relationships with things external. Sensation turns in upon itself and represents itself. The ending of the poem has often been considered perfunctory as a description of new commitment and identification with that beyond self:

'Make me a cottage in the vale,' she said,
   'Where I may mourn and pray.'

                                                            (290–1)

Another reading is that the poverty of the ending comes about because there is no solution to the complex condition of alienation in the poem, least of all a misguided, punitive course of Christian self-abnegation, which is simply to reverse lordship and repeat the abstract patterns of the Soul's experience of externality in another form.

'The Lady of Shalott' can be a useful transition from 'The Palace of Art', with its empty and pathologized culture, to 'The Lotos-Eaters', for it configures concerns which appear separately in the other poems – feminine sexuality, art and language, oppressed labour, race. It is almost always seen as a critique of the isolated artist, cut off from life, and elided with 'The Palace of Art'. The Lady is thought of as retreating into the aesthetic world of infinite regression designated by the weaving which reproduces the mirror reflections which reproduce the world. 'The Lady of Shalott' is also identified with the sensuous withdrawal of 'The Lotos-Eaters.' But such a regress is alien to both 'The Palace of Art' and 'The Lotos-Eaters', and the categories of art and life are inadequate to all the poems if only because they are precisely what is being questioned in them. Even the more sophisticated Lacanian version of traditional accounts of 'The Lady of Shalott', as the failure of the primal consciousness of the mirror phase to recognize the radical disjunction of the symbolic order which constitutes the social order of the law, simply expresses this rigid opposition in a different language. 'The Lady of Shalott', which has no source, and is in fact the conflation of a number of mythic structures, is a modern myth, sealed off from interpretation with all the mysteriousness and inaccessibility of myth as surely as the Lady is sealed in her tower. As in 'The Palace of Art', breakdown and trauma are at the centre of the poem as the 'fairy' Lady breaks the taboo on access to the human world when she sees Lancelot, and dies. Fusing the many myths of the weaving lady, from Arachne to Penelope, with the myths of reflection carried by Narcissus and Echo (in 1842 her song 'echoes cheerly'), this is a poem of longing for sexual love, change and transformation, which is denied change. The Lady is a doomed victim, and dies a sacrificial death, failing to come into sexuality and language.

As with so many of the early poems, two readings are simultaneously at work. In one the Lady is locked into rigid oppositions, between the rural and the urban, an older order of labour by hand and mercantilism and trade, an organic, integrated world and a fragmented commercial world, between isolation and community, between passivity and action and aggression, female and male, the aesthetic and the 'real'. Unable to mediate these oppositions she appears to be condemned to passivity and death. In 1832 these oppositions are consolidated through the Lady's final message, '*The charm is broken utterly*' (169), which in 1842 was replaced by the wondering gaze of the knights and Lancelot's uncomprehending speech. Despite the tragic poignance of the Lady's death, the condemnation of woman to passivity seems deeply repressive, just as the rigid oppositions are deterministically conservative in their fixity.

Read as an expressive poem in which an assent to the experiencing subject's affective understanding of its predicament is foremost, the poem avails itself of this oppositional reading. George Eliot, who liked the poem, re-read it in exactly this way when, in *The Mill on the Floss*, she made Maggie's tragic predicament, an unsuccessful attempt to break out of restriction, echo that of the Lady. Read as analysis beyond what the perception of the experiencing subject can encompass, as critique which is precisely concerned with the limits of expressive representation and representation itself, a second poem emerges which dissolves and interrogates the fixed positions and oppositions of the first and redefines its aesthetics and politics. This second reading is present both in 1832 and 1842, but 1842 exposes the problematic nature of the Lady's position more emphatically.

It must be remembered that this consummately arcane and beautiful poem is the latter-day poet's reconstruction of mythic representation. As well as discovering in Keightley's *The Fairy Mythology* that myths are part of a primal, indigenous peasant culture where the imaginative life of a nation resides, an intuitive form of thought which possesses an organic wholeness prior to thought, and in particular to artificial society, Tennyson would also have read that myths are instruments of power and ideology, used by a ruling class to coerce the ruled, and frequently changing with a change of power. Keightley wrote that myths are a 'poetic fiction' and that 'all the ancient systems of heathen religion were devised by philosophers for the instruction of rude tribes'.[14] Changes of religious faith transform the meaning of myths. So they become the instrument of the 'artificial' world. What is the status of myth? What is the relation between myth and power? What are the conditions of change? These are central questions in the analytical poem, the second lyric within the lyric.

The Lady is subject to a coercive taboo whose source and meaning she does not understand. 'She has heard a whisper say, / A curse is on her if she stay / ... She knows not what the curse may be'

(39–40, 42). One of the conditions of the threat of the curse is that she does not 'stay' or cease from labour. For all its magical aesthetic quality, the weaving of the web is ceaseless work without escape and without *pleasure*. In 1832 the Lady worked without extremes of feeling – 'She lives with little joy or fear' (46). The Lady works just as the agrarian reapers work (they were pluralized in 1842). This affinity is illuminated by Carlyle in *Sartor Resartus* when he brings women and workers together, relating weavers at 'Arkwright looms' and 'silent Arachne' weavers who are all, he says, subject to and subjects of different kinds of cultural myth.[15] It seems that Tennyson is manoeuvring together the constraints working on women and the compulsions working on other forms of labour. The reapers and the Cambridge rick-burners reacting to the corn laws, the starving handloom weavers who were being displaced by new industrial processes, these hover just outside the poem and become strangely aligned with the imprisoned Lady. The possibility of change is explored through her psyche, as she becomes a representation of alienation and work.

She is unaware of the constraints worked upon her and obedient to the mysterious power until the appearance of lovers in the mirror forces her to reconceptualize her world as phantasmal and secondary, mere representation. It has not seemed so to her until this point: 'I am half sick of shadows' (71). The appearance of Lancelot brings the shock of a radically changed perception. Indeed the poem works structurally as a series of shocks and disjunctions. The shock of Lancelot's appearance, the violent shattering of the mirror, the disintegration of the web, the Lady's death. A correlative of these physical shocks are the gaps and disjunctions of the narrative which have the same effect, creating discontinuity and unsettling interpretation, just as the brilliant colours of the poem dazzle and confound. (The poetry of sensation is brilliantly at work here.) The powerful sexuality of Lancelot, physically close – 'A bow-shot from her bower-eaves' (73) – but oddly distanced by the dazzling double reflection of him and his image in the water refracted in the mirror, brings the culminating sense of lack which forces the Lady into action. The curse, suggesting the biblical curse of labour and sexuality, is invoked. But there is a strange irony here: if this is the curse of labour and sexuality the Lady was already subject to these in her isolated life in the tower. What was lacking was the sense of lack which forces a *realization* of estrangement and oppression. The curse is the myth of power, a representation, which kept the Lady subject. But the double irony is that the curse comes 'true' as the condition of her realization, at the very moment when she redefines her life as a condition of lack. Thus myths do materially organize experience.

It seems that in the simultaneous second poem which is critique rather than expressive experience, Tennyson is exploring not so much the passivity of the suffering subject but the recognition of lack as the precondition of a changed perception of the world which precipitates action. It is the moment when myth is recognized *as* myth, or as ideology, which enables action, and the construction of a new myth. The repercussions for feminine sexuality and for oppressed labour are the same. They are not caught in a determined world of rigid opposition but can transform it. In the first, expressive poem, however, the revolutionary moment fails. In the second, analytical poem, its failure is contradictory and ambiguous. The second poem loosens and reconfigures the rigidity of the first. The structural oppositions set up do not fall into a symmetry of positive and negative attributes. Power operates in the world of Camelot as much as in the tower of Shalott. If the world of the Lady is affective and passive in contrast to the world of action, that world of action is an aggressive one. The world of Camelot which the Lady sees in her mirror is hierarchical, aristocratic and organized by religious feeling. It is an archaic world of simple exchange and barter. It is strangely mismatched with the sophisticated culture of Camelot as it is presented at the end of the poem. The mirror itself, far from being a static reflecting entity, changes from blue to crystal. Indeed it is not clear whether the pictures in the mirror are always reflections of externality or the figures woven in the fabric and returned to the mirror, and thus may be constructs of the Lady's mind. The mirror is contradictory, and breaks down the opposition between art and 'reality' and with it the two opposing worlds. The world outside the tower is equally a confusion of reflection, image and figure. The Lady takes on the function of the mirror with her 'glassy countenance' as she floats down the river to Camelot. It is not clear whether her new song is a song of triumph or defeat. In 1832 she is compared to the swan whose death in the pagan mysteries Tennyson read of would have been the beginnings of transformation.[16] The Lady moves from picture to writing, abstract signs which confirm absence because they are substitutive symbols. But whether this is a liberation into the representative freedom of the sign or the dissociation of a unified mode of figuring is an open question. One thing is clear: she does not name herself but places herself in a pregiven hierarchy when she writes that she is 'The Lady of Shalott'. The 1842 revisions increase the sense that she is struggling with the need to represent herself but constantly deprived of this capacity. Lancelot speaks *for* her at the end of the poem, just as she earlier mirrors not herself but him. In 1842 Tennyson swept away the descriptive material which decorated her in jewels and colours, replacing these with images of work and toil and making her blanker, more empty, the mysterious other who defeats signification. No one has seen her. She is metonymically the blank space of flowers figured in the second stanza of the poem which displaces her at the moment when she is expected to appear. The sexual politics of the poem suggest that the sensuous freedom of femininity which can break the bonds of custom is severely restricted, and has repercussions in the wider politics of oppression. Like 'The Lotos-Eaters' the poem ends with a revolutionary situation *without* revolution. Turning from 'The Lady of Shalott' to that poem, it becomes evident that in 1842 this was Tennyson's most intense critique of oppression – but this time in a male world which uncannily seems to contain only one gender.

It is arguable that in many cases the revisions of 1842 create two incompatible texts within the same poem. This is a perfectly reasonable assumption. The 1832 poems, however, work by positing contradictions. The 1842 revisions tend to shift these more emphatically in the direction of critique, consciously textualizing and exposing them and forcing contradictions into the open. This can be seen particularly in 'The Lotos-Eaters' and its heavy, luxuriant passivity, where Tennyson returns to the life and language of sensation.

The poem rolls its orchestration of enervated, slumbrous cadences to end, in 1832, in delirium, and in 1842 in the careless retreat of Epicurean gods. It is at once the culminating expression of the poetry of sensation and its greatest critique. Its motive is from Homeric myth, the enchanted fruit of the Lotos given to Odysseus' sailors. As a modern myth it carries along in its waves of sound the great literary testimonies against sloth, reminiscences of Spenser's *The Faerie Queene*, and virtual quotation from Thomson's *Castle of Indolence*, and subjects them to unsettling investigation. The 'sultry toil' of 'The Palace of Art' reappears as the mariners repudiate labour. The analogue of the Lotos-Eaters is, of course, the opium-eater, as the drugged, semi-conscious cadences and their paradoxical intensity suggest – 'And deep-asleep he seemed, yet all awake' (35). It is no accident that the mariners' need for the Lotos is to allay the horrors of labour, for opium was often taken by industrial workers for the same reason.[17] Characteristic of the double poem, 'The Lotos-Eaters' is both the *expression* of the addictive desire in which drug requires further drugging, and an *analysis* of the conditions under which the unhappy consciousness and the unhappy body come into being. The unhappy consciousness is forced to construe experience in terms of passivity and consumption, a consumption which becomes consuming. In one reading a passive consciousness is the *result* of eating the Lotos. In the second reading exhaustion *causes* the addictive need to forget, rather than being the result of consuming the magic fruit. Behind the second reading is the cruelty of work, brute, mindless labour. This reading considers the conditions which *constitute* consciousness, volition and labour in passive terms, the conditions which force the need for the Lotos upon the mariners, and which necessitate the exhausted, semi-conscious reverie of forgetting, the longing for mindless life.

Tennyson brilliantly makes strange the postulates underlying mechanized labour and exploitation by transposing them to a 'colonial' island strangely like John Wilson's Isle of Palms. In circular fashion these postulates bring the world of mechanized labour into being as well as being generated by these very things. The contradictory terms of exploitation, in which natives offer resources which the intruders interpret as the magical release from toil, but which turn out to belong to the very conditions of labour, are disclosed by the simple move of allowing them to occur in another 'place', Homer's Greece. The colonial dream of magical consumption is located exactly in the mythological landscape from which its fantasies of obliterating the connection between labour and consumption derive, the untouched exotic island waiting for sailors to arrive.

It is important to see that the poem is not concerned with the literal, physical conditions of labour, but (true to Hallam's propositions) with the physical and mental world of *sensations* which emerges from oppressed labour. Moreover, as the poem proceeds, the material sensations which are so amazingly lyricized are seen to be inseparable from an account of consciousness which is both cause and effect of the experience of crushing passivity and toil. In other words, Tennyson is writing of the postulates on which the world of mechanized labour is founded, and which have changed the material world, as well as portraying the psychological state which arises from it. The poem works with four interrelated postulates in order to construe a world of alienation in which labour must be *the* consuming and destructive force. These are disclosed in the Introduction to the Choric Song and are, first, a world without the *a priori* category of time, so that acts of mind are the discontinuous fragments of being which so interested Hallam. Secondly, a world without agency is posited (partly a consequence of the world without time), a passive reaction to external powers. Thirdly, the poem posits a world in which consciousness is the reproduction of internal genetic physical sensations which echo in the caverns of the ear – 'And *music* in his ears his beating heart did make' (36) – so that consciousness is a sound system produced from the pulses of the blood, from sensation itself. Lastly it posits a world without language.

The voices of the mariners become thin and sink to whispers. As
the organization of the Choric Song suggests, it seems to be a language
without reference except to itself. In 1842, in the added coda about the
gods, language has reached the state of pure aural signifier, a 'tale of
little meaning', though 'the words are strong'. Why do these
conditions belong together?

As we have seen, the postulates about consciousness, labour and
language are circular and cause and effect of one another. The
structure of the Introduction predetermines that of the Choric Song
even though the Choric Song supposedly follows the changed
condition which succeeds to the eating of the Lotos. In fact the
Introduction, with a strange backwards relationship to the song, is
an intensification of it, and the song adumbrates the elements of its
preface rather than allowing the preface to explain the song. It is a
condition without sequence, of repetition without progression and
disjunction without change. Repetition, a feature of the new form
of labour, is the key to the postulates of the Introduction. It is
produced out of mesmeric repetition as parallelism and pattern take
precedence over reference: 'The Lotos *blooms below* the barren peak: /
The Lotos *blows* by every winding creek' (145–6) (my emphasis).
Repetition reconfigures the same sound elements and destroys
sequence as the Lotos flowers and falls, blooms and blows,
simultaneously. Opposite conditions coexist and turn out to be forms
of one another. If this is 'A land where all things always seemed the
same!' (24), temporal conditions are suspended and all experience
exists simultaneously (and logically not at all) as afternoon, moon and
sunset occur together. Perceptual contradictions arise from this: the
stream is intermittently in motion and still, creating that heightened
nervous tension and uncertainty by which the poetry of sensation
dissolves habitual associations and dislocates the sign. Water like a
'downward smoke' (8) reverses attributes (for logically it could flow
upwards if smoke can fall downwards) and is 'Slow-dropping' (11).
The correlative of this is both a frightful intensity and a dulled half-
awareness which is projected into the Choric Song in the 'half-dream'
(101), the 'half-drop't eyelid' (135) and the continual repetition of
falling water, breaking waves and echoing caves which echo and
repeat so continuously that experience takes place as a world of
secondary reverberation, a kind of aural disorder. A 'modern'
internal, psychological language in which objects are projections or
evolve in correspondence with a state of mind – 'languid air' (5),
'weary dream' (6), 'slumbrous sheet of foam' (13) – exists side by side
with an external world expressed through formal, archaic and
artificial diction – '*Up-clomb* the shadowy pine against the *woven*
copse' (18) (my emphasis). The historical disjunctions effected by

this linguistic misalignment make both internal and external exist in hallucinatory estrangement from one another. Though it flagrantly borrows, sometimes almost word for word, from Thomson's *Castle of Indolence* (1748), the poem dissipates Thomson's rational and moral order, just as it dissolves the highly organized Spenserian stanza.

> And up the hills, on either side, a wood
> Of blackening pines, ay waving to and fro,
> Sent forth a sleepy horror through the blood;
> And where this valley winded out, below,
> The murmuring main was heard, and scarcely heard, to flow.
>
> A pleasing land of drowsyness it was:
> Of dreams that wave before the half-shut eye;
> And of gay castles in the clouds that pass,
> Forever flushing round a summer sky:
> There eke the sweet delights that witchingly
> Instil a wanton sweetness through the breast,
> And the calm pleasures always hovered nigh;
> But whate'er smacked of noyance, or unrest,
> Was far far off expelled from this delicious nest.
>
> (*The Castle of Indolence*, v, vi)

Just as Tennyson's poem disorganizes the syntax and perceptual order of Thomson's poem, so he disorganizes the rationally paired moral opposition between indolence and industry and shows it to be incoherent. The dichotomy between withdrawal and toil is an antithesis produced by and producing the passive account of consciousness and labour which is the condition of the Lotos-eating existence. It is predicated on the erasing of the link between labour and the objects of consumption, which is why the magical lethargy of the Lotos-Eaters is as uncomfortable and alienating as mechanical labour itself. Like Thomson, Tennyson allows the Lotos-Eaters to believe that labour is the differentiating characteristic of consciousness in that unlike animals or plants it *knows* that it exists and labours.

> All things have rest: why should we toil alone,
> We only toil, who are the first of things,
> And make perpetual moan,
>
> (60–2)

But labour here is marked by neither self-creation nor exertion or agency. It is suffering rather than labour, because it is imposed on a passive recipient, which is defined and defines itself as passive. To labour on the sea is to be driven to labour by the rocking waves, inert external force – 'Is there any peace / In ever *climbing* up the *climbing* wave?' (94–5) (my emphasis): 'We have had enough of action, and of motion, we, / *Rolled* to starboard, *rolled* to larboard, when the surge was seething free' (150–1) (my emphasis). The surge is not 'free', any more than the sailors are, but this is a way of denoting the structural conditions of work which Carlyle was recognizing at the same time. 'The sailor furls his sail, and lays down his oar', just as 'the shuttle drops from the fingers of the weaver'.[18] Work was passive and mechanical, Carlyle recognized, because the conditions of labour had structurally changed, as the *results* of work no longer returned to the labourer, the great differentiating feature of the new systems of the division of labour from earlier forms of work. Tennyson brilliantly renders, not the literal relation of worker and product, but the psychological state the new indirect relations create. For the Lotos-Eaters all experience is always emptying out, because identity itself is transformed, 'taken from us' (91), into an estranged past when consciousness has no direct access to what it makes: *production*, materially and psychologically, is a *subtraction* from identity; 'ah, why / Should life all labour be? . . . Let us alone. What is it that will last? / All things are taken from us, and become / Portions and parcels of the dreadful Past' (86–8, 90–2). Experience loses its immediacy and belongs to the phantasmal past, 'dreadful' because the past itself is a series of disintegrated 'portions' which have been 'taken from' the ever disappearing present.

A 'genetic history of what we see *in* the mind', Carlyle says, not an understanding of the nature of consciousness itself, is the consequence of a passive, materialist theory of mind; and a mechanical account of labour is a postulate of this epistemology; they bring each other into being.[19] 'And music in his ears his beating heart did make' (36), Tennyson writes of the Lotos-Eaters who have been reduced to creatures of the history of their own physical sensations. The associationist philosophers, according to Carlyle (Locke, Hume and Reid in particular), ignore the metaphysical questions of necessity, Free will, Mind and Matter, and produce an incoherent epistemology in which the lethargic consciousness fragments into sensation. This is dangerously close to Hallam's 'fragments of self'. Tennyson is concerned with the incoherence of such a consciousness and with its symptoms. The reduction of experience to the genetically produced 'music' of sensation in the ear means that the physical basis of mind develops a longing for the 'pure' sensation, its own physical essence divorced from thought. For if labour manifests itself in the unhappy awareness of a depleted consciousness, pleasure can only be found in immediate physical

experience. But 'pure' sensation, is impossible except in a condition
where one could not by definition be aware of it – hence the yellow
leaf and the overmellow apple grow and drop to the ground without
volition (iii). Or if the passive consciousness cannot consume itself in
the narcotic of forgetting it is forced to posit the present as a
continual act of memory. For if consciousness is divided into lost
experience and awareness of that loss, it is continually ahead of (or,
by the same token, behind) its 'real' essence or immediate life, which
it is forced to reconstruct as the past to constitute identity. Even the
future will be a future memory, as the subjunctive here suggests.

> How sweet it were, hearing the downward stream, . . .
> To muse and brood and live again in memory . . .
>
> (99, 100)

Experience as memory is the correlative of a mechanistic order. Hence
the language of non sequitur and, in fact, the disappearance of
language – voices are 'thin' and speech is 'whispered' – because the
music reproduced in the ear is not only secondary but turns back
on itself to reproduce a past sound again. The 'dewy echoes calling /
From cave to cave' (39–40) re-sound through hollow spaces, as in
the ear, as ever receding simulacra of themselves. In this reading
language always represents a prior representation in a regress which
is further and further from the experience which generates it. That is
why the sounds of the island are scarcely heard. The music of the
island (Tennyson never ceased to work upon *The Tempest*) falls almost
soundlessly upon the ear. Language finally becomes pure sound
only representing itself. The descriptive strategy of the poem is to
bring this condition into being by displacing one comparison with
another, which thus recedes from its source in the world. Music is
softer than falling rose petals and then as soundless as condensing
dew on granite (46–9). The mutual regress of language and
consciousness here reminds one of Hallam's analysis of the modern
self which withdraws into consciousness, issuing in melancholy and
the sense of loss. The subject becomes a representation which only
it can read. The loss of reference runs parallel to the dissociation of
consciousness from what it has made in the world.

Fatalism is the necessary condition of a subject without continuity
and volition, Carlyle believed. It is this which is emphasized in 1842
with the addition of a passage in which the mariners find the
possibility of returning to make an intervention in the 'confusion' (128)
of their island home unthinkable. By definition a return to the past is
literally unthinkable, because it can only be a new representation.
The Lotos-Eaters imagine themselves to be horrendously posthumous

to their social world, already part of history and art, somebody else's fictions, as their 'great deeds' (123) are sung by minstrels. The 'long labour' (130) of return is impossible. The failure to participate in history becomes critical in 1842, when the question of the will as agent is introduced and with it a set of directly moral and social issues. Carlyle's reference to Hume and Reid is part of a debate which is theological in essence. It was begun in 1830 by Sir William Hamilton, who attempted to rehabilitate the thinking of Reid by differentiating him sharply from Hume.[20] J. F. Ferrier continued this discussion in 1838–39, in a series of essays in *Blackwood's Magazine*, 'An introduction to the philosophy of consciousness'.[21] For Ferrier consciousness is locked into relationship with the world, since the mind brings its own categories to objects in the world, and frames them with its perceptual constructions, which cannot be divorced from things. Agency is created by the will, which is the antagonistic principle intruding on the life of simple sensation. Its struggle to exist and control the immediacy of experience through a reflexive act constitutes freedom. Otherwise the self must exist as 'reverie' without action in a world which is essentially violent because, like a being in the sea, consciousness is at the mercy of what is external to it. Here Ferrier oddly reproduces the violence done to the Lotos-Eaters by passive toil, for in avoiding the violence of the external world of sensation the will resorts to an equally violent act of domination over the senses.

> Nature and her powers have now no constraining hold over him; he stands out of her jurisdiction. In this act he has taken himself out of her hands into his own; he has made himself his own master. In this act he has displaced his sensations, and his sensations no longer monopolise him; they have no longer the complete mastery over him. In this act he has thrust his passions from their place, and his passions have lost their supreme ascendancy.[22]

Ferrier's argument is subtle and transforms sceptical argument into affirmation. In another part of his discussion he writes of sceptical philosophy:

> What sort of picture have their researches presented to our observation? Not the picture of a man; but the representation of an automaton, that is what it cannot help being, – a phantom dreaming what it cannot but dream – an engine performing what it *must* perform [cf. the violence done to the Lotos-Eater in passive toil] – an incarnate reverie – a weathercock, shifting

71

helplessly in the winds of sensibility – a wretched association-machine, through which ideas pass linked together by laws over which the machine itself has no control – anything, in short, except that free and self-sustained centre of underived, and therefore responsible activity, which we call *Man*.[23]

As 'dreaming phantoms' or 'incarnate reverie' the mariners have been made incapable of 'mastering' their world. And yet Ferrier's intervening 'will' is an oddly uneasy and external faculty. 'Underived' from genetic history and intruding *sui generis* upon it, it is an idealist will, brought in to redress a materialist psychology. The ending added to 'The Lotos-Eaters' in 1842 pulls the poem in this direction, as the irresponsible Epicurean gods refuse to intervene in history. It appears to support a hypothesis which assumes the critical necessity of will, yet exposes its actual externality and idealism among the slothful gods. In 1832 the Lotos-Eaters propose to 'abide in the golden vale / ... till the Lotos fail' (26–7) in delirious ecstasy. So, in the Malthusian dread of scarcity which is not the dialectical opposite but the complement of the fantasy of the exploitation of magical fecundity, nature's stocks can be exhausted. The drug is a commodity which will inevitably, and disastrously, run out, leaving the Lotos-Eaters to their suicidal frenzy. The shock of this ending is extraordinarily appropriate both to the fantasy of endlessly exploitable colonial resources in the South Pacific and to the despair which Carlyle saw as the terminal moment of scepticism. It is also appropriate to a poem which was to be revised in the hungry 1840s, the era of cholera, starvation and massive hardship for an overcrowded and impoverished populace. But Tennyson altered it. The Lotos-Eaters reverse their oppressed position by an imaginary act in which they become gods, 'careless of mankind' (155) and dissociated from human life, regarding the catastrophes they actually create as things which happen without their responsibility – 'and the bolts are *hurled* / Far below them' (156–7). Gods repudiating agency and power: these are the mirror images of the oppressed consciousness without power. The gods turn away from the damage they wreak upon men, seemingly unaware of the relationship of exploitation between deities and men, who supplicate and sacrifice to the gods to no avail. Men, victims of famine, plague, war and natural disaster, caught up in a deluded religion which constructs divinity as a power to be appeased, a power which will intervene if the 'praying hands' (161) of the suffering persist in sacrifice, are caught up in a mystified relationship to the powers above.

Suffering men and careless gods are predicated on one another. The 1842 ending is fiercely ideological as the passage from Lucretius which is the basis of this coda is transformed into a master–slave nightmare. The ending does, paradoxically, return the mariners to the divided 'confusion' of human society, but human society is made strange in the act of imagination which sees it from another place, from the heaven of the Epicurean gods. Aristocratic detachment and the refusal of action and agency, oppressed toil and exploitation, are here forms of one another. It is a fierce analysis of the structure of an existing political situation. The coda introduces a critique which goes far beyond 1832 as it envisages a universe which conceives the idealist will as external to it and irrelevant to its affairs, 'underived' from experience indeed. Neither art nor language have a place here. The gods may aestheticize the 'doleful song' (162) of suffering and lamentation, but it is 'Like a tale of little meaning, though the words are strong' (164). The lamentation is uninterpretable as sign and meaning split apart, a consequence of the mariners' alienated music of the beating heart, where sound only refers to itself, and the object of signification slips into oblivion, just as the result of their labour upon the world is 'taken from' them and passes over into the memory. The coda is a strange place in which to find Hallam's poetry of pure sound. The life of pure sensation, Ferrier said, is blind – and deaf.[24]

The slumbrous cadences of 'The Lotos-Eaters' betray a real anxiety, as they struggle to represent a materialism which actually makes consciousness more and more phantasmal and to change the opposition between escape and toil by giving it a new political content. It can quite rightly be read as an overwhelming threnody on the desire to escape into forgetting, but that very desire constitutes an analysis and critique of deep contradictions. The additions of 1842 consolidate the critique. They are an extraordinary response to the worsening social conditions of the 1840s and turn the poem of 1832 virtually into a new text as the brutalizing suffering of the 1840s finds a place in it. Change without change, engagement simultaneous with detachment, the continuity of the past as against the rupture of the present, a poetry of sound where meaning is the history of that sound rather than new signification – the risky, paradoxical subversiveness of the Apostles seems to have become increasingly difficult to hold as political and aesthetic positions and breaks down under the pressure of the 1840s.

Notes

1. *The Poems of Tennyson* (Longman Annotated English Poets), CHRISTOPHER
   RICKS, ed., 3 vols, 2nd edn, London, 1987, I, 436.
2. Ibid.
3. The tradition of debating Coleridge's poems began in the Cambridge Union
   in the late 1820s. PETER ALLEN, *The Cambridge Apostles: The Early Years*,
   Cambridge, 1978, 47.
4. WILLIAM WHEWELL, *On Astronomy and General Physics considered with Reference
   to Natural Theology*, Bridgewater Treatises III, London, 1833, 182.
5. Hallam on the Greeks, *The Writings of Arthur Hallam*, T. H. VAIL MOTTER, ed.,
   London and New York, 1943, 145–7.
6. *Victorian Scrutinies: Reviews of Poetry 1830–70*, ISOBEL ARMSTRONG, ed., London,
   1972, 123–4.
7. *The Excursion*, Preface of 1814, 63–7, in WILLIAM WORDSWORTH, *Poetical Works*
   (Oxford Standard Authors), Thomas Hutchinson and Ernest de Selincourt,
   eds, 1936, 590.
8. 'On sympathy', MOTTER, *Hallam*, 133–42: 137, 138.
9. Ibid., 138, 139.
10. 'Theodicaea Novissima', ibid., 198–213: 204.
11. Ibid., 205.
12. Ibid., 66. But though 'reasons thrive' on the five senses, knowledge, and nature,
    'hath never a bound'.
13. 'Lines addressed to Alfred Tennyson' (1830), ibid., 67.
14. THOMAS KEIGHTLEY, *The Fairy Mythology*, 2 vols, London, 1828, I, 7. See also
    21; and Preface, xii, for Keightley's belief that popular legends affect 'the feelings
    of a nation'.
15. THOMAS CARLYLE, *Sartor Resartus: The Life and Opinions of Herr Teufelsdröckh*
    (1831), *Thomas Carlyle's Collected Works* (Library Edition), 31 vols, London
    and New York, 1869–71, I, 65.
16. W. D. PADEN, *Tennyson in Egypt: A Study of the Imagery in this Earlier Work*,
    University of Kansas Publications, Humanistic Studies, 27, Lawrence, 1942,
    155.
17. MRS GASKELL describes the resort to opium by working men (to dull the pain
    of hunger) in *Mary Barton* (1848).
18. THOMAS CARLYLE, 'Signs of the times' (1829), *Critical and Miscellaneous Essays*,
    6 vols, II, 313–42; 317 (vol. VII, *Thomas Carlyle's Collected Works*, Library
    Edition, 31 vols, London and New York, 1869–71).
19. Ibid., 322.
20. 'Philosophy of Perception: Reid and Brown', *Edinburgh Review*, LII (1830–1),
    158–207.
21. J. F. FERRIER's articles on consciousness were published in *Blackwood's
    Edinburgh Magazine*, XLIII (1838), 187–201, 437–52, 784–91; XLIV (1838),
    539–52; XLV (1839), 201–11, 419–30. W. DAVID SHAW first made the connection
    between Ferrier and Tennyson in his *The Lucid Veil: Poetic Truth in the Victorian
    Age*, London, 1987, 48–53.
22. *Blackwood's Edinburgh Magazine*, XLV (1839), 204.
23. Ibid., 202.

24. Since sensations are 'enslaving powers of darkness', without being under the control of the will, the paradox is that reliance on sensation leads to a *dearth* of perceptual experience. Ibid., 203.

4 Tennyson: Politics and Sexuality in *The Princess* and *In Memoriam**

TERRY EAGLETON

Terry Eagleton is another important critic who is committed to uniting cultural practice and political practice. In 1983 in *Literary Theory: An Introduction* he argued that literary criticism should enrich our lives through the transformation of a divided society by showing how particular discourses are used for particular ideological ends. This he likens to the classical study of rhetoric as a study of linguistic devices used to persuade, incite or plead. In this essay, written in 1978, Eagleton unites Lacanian analysis and Marxist literary theory to argue that Tennyson's *In Memoriam* and *The Princess* are an attempt to resolve the mid-century 'Oedipal' crisis of the bourgeois state brought about by the class struggles of the 1840s and the spectre of revolution in Europe. Such a process in the poems involves a transcendence of feminine grief and a reconsolidation of the symbolic order in a celebration of bourgeois sexual reproduction, thus resolving the oedipal complex and the struggle for manhood. (See Sinfield's critique of this reading in *Alfred Tennyson*, pp. 135–6: for Sinfield the blurring of gender roles is part of a dissident strategy, for Eagleton it is means to restabilize such roles and thereby affirm the dominant order.)

Perhaps I could begin by suggesting, rather frivolously, that the mid-nineteenth century bourgeois state had problems in resolving its Oedipus complex. In striving to achieve its manhood – that is to say, to secure that full political dominance which I will designate as 'masculine' – it needed to settle a certain envying hostility towards its own repressive 'father' – towards that other form of state power figured in Tennyson's *The Princess* by the hermaphroditic Prince's own father, the barbaric, nakedly militaristic, blatantly sexist king. Such iron political repression continues, of course, to be a necessity for the mid-nineteenth century state; but in so far as this brutally explicit *dominance* fails to secure the conditions of ruling-class *hegemony*, the admiring identification with the strong father must be

---

*Reprinted from *1848: The Sociology of Literature*, ed., Francis Barker *et al.* (Colchester: Essex University Press, 1978), pp. 97–106.

tempered and complicated by a sustained Oedipal allegiance to the 'mother' – that is to say, to those 'civilizing' values of 'sweetness' and 'moral nobility' which are paradigmatically 'feminine'. There is, however, an additional contradiction here. For if sexual reproduction is to be continued, and the social relations of capitalist production correspondingly perpetuated, the Oedipal relation to the mother must be repressed and transcended; yet how is this then to avoid the irruption into the social formation of that heterogeneous flux, process and production of sexual *desire* which is potentially subversive of the social order? If this threat is to be avoided, the woman must naturally be desexualized: all women must become 'mothers'. (I shall suggest later that, in marrying Ida, the protagonist of *The Princess* is among other things marrying his mother.) But if the woman is desexualized, how is the bourgeois social formation to survive by the progenitive reproduction of its individual agents?

I read the ideological project of *The Princess* as an imaginary 'resolution' of these contradictions by a re-fashioning of what we may call, after Lacan, the 'symbolic order'. And although I am far from suggesting that the sexual 'code' of the text is purely phenomenal – that the poem is not 'really' about sexuality – I want to argue that this dominant semiotic code does indeed, in its turn, encode other ideological motifs, one of which I have already adumbrated – the question of a certain transitional crisis in the nature of state power, occasioned most directly by the sharpening of the class struggle in the 1840s, by the stage of development of the productive forces, and by the minatory spectre of the events in France. As what we may risk calling a 'psychoanalysis of the bourgeois state', the text subtly imbricates the questions of the production of sexuality and the production of political power – the reshaping of the symbolic order and the qualified recasting of the structures of bourgeois dominance. (And there are other codes also, as I will show later – most notably, the problem of the nature of literary production itself, of which the text's strikingly bizarre *form* is at once index and attempted resolution.)

That *The Princess* concerns a severe disturbance in the symbolic order – that is to say, in that distribution and stabilization of sexual roles which rests upon the post-Oedipal acceptance of difference, opposition and exclusion – is obvious enough on even the most cursory reading. The bare bones of its narrative, after all, concern a 'feminine' male assuming female disguise in order to woo a 'masculine' female to whom he plays the roles of both child and lover. The poem's ideological project will then be to 'resolve' this socially subversive androgyny by re-establishing that 'otherness' of sexual roles essential for socio-sexual reproduction, while simultaneously effecting that controlled *transference* and reciprocity of sexual characteristics (power and gentleness, knowledge and wisdom, etc.) essential for the 'humanization', and so consolidated hegemony, of the bourgeois state. To put the matter another way: the ceaselessly heterogeneous, polyvalent flux of *desire* must be caught up, trapped and stabilized in a regulated symbolic exchange of discrete, reified 'sexual characteristics'.

A good many Tennysonian texts are marked by a notably ambivalent attitude towards the 'otherness' of the woman. That the woman should be 'other' is, as I have argued, naturally essential for socio-sexual reproduction; but it is precisely this 'otherness' which is also at the root of Tennyson's profound fear of the woman. (And 'Tennyson' here is no more than a name for the mid-Victorian ideological formation, whatever pathological problems he may himself have endured.) Sexuality is commonly associated in Tennyson with violence and death; the sexual strife between the Prince and Ida triggers off a war, and inscribed on the gate of Ida's feminist college is the motto: 'Let no man enter in on pain of death'. To penetrate the mysterious female stronghold, to enter the *vagina dentata* of the woman, is to risk that symbolic death which is castration. Tennyson fears women because they signify the potentially subversive flux of desire, and so unmask the guilty secret of the sublimated allegiance to the mother; but he fears them also because they represent the repressed 'female' in himself – the erotic, privatized, psychically 'estranged' literary producer impermissably at odds with the 'masculine' state ideologue, the poet whose texts must ceaselessly displace their sensuality into sensuousness. The distance between, say, 'Mariana' and the 'Ode on the Death of the Duke of Wellington' is an exact measure of this 'feminine'/'masculine' contradiction, which is no mere question of clinical biography, but an objective contradiction traversing the places of the mid-Victorian poet within the social formation. For on the one hand, given the necessary marginalization of poetic production within Victorian ideological production as a whole, the poetic text becomes the repository of those 'feminine' elements expelled by the crass 'masculinity' of the dominant utilitarian ideology – becomes, in a phrase, the locus of 'lyrical sensibility'. Yet on the other hand, the poetic producer must necessarily remain bound by the 'masculine' propositional discourses of that ideology. Alfred Lord Tennyson, private lyricist and Poet Laureate, is a name which marks one particular nexus of this contradiction within aesthetic ideology. Indeed it is a striking index of that fact that the 'public', 'masculine' text which unquestionably confirms his function as literary state-lackey (*In*

Memoriam) is no more than a restless congeries of private ('feminine')
lyrics.

It is as an attempted resolution of this (and other) contradictions
that I read *The Princess*. For if it is faintly frivolous to suggest that
the Victorian state had Oedipal problems, it is flagrantly obvious to
point out that the Prince in this poem does so. Overshadowed by
his ravingly sexist father, and devoted to the image of his mother
('No Angel, but a dearer being, all dipt / In Angel instincts,
breathing Paradise'), the sexually indeterminate Prince ('blue-eyed,
and fair in face . . . With lengths of yellow ringlet, like a girl') has
yet to achieve his manhood; his tediously frequent hallucinations, in
which reality dissolves into mocking illusion, signify, in Lacanian
terms, his inability properly to enter into the symbolic order. They
involve a 'swooning' which is, symbolically, sexual impotence and
castration; and to overcome this symbolic impotence (which is, as we
shall see, 'ideological' as well as sexual), the Prince must confront,
in displaced and mystified form, the repressed 'femininity' in his
personality. The way he achieves this in the first place is by assuming
female dress and personality – that is to say, by symbolically castrating
himself, and so acting out in fiction and charade his actual,
symbolically castrated condition. In thus 'fictionalizing' and
'mythifying' that condition, the assumption of female dress and
voice has, one might say, something of the structure of the neurotic
symptom: it allows the Prince at once to express his psychological
disturbance and yet to conceal it (since it is farcically obvious that he
is in fact a man). The disguise, as it were, reinforces his maleness in
the very act of dissembling and displacing it.

But the Prince's true fulfilment of his manhood is, of course, his
winning of the Princess Ida, for which the female disguise is merely
instrumental. If the Prince is a feminine male, Ida is a masculine
female; and one might write the ideological equation of the poem
thus: feminine male × masculine female = masculine male + feminine
female. (Although this, given the ideologically essential transference
of 'sexual characteristics' which I have already discussed, will do only
as a partial, provisional formulation.) As a 'masculine' woman, Ida
symbolizes for the Prince the fearfully emasculating power of female
sexuality; this, indeed, is one of the text's multiple sexual
ambiguities, since although Ida's feminism in one sense 'desexualizes'
her (thus rendering her less of a sexual threat to the Prince), that
feminism also signifies the full achievement of her womanhood. If
the Prince can 'feminize' a 'masculine' woman, then he can gain his
own manhood by having confronted, and conquered, the fearful
'masculine' power of female sexuality. In this sense, Ida is the
Prince's own alienated masculinity, the 'ideal ego' (in Lacan's term)

to which his relationship is the 'imaginary' one of simultaneous identification/estrangement. But at the same time, since this 'ideal ego' is in fact a woman, the Prince, in winning her ('Lay thy sweet hands in mine and trust in me'), is, so to speak, incorporating the female into himself, and thus coming to terms with the 'feminine' aspects of himself in ways fully acceptable to the symbolic order (i.e. in marriage).

The text, then, has fulfilled its ideological function. The symbolic order has been re-consolidated, although in suitably refurbished form. The ideologically unacceptable sexist coerciveness of the Prince's father ('Man with the head and woman with the heart, / Man to command and woman to obey') has been qualified by a judicious incorporation of certain 'feminine' qualities into the sexist bourgeois state, for the purpose of buttressing its hegemony. For if women are excessively subjugated, the genetic effects of this upon their sons, and the 'spiritual' effects of it upon their husbands, may well prove socially and politically disastrous. 'If she be small, slight-natured, miserable, / How shall men grow?' Women should not be excessively subjugated, then, in order that their sons and husbands, as members of the hegemonic class, may be better equipped to subjugate them more efficiently. Part of the apparatus of that repression is, of course, the ideological practice of 'literature' itself, which includes *The Princess*. I do not mean by this merely that the poem's blatantly sexist 'content' reinforces the oppression of women; I am referring also to what the poem achieves in *the material practice of its writing*. For we must remember that Ida is a '*Poet*-Princess', who recognizes that a crucial condition of women's liberation consists in the wresting of the educational and 'cultural' apparatuses from male domination. She and her comrades have conquered, and transmuted, the 'masculine' discourses of science, learning, history, mythology – in brief, those discourses which Tennyson himself, as 'feminine' poet, finds so difficult to introduce, other than nervously and obliquely, into his own poetic production. (One might say of his texts that their 'thought' consists at best of feelings tremulously tinged with concepts.) In appropriating Ida, then Tennyson/the Prince have recovered their aesthetic-ideological, as well as sexual, potency, united with their poetic, as well as 'masculine', ideal-ego. That recovery *is* the textual practice known as *The Princess*; inexpropriating the women of their learning and smashing up their college, the Poet Laureate has provided himself with the materials for a 'masculine', 'public' poem.

It would be mistaken, however, to conclude that *The Princess* triumphantly resolves the contradictions which are the very process of its constitution. It is true that the text transforms the college into a hospital, thus returning its inmates to their proper roles of ministering tenderly to fevered males; it is true also, in a crucial symbolic act, that Ida is persuaded to return Psyche's child to her, thus confirming the sacredness of maternity and the priorities of familial sexual reproduction. Yet for all that, the Prince himself remains locked to the end in his Oedipal problems in a way which profoundly disturbs and interrogates the poem's attempt to re-constitute the symbolic order. For one of the text's deepest ironies is that the Prince finally wins Ida, and so achieves full manhood, only by a process which involves his regression to a childlike dependence on her 'maternal' ministrations, when he lies, injured after battle, in that state of 'psychotic' hallucination which signifies his inability fully to enter the symbolic order. It is no accident that the hymn of praise to his mother I quoted previously occurs just before he successfully concludes his wooing; the Oedipus complex has, so to speak, merely been transferred. Or perhaps it would be more accurate to say that the true contradiction lies in the fact that the complex has been at once transcended and preserved; the Prince has achieved his manhood in love and battle, yet remains tied as a child to his maternal mistress.

It is the necessity of this contradiction which it is important to emphasize. If the social relations of production are to be perpetuated, the Oedipus complex must be overcome in the name of a mature sexuality; but if the disruptiveness of desire is to be curtailed, the woman must be 'desexualized' to a mother-image which will then induce impotence in the male. The poem is scored through by this contradiction, as it is by the related one I have described: that, precisely at the point where the capitalist social formation needs to assert the stringent discipline of the 'masculine' principle, it needs also to qualify that principle with the virtues of 'femininity'. This, indeed, is the note of compromise on which the poem ends, in its explicitly political comments on the upheavals in Europe. The Tory member's son makes his chuckle-headed chauvinist contrast between British stability and European turmoil, and there is no doubt that the comments are textually endorsed; yet the author's persona then instantly inserts his tempering, reformist, 'feminine' caveat, recalling the 'social wrong' of Britain itself and the need for political patience.

Formally speaking, *The Princess* is, of course, a narrative within a narrative – a mythical tale concocted by seven mindless Oxford undergraduates lolling indolently within an aristocratic country seat. The entire poem, in other words, is precisely a sport, an idle frivolity, a distracting device, a light-hearted piece of ritualized upper-class self-indulgence. The whole text is officially no more than a verbal game, uncertain how seriously to take itself; and it is important to register the ideological necessity of this fact. For if the Prince himself, in his hallucinatory fits, is unable to 'know the shadow from the substance', finding reality a 'mockery' and 'hollow show', exactly the same is true of the poem itself. Indeed one of its most curious features is its constant undertone of farce – a farce which seems to consist in nothing less than the poem's sporadically sending itself up. I am thinking, for example, of the absurdity of the disguised Prince's piping up in a female treble, or of that strikingly dissonant moment when, fleeing for his life from an enraged bunch of feminists, he tells us that 'secret laughter tickled all (his) soul'. It seems to me difficult to see these devices as anything other than 'defence' and 'displacement' mechanisms, analogous to the Freudian joke, whereby disturbing material almost too painful to be admitted into consciousness is allowed through only in 'emasculated' form. The poem, in short, can 'succeed' (not that it does) only partly, cancelling and 'castrating' its own serious, 'masculine' substance – repressing its own material reality as a writing practice, as sober Victorian epic, and displacing itself instead into the 'feminine' modality of frivolous sport.

Yet there is an additional contradiction here, for if it is true that the poem casts itself into such 'feminine' modality, it is nonetheless imperative that the 'masculine' voice maintains its dominance – that, within the interplay of voices which speak or sing the text, the women are subordinated to the lowly status of intermittent lyrical 'punctuations' of the men's narrative ('To give us breathing space', as the authorial persona generously remarks.) So that while the formal frame of the text is 'feminine' sport, and the 'feminine' thus 'officially' dominant, this frame is in fact no more than the support of 'masculine' discursive dominance. It is, however, in any case somewhat misleading to speak of the poem as characterized by an 'interplay of voices'. For what is most graphically evident is that the poem displays no *dialectic* of discourses whatsoever; the seven male voices are in no sense differentiated, rigorously subjected as they are to a single, dominant narrative discourse whose only alterity is 'feminine' lyrical interlude. There is no sense in which one discourse inheres within, contradicts, interrogates or 'de-centres' another, as there is with both Clough and Browning. So if the ideological motifs of *The Princess* concern, in the Lacanian sense, the 'symbolic', the sealed closure of its inexorably 'centred' form is, again in Lacan's sense, classically 'imaginary'. Which is no more than to remind ourselves that the substance of the poem is *myth* – for myth is precisely that self-enclosed order of plenitude whose opposite is the open dialectic of history. Myth, one might argue, is 'metaphorical', in that it represents a substitute structure of significations for the historical; and the deepest formal irony of the poem is then that, myth though it is, its actual 'content' is *metonymic*, concerned with the movements and displacements of narrative/desire. This metonymic movement is enclosed, stabilized within the metaphorical; and one index of this stabilization is precisely the regular recurrence of the 'feminine' lyrics within the narrative. For if narrative is predominantly metonymic, lyric is predominantly metaphorical. The 'metaphorical' females are thus allowed from time to time gently to supervene on the 'metonymic' males, to recall and recuperate their turbulent narrative into the securing, anchoring, 'timeless' mythological themes of love, sorrow, parting, reunion and so on.

If *The Princess* is a 'full' poem, constituted by a highly wrought, gorgeous density of language, *In Memoriam* is a notably 'empty' one, whose language seems listlessly to turn around some central elusive negativity. That negativity, formally speaking, is the absence created by the death of Hallam – a death which for Tennyson is nothing less than the striking from the world of the 'transcendental signified'. Emptied of this ideological bedrock of senses, all that *In Memoriam's* own signifiers can do is set up subliminal resonances between each other, in order to generate some mood or context which might capture some substantive signified which forever evades them. The text's language thus involves a constant displacement of meaning: it becomes a kind of narcotic or masturbatory act, a melancholic self-drugging:

> In words like weeks I'll wrap me o'er
> Like coarsest clothes against the cold,
> But that large grief which these enfold
> Is given in outline and no more.

But it is not quite the conventional proposition that the poem has a meaning but cannot express it: the 'grief' the text speaks of is no less than the *grief of a whole crisis of language*, which is in turn the grief of a whole crisis of mid-nineteenth century bourgeois ideology. For Hallam, as I have argued in *Criticism and Ideology*, is nothing less than the empty space congregated by a whole set of ideological anxieties concerned with science, religion, the class struggle, in short with the 'revolutionary' de-centring of 'man' from his 'imaginary' relation of unity with his world. Tennyson's relation with Hallam was of this classically 'imaginary' kind (he describes the relation at one point as that of mother and child); but Hallam's death has dislodged the poet from that 'imaginary' narcissistic plenitude of identity and left him dolefully stranded in the 'symbolic order', marooned in that ceaseless play of difference, loss, absence and exclusion which is part of the very linguistic form of the text. To enter the symbolic order is to recognize that the world is independent of one's consciousness, that its continued existence does not depend upon oneself, and thus that one can die. Indeed as Tennyson writes, in a passage which unquestionably proves that he had read Lacan's *Ecrits*:

> The baby new to earth and sky,
> What time his tender palm is pressed
> Against the circle of the breast,
> Has never thought that 'this is I':
>
> But as he grows he gathers much,
> And learns the use of 'I' and 'me',
> And finds 'I am not what I see,
> And other than the things I touch'.

The contradiction of *In Memoriam*, however, is that while Hallam's death has forced it into this consciousness of differentiation and opposition (and evolutionary science has, of course, demonstrated 'man's' contingency to the universe), the text also finds it ideologically impermissible to accept this shattering of 'man's' metaphysical centredness. If the baby of the above stanzas is slowly emerging from the 'mirror-phrase', Tennyson himself is still trapped within it, or is even prior to it:

> So runs my dream: but what am I?
> An infant crying in the night:
> An infant crying for the light:
> And with no language but a cry.

In Lacan's parlance, 'demand' has not yet been mediated through language into 'desire'. The poem's ideological strategy, then, must be to come gradually to terms with the loss of Hallam, but then mythically to reconstruct the symbolic order into a 'higher' version of the lost 'imaginary'.

As the 'transcendental signifier' of *all* losses, Hallam, in Lacanian terms, represents the phallus for Tennyson. In order to 'enter into its manhood' – that is to say, to overcome its 'feminine' and 'infantile' grief and grow into a 'masculine', affirmative and thus ideologically efficacious text – the poem must recognize the necessity of the absence and opposition which the phallus signifies. But this recognition is constantly forestalled by the fact that the text's relation to Hallam is not only 'imaginary', but also Oedipal, fraternal and homosexual. Indeed, in a bafflingly complex series of slippages, Hallam figures for the text at various times as mother, brother, lover, wife and husband. The significant missing term is, of course, 'father'. If the poem can give up wishing to marry Hallam (either as mother, wife or husband) and establish him instead as the type of 'masculine' authority, then it can establish its own sexual identity as his admiring yet strong and separate son, or younger brother. The determinants which effect this transposition in the text are political ones. Given the threat of revolutionary upheaval, the poem must transcend its private 'feminine' melancholy and turn instead to the problem of 'masculine' political dominance:

> . . . Is this an hour
> For private sorrow's barren song,
> When more and more the people throng
> The chairs and thrones of civil power?

Hallam, had he lived, would have become a good counter-revolutionary politician,

> . . . A potent voice of Parliament,
> A pillar steadfast in the storm,
>
> Should licensed boldness gather force,
> Becoming, when the time has birth,
> A lever to uplift the earth
> And roll it in another course . . .

But even as a corpse he remains a powerful symbol of bourgeois hegemony: 'A deeper voice across the storm',

> Proclaiming social truth shall spread,
> And justice, ev'n tho' thrice again
> The red fool-fury of the Seine
> Should pile her barricades with dead.

To put the matter a little crudely: what has enabled the text to overcome its Oedipus complex is 1848.

It is in this way, then, that *In Memoriam* is finally able to enter the symbolic order – to become itself the ideologically potent, fully-sexed son of its dead father. Instead of wishing to marry Hallam, it celebrates the marriage of Tennyson's own younger sister, in a triumphant reaffirmation of bourgeois sexual reproduction. And yet for all that, the poem does not abandon the 'imaginary'. I argued earlier that the poem's language partook of the 'symbolic'; but it does not, naturally, press that all the way into the full-bloodedly *symboliste* discourse of a Mallarmé, where the evaporation of the signified into an infinite play of signifiers becomes the basis for a radically new poetic. *In Memoriam* is still ideologically constrained by the demand to produce a coherent propositional realism; so that while the bond between signifier and signified has certainly loosened, a 'mirror-relation' between 'word' and 'thing' is nevertheless preserved. And if the poem sustains the 'imaginary' at its linguistic level, it does so also, in the end, at the level of 'content'. Hallam is finally elevated to a cosmic type of some future human unity, reverently installed as a privileged subject within the life of that divine Subject of subjects on which the whole of creation centres. The closing stanzas of *In Memoriam* would seem powerfully to validate Louis Althusser's claim that the 'model' for all ideology is fundamentally theological.

I want to end on what the liberal critics call a 'personal note'. Given the ideological conditions within which this paper is produced, it would be surprising, since I am male, if it did not contain residual elements of sexism. One such element I thought I had spotted, in re-reading what I have written – that I give a good deal more attention to the Prince in *The Princess* than to Ida herself. But this seems to me to reflect a significant fact about the poem. The poem is mistitled: ostensibly 'about' Ida, it in fact concerns problems of 'masculine' hegemony. There is a revealing discrepancy between the poem's title (which, as with all literary texts, is part of its meaning) and the substance of the poem itself, which the title displaces. In this case, at least, it would seem that the sexism is the text's, rather than my own.

5 Woman Red in Tooth and Claw: Nature and the Feminine in Tennyson* and Darwin

JAMES ELI ADAMS

Adams here takes an interdisciplinary approach to show how new ideas about nature brought about by Victorian science came to unsettle traditional archetypes of womanhood. Both Darwin and Tennyson (in *In Memoriam* and *The Princess*) are shown struggling with such archetypes unable in the end to hold them in place as feminine Nature came gradually to be seen not as a nurturing agent but as a potentially monstrous destroyer of her offspring in the processes of natural selection: 'Nature, red in tooth and claw'. Once again Adams is interested in ideology and discourse, concerned to reveal how Tennyson's poetry works to challenge or smooth over Victorian ideological problems. Like Eagleton, Adams shows how important the construction of a notion of 'woman' is to mid-century conservative ideas, how an ideal of a maternal femininity came to be representative of the forces of continuity and vigilance in a moment of crisis and punctuated by revolution. New scientific theories about the nature of Nature, then, were to prompt a new recognition of the significance of the feminine, not only as a biological category but as an organizing principle of Victorian discourse and thus to threaten the stability of such notions of gradual, rather than revolutionary, change.

One can easily imagine Tennyson's satisfaction at the fate of his phrase, 'Nature, red in tooth and claw': a mere six words have been vested by historians with power to sum up nothing less than the impact of evolutionary thought on Christian humanism. But of course the transformation of poetry into a slogan has its costs. Tennyson's phrase has been profoundly diminished by the effacement of its original context – in particular, by the neglect of the fundamental poetic device within which the phrase functions. Tennyson's 'Nature', so commonly invoked as a transparent scientific concept, appears in the famous sections LV and LVI of *In Memoriam* (1850) as a personification – an extended, strikingly elaborate

---

*Reprinted from *Victorian Studies* **33** 1 (Autumn 1989), pp. 7–27

personification of the world-image Tennyson derived from contemporary science. Curiously, this fact is almost never remarked upon by commentators. Perhaps the feature seems unremarkable, since the idea of nature is so deeply engrained in Western culture and its languages as a feminine agent with volition and purpose. Yet the very point of Tennyson's personification is to unsettle this traditional figuration. His Nature remains feminine, to be sure, yet his night thoughts on modern science are focused by the dread that the character of this feminine being has changed utterly – that 'Mother Nature' has become a mocking, savage oxymoron.

Tennyson's personification of nature, so often cited to illustrate the impact of science on religious faith, thus suggests that evolutionary speculation also rendered newly problematic a deeply traditional and comforting archetype of womanhood. In registering this disturbance, the 'scientific' sections of *In Memoriam* suggest an important relation between science and gender not only in Tennyson's poetry but throughout early Victorian discourse. It is a relation articulated by Darwin (albeit more obliquely) when he, too, acknowledges new pressures on traditional figurations of nature. Responding to critics who complained of his figurative language in *The Origin of Species*, Darwin protested, 'It is hard to avoid personifying the word Nature' – a somewhat impatient objection, it might seem, but one which goes to the heat of debates about the very concept of nature.[1] Darwin's theory ostensibly dealt a final blow to anthropomorphic understandings of the natural world – and hence to personifications of nature – yet in the famous work setting forth that theory Darwin clearly and persistently depicts the natural world as a feminine, nurturing being. To be sure, anthropomorphism had been logically suspect at least since the rise of Baconian empiricism, which rejected the notion of final cause in scientific explanation, and Darwin was hardly the first scientist to fail to live up to the descriptive norms of a thoroughgoing positivism. Yet in light of the growing authority of this sceptical tradition – of which the *Origin* is in some respects a culmination – personifications of nature increasingly come to represent a reactionary, even archaic mode of discourse. Tennyson's trope in particular can be viewed as a desperate effort to humanize the results of science by envisioning nature even in its bleakest aspects as a conscious, designing being, however perverse. In representing an older, anthropocentric world-view, however, the personification also allowed Tennyson to contemplate the destruction of that older view as a transformation in conceptions of gender. To question the nature of 'Nature' as *In Memoriam* does is inescapably to question the nature of woman. More precisely, it is to ask what has become of

those conventionally feminine attributes that have so long
distinguished 'Mother Nature'.[2]

Throughout history, of course, the 'conventionally feminine' has
been constructed antithetically. There is no figurative image of
woman, Simone de Beauvoir has contended, that does not
immediately evoke its opposite.[3] Indeed, the archetypal doubleness
of the feminine (and hence of nature) clearly informs a work by one
of Tennyson's contemporaries that may well have suggested the
figure of 'Nature, red in tooth and claw'. In the chapter of *Past and
Present* (1843) entitled 'The Sphinx', Carlyle proclaimed that

> Nature, like the Sphinx, is of womanly celestial loveliness and
> tenderness: the face and bosom of a goddess, but ending in
> claws and the body of a lioness. There is in her a celestial
> beauty ... but there is also a darkness, a ferocity, fatality, which
> are infernal ... Answer her riddle, it is well with thee. Answer it
> not, pass on regarding it not, it will answer itself; the solution is a
> thing of teeth and claws.[4]

By virtue of the desire invested in the image of nature as a maternal
agency, the image always holds in reserve a terrible double
associated with the withdrawal of that agency. But such doubleness
(and duplicity) seems to have become an especially urgent and
threatening reality in early Victorian discourse, which shaped the
long gestations of both *In Memoriam* and *The Origin of Species*, as
well as the feverish production of *Past and Present*. On the one hand,
during the 1830s and 1840s, conservative voices in the debate over
woman's place – such as Sarah Ellis, author of the immensely popular
Women of England (1837) – were codifying an ideal of womanhood
as a quasi-redemptive agency that operated almost entirely within
the sphere of maternity and domestic life. Woman's very being, it
seemed, was constituted by her role of tending to the physical and
emotional needs of men and children.[5] This is precisely the maternal
idea which Tennyson's Nature confounds – and from which that
figure would have drawn a special power to disturb its original
audience. Of course the very fervour with which motherhood is
celebrated in this period makes plain the role of the ideal as a response
to a wealth of adversarial forces.[6] But Tennyson's poetry, like Darwin's
science, reminds us that the maternal ideal assumes its urgency in
Victorian culture at the same moment that the claims of science are
finally undermining one of the culture's most powerful icons of
maternity: the very conception of nature as Mother Nature. Hence it
is that Tennyson's poetry can articulate a direct and substantial bond
between evolutionary science and an image that, in its subversion of

the domestic ideal of womanhood, haunts the Victorian consciousness: the figure of the femme fatale or demonic woman.[7] In personifying nature, Tennyson envisions the subversion of the maternal archetype as an act of feminine betrayal. When Nature's maternal solicitude gives way to indifference, the male poet regards the withdrawal as an act of open hostility toward mankind.

This startling metamorphosis of a feminine Nature defines a powerful congruence between *In Memoriam* and *The Princess*, the latter of which is largely constructed around Tennyson's association of evolutionary nature with feminine betrayal. But I also will suggest, in a more speculative vein, that this conjunction within Tennyson's poetry helps to explain the prominence and persistence of the demonic woman as a motif of Victorian culture generally. 'Nature never did betray the heart that loved her', Wordsworth declared – a profession of faith that suggests how manifold and complex could be the personal and cultural investment in a feminine Nature. The femininity that Tennyson finds betrayed, and that betrays Tennyson, is likewise not only maternal and erotic, but cognitive as well. His poetry demonstrates how intricately and profoundly the intellectual and symbolic order of the early Victorian period depends on a typology of woman as an agent of continuity, restraint, and coherence in a world in which schemes of history, political structures, and meaning itself are constantly threatening to fall apart. In this regard the plaintive, self-baffling plea in *The Princess* (1847) for a via media in 'the woman question' unexpectedly converges with Mill's radical stance in *The Subjection of Women* (1869). Both works rely on a tacit identification of woman with a particular mode of knowing and acting shaped by female domesticity, a 'woman's wisdom' that uniquely guides and supports the impetus of male action and speculation.

I

Darwin's response to critics of his figurative language – 'It is difficult to avoid personifying the word Nature' – appeals to the inherently figurative character of language itself. But the rejoinder, as many commentators have objected, hardly explains Darwin's reluctance to surrender his intricate and emphatic personifications of nature:[8]

> As man can produce and certainly has produced a great result by his methodical and unconscious means of selection, what may not nature effect? Man can act only on external and visible

characters: nature cares nothing for appearances, except in so far
as they may be useful to any being. She can act on every internal
organ, on every shade of constitutional difference, on the whole
machinery of life. Man selects only for his own good; Nature
only for that of the being which she tends. Every selected
character is fully exercised by her; and the being is placed under
well-suited conditions of life.

(Origin, p. 132)

Darwin's crucial analogy between natural and artificial selection is
thus presented in a form that defies the explanatory norms enforced
by a rigorous positivism. As recent Darwin scholars have pointed
out, however, his metaphors generally perform what Edward
Manier has called 'a full job of scientific work'. This particular
personification, Manier argues, has a crucial function as a heuristic
device that enabled Darwin to outline his theoretical framework in
some detail, even though he could not precisely specify the
mechanisms that would account for natural selection. Ironically, this
'logic of possibility' – like Darwin's image of nature as a conscious
agent – is deeply indebted to the discourse of natural theology.
Indeed, in Darwin's earlier drafts of his theory nature seems to
verge on divinity: in the *Sketch* of 1842, it is 'a being infinitely more
sagacious than man', in the *Essay* of 1844 'a Being with penetration
sufficient to perceive differences quite imperceptible to man'.[9] But
why, then, should Darwin in the *Origin* present nature's sagacity as
an emphatically feminine wisdom?

It is not entirely surprising that Darwin's central analogy between
natural and human selection would articulate an ideology of gender,
since the analogy is so readily associated with the dualism of nature
and culture, which in turn is almost universally aligned with a
cultural opposition between male and female attributes.[10] Yet the
particular attributes Darwin assigns to nature are revealing. The
leading characteristic of this female agent is not the sheer fecundity
one might associate with Mother Nature, but rather a peculiarly
domestic femininity, an attribute closely identified with rearing offspring and ministering to the needs of individuals. The activity of
man's selection is, by comparison, rather crude, shortsighted
(governed solely by external characteristics), and selfish: man selects
only with an eye to what benefits man. But Nature is more discerning
and more generous. She has an intuitive grasp of, and can minister
to, subtleties of inner being that elude the coarser sensibility. She is
careful, vigilant, disinterested, even selfless in her responsibility for
'the being which she tends'.[11] Clearly this personification responds to
and underscores Darwin's apprehension of nature as a marvel of

intricate adjustment to changing conditions. The special aptitude with which species seem to have adapted (or been adapted) to those conditions suggests an agency whose attentiveness to the individual needs of each being is distinctively feminine. Moreover, the personification offers a speculative balm which anticipates the anxieties of Darwin's audience, and perhaps responds to those of Darwin himself. As forbiddingly impersonal and inhuman as evolution might seem, the fact that natural selection might be plausibly presented as a constructive, nurturing power implied that the process need not be profoundly alien to human aspirations and desires (Manier, p. 186, notes this hint of consolation).

To note these associations is not to argue, as does Stanley Edgar Hyman, that Darwin's personification is the centrepiece of a fully developed teleology, which replaces God the Father with Mother Nature. On the other hand, it is facile to object in response, with Walter Cannon, that Darwin's figure merely draws on the vocabulary of 'old-fashioned' British naturalism, which 'had been speaking of "Nature" without believing in her for a hundred years or so'.[12] What is at issue is not a simple dichotomy of belief and unbelief: it is the way in which Darwin's thought depends upon and embodies a symbolic economy of gender, the dynamics of which are brought into focus by a scepticism that challenges the traditional association of nature and maternity – in part simply by bringing it to consciousness. Darwin was reluctant to surrender his personification of nature, at least in part because a feminine Nature seemed especially suited to convey his sense of the richness and intricacy of natural selection, as well as to impart a consolingly benign view of the moral implications of his theory.

That gesture of consolation, however, is most clearly apparent in its incapacity to disarm another, more plausible inference to be drawn from Darwin's theory. In personifying nature as a nurturing mother, Darwin indulges in a reassuring ambiguity of the term 'being'. As that term is employed in the *Origin*, it most often denotes, not a particular individual, but a particular *variety* or species. In retaining the traditional model of Mother Nature, Darwin resists a central feature of his theory, a feature that aligns it with much nineteenth-century radical speculation: the subordination of individual needs to the dynamics of a group. Within the dynamics of these larger *types* of being, the 'good' can no longer be adjusted to the demands of a particular individual: it is whatever enables a particular species to become established and to survive – invariably at the expense of some of its own members – within an intricate, dynamic biological equilibrium. We must 'keep steadily in mind', Darwin urges, 'that each organic being is striving to increase at a geometrical ratio; that each at some period of its life . . . has to struggle for life, and to suffer great destruction. When we reflect on this struggle, we may console ourselves with the full belief, that the war of nature is not incessant, that no fear is felt, that death is generally prompt, and that the vigorous, the healthy, and the happy survive and multiply' (p. 129). It taxes scientific logic to conceive of an amoebum or a lichen as 'happy', save in the weak sense of 'fortunate'. But there is more than a hint of straining for consolation here, and in the context Darwin can hardly personify nature as a nurturing mother. At best one might imagine a being rather like Florence Nightingale, a nurse who eases the pain of the dying. Yet the vision of incessant struggle also invites a more somber image of nature: not a nurse, but an angel of death, a monstrous agent that rigidly and impersonally lays waste its own dependents.

Ten years before the publication of the *Origin of Species*, Tennyson in *In Memoriam* had imagined just such a sinister nature. Like Darwin, Tennyson personifies nature as a female being whose characteristics clearly owe much to the domestic norms of Victorian femininity. Tennyson's Nature, however, acknowledges those norms by defying them. Whereas Darwin conceives of nature as a marvel of intricate adaptation – adaptation that suggests the activity of a feminine agent attentive to individual needs – Tennyson is most deeply engaged by the idea of a Nature indifferent to its own creatures, a nature which fails to display the maternal character that even Darwin is anxious to preserve. Responding to the claims of early Victorian science within the traditional conception of Mother Nature, Tennyson transforms the discrepancy between the two views of nature into a startlingly vivid and sustained portrait of feminine betrayal. Over the course of the famous sections LV and LVI, a remote, enigmatic 'nature' turns into a predatory being, 'Nature, red in tooth and claw/With ravine'.

> LV
> The wish, that of the living whole
>   No life may fail beyond the grave,
>   Derives it not from what we have
> The nearest God within the soul?
>
>
> Are God and Nature then at strife,
>   That nature lends such evil dreams?
>   So careful of the type she seems,
> So careless of the single life;

That I, considering everywhere
    Her secret meaning in her deeds,
    And finding that of fifty seeds
She often brings but one to bear,

I falter where I firmly trod,
    And falling with my weight of cares
    Upon the world's great altar-stairs
That slope through darkness up to God,

I stretch lame hands of faith, and grope,
    And gather dust and chaff, and call
    To what I feel is Lord of all
And faintly trust the larger hope.

LVI
'So careful of the type?' but no.
    From scarped cliff and quarried stone
    She cries, 'A thousand types are gone:
I care for nothing, all shall go.

'Thou makest thine appeal to me:
    I bring to life, I bring to death:
    The spirit does but mean the breath:
I know no more.' And he, shall he,

Man, her last work, who seemed so fair,
    Such splendid purpose in his eyes,
    Who rolled the psalm to wintry skies,
Who built him lanes of fruitless prayer,

Who trusted God was love indeed
    And love Creation's final law –
    Though Nature, red in tooth and claw
With ravine, shrieked against his creed –

Who loved, who suffered countless ills,
    Who battled for the True, the Just,
    Be blown about the desert dust,
Or sealed within the iron hills?

No more? A monster then, a dream,
    A discord. Dragons of the prime,

That tare each other in their slime,
Were mellow music matched with him.

O life as futile then, as frail!
    O for thy voice to soothe and bless!
    What hope of answer, or redress?
Behind the veil, behind the veil.[13]

'That strange abstraction, "Nature" ', T. S. Eliot commented, 'becomes
a real god or goddess, perhaps more real, at moments, to Tennyson,
than God.'[14] Although condescending, Eliot's remark is faithful to the
extraordinary intensity and vehemence of Tennyson's
personification. Yet the distinction between a god and a goddess
should not be so glibly elided. When the phrase is read out of
context (as it usually is), 'Nature, red in tooth and claw' may not
even suggest an anthropomorphic being; it might suggest a field of
bloody combat or a single beast of prey. But if one attends to the
details of the personification, the beast of prey gives way to a more
startling and more complex image. Nature is a woman red in tooth
and claw – not a mere female animal (a lioness, say, could hardly
cry out to the anxious poet with such articulate violence), but a
woman in demonic form, a Fury.

By inverting one archetype of woman, Tennyson arrives at another.
Yet the deeply traditional image had in this particular cultural and
poetic context an unusual power to shock. As befits the poet's
anxieties, 'Nature' as he envisions her is more 'unnatural' than any
beast of prey – and she is so precisely by virtue of being female. This
Nature confounds that traditional figure of Mother Nature, with its
embodiment of a sympathetic moral order in the natural world.
Moreover, that figure rests in turn on an identification of woman with
maternal care that is particularly insistent in Victorian discourse, but
which Tennyson's Nature likewise resists. The nature of 'Nature' –
its character as both a moral and a physical order – is thus intricately
bound up with the nature of woman and the conventions of gender
that define the feminine.

The significance of the bond between nature and the feminine is
subtly but powerfully articulated in the simple phrase, 'I care for
nothing'. As a disembodied utterance, the phrase immediately
suggests the meaning, 'I value nothing'. But the words are the
defiant cry of a female Nature renouncing her traditional maternal
function, denying man's 'appeal' for solace and comfort. In this
context, 'care for' is charged with the further associations of Darwin's
verb, 'to tend' ('the being which she tends'). To care for is to take
care of, to nurture, particularly as one would care for a child or a

delicate plant. As in the phrase 'Nature, red in tooth and claw', the meaning and emotional force of Tennyson's language is again crucially dependent upon gender. In this instance, the poet regards the newly alien character of Nature as a repudiation of the most intimate, most elemental human needs. With her cry 'I care for nothing', the traditionally maternal Nature rejects the poet who has just imagined himself (in section LIV) as 'An infant crying in the night'.

Tennyson's meditation upon early Victorian science thus draws much of its intensity from the erotic significance latent in the conception of nature as a feminine being. The conceptual impact of that science is felt in the most intimate aspects of (male) social and psychological being, in that the figure of Nature identifies a new conception of the natural world with the enigma of a femininity that withdraws from, or openly defies, male desires. That desire and its frustration are in turn played out in two distinct but related spheres: as the collective male desire that enforces dominant conventions of femininity, and as an individual male's demand for a more personal responsiveness on the part of a particular woman. Within this sexual dynamic, the poem's central but diffuse meditations on teleology assume unexpected focus as responses to an enigma of feminine will. What is it that prompts Nature to betray her conventional role (and the infant crying in the night) with a violence at once symbolic and physical? Were Nature figured simply as a beast of prey, the question would be pointless, since the term would conjure up mere instinctive ferocity. But woman red in tooth and claw startles the reader into pondering intentionality. What is 'the secret meaning in her deeds'? Behind the veil, behind the veil: the poet's quest for solace is thwarted by that seductive yet disturbing emblem of feminine mystery.

She mysteriously withdraws the care the poet has come to expect, leaving him baffled, abandoned, and fearful: clearly this Nature incarnates that strangely tenacious and central theme of nineteenth-century literature and art, the demonic woman. In Tennyson's personification, as in Carlyle's evocation of a Sphinx-like Nature, the male observer is held in thrall when a feminine Nature, formerly beautiful and benign, discloses an unexpected and terrifying enigma of violent purpose. Of course the conjunction of nature with feminine mystery is as old as Western culture itself (as Carlyle's figure reminds us). Yet the archetype seems to take on new urgency in early Victorian discourse, when newly problematic conceptions of nature coincide with prevailing norms of gender that cannot easily accommodate associations of woman with mystery.

The growing debate over 'woman's place' consolidated a peculiarly strenuous and narrow ideal of femininity, which dictated not only that woman ought to be devoted to and dependent upon man, but also that such devotion was wholly rooted in emotion and instinct. Within the crude dichotomy of head and heart, to which the dualism of male and female was often reduced, there is no place for woman to formulate and pursue intellectual designs independent of male desires, or inaccessible to male understanding.[15] If there is mystery in such a model of femininity, it is the enigma of an intellectual void rather than of a hidden design. But when glimmers of independent purpose complicate the categories, they also open up a new and disturbing enigma: what could lead a woman away from her 'natural' maternal and domestic function? (As the question would be phrased in explicitly political debate, 'What does woman want?') This is precisely the unsettling question Tennyson poses when he brings evolutionary conceptions of nature into juxtaposition with the traditional conception of nature as a maternal agency. He aligns the two discourses by personifying evolutionary nature as a female who subverts all the 'natural' attributes of femininity and thereby confounds male desire both individual and collective. In this light, if one reflects anew on the significance of 'I care for nothing', the phrase suggests not only an impersonal nihilism or a repudiation of maternal roles, but a specifically personal, erotic rejection: I care for nothing, and I don't care for you. The infant crying in the night merges with the spurned lover, and Nature more clearly than ever seems to assume the role of the femme fatale.

It is clear, I think, how such associations could be mapped within the larger designs of *In Memoriam*, where the recovery of Hallam brings with it, among other things, a recuperation of the feminized, nurturing, almost domestic cosmos displaced by evolutionary nature. (Hallam, as Terry Eagleton has pointed out, figures in virtually every familial relation to the poet – save, tellingly, that of the father.)[16] But Tennyson's association of contemporary science and feminine betrayal is even more palpable and central in the other long poem he wrote during the composition of *In Memoriam*: *The Princess*.[17] In *In Memoriam*, I have suggested, Tennyson engaged the claims of Victorian science by imagining its world as the work of a feminine Nature that had betrayed its conventional nurturing role. In *The Princess* the same identification is established from the opposite direction: Tennyson imagines a woman's resistance to male desire in forms that align feminine betrayal with the mechanisms of evolution.[18]

II

Why, for Tennyson, should affairs of the heart be so intimately bound up with the results of early Victorian science? With respect to *In Memoriam* there is a familiar and obvious answer: the poet wishes to believe that he will be reunited with Hallam in an afterlife, but that faith is challenged by the fearful materialism incarnated as 'Nature, red in tooth and claw'. But science more immediately engages the poet's imagination and energizes his despair as narrative rather than as theological argument. Geology in particular articulates a history whose broad outlines mirror the history of the poet's own life. To be sure, the two narratives seem radically incommensurate in timescale and scope: the geological operates over eons and continents, the personal in fragments of days and weeks – years at most – within intensely localized and personalized settings. But for Tennyson the two histories are hauntingly conjoined in 'the evidence of the rocks', those layers of fossilized sediment that were so powerful an emblem in the period. In 'scarped cliff and quarried stone' Tennyson found an image of a long history startlingly fore-shortened, compressed into abrupt juxtapositions of presence and absence. In effect, Tennyson saw in the fossil layers irruptions of catastrophe within a uniformitarian scheme of history.[19]

Hallam's death had caused just such a disruption in the steady, continuous pattern of the poet's own existence. In this context, the rock strata body forth something like an anatomy of memory itself – more precisely, of the telescoping effects of memory as it responds to loss. With Hallam's death, the life he had shared with the poet, which now seems to survive only in the poet's memory, is likewise foreshortened, abruptly sealed off, summed up, yet summoned forth with all the preternatural vividness and haunting sense of finality that inheres in the record of a being irrevocably lost. Like the forces inscribed in scarped cliff and quarried stone, Hallam's death ruptures the continuity of a larger history. And with that rupture the sense of identity constituted and sustained by a sense of coherent personal history, of fundamental continuity in one's experience, is likewise shattered into discontinuous moments of being.[20]

> But thou art turned to something strange,
>   And I have lost the links that bound
>   Thy changes; here upon the ground,
> No more partaker of thy change.

XL, (5–8)

The consoling narrative of progress, in which every loss discloses a redeeming gain, collapses when one loses the links that bind the changes. The impact on the poet is delicately registered by one of the most insistent and poignant of Tennysonian rhymes. 'Change' is especially 'strange' when it is experienced as an abrupt and irreparable breach of historical continuity – whether as devastating loss in one's life, or as the disappearance of a species recorded in the fossil record. Just such a ruptured narrative is writ large in rock-pits and quarries. Nature blazons the very hillsides with emblems of irreversible loss – not merely of particular individuals, but of whole 'types' of being.

In this light, one must appreciate that Princess Ida is a feminist of a peculiarly Victorian sort: she conceives of her goals and of social progress generally in evolutionary terms. Her vocation is not so much that of an educator as of a sort of evolutionary demiurge: she will 'raise' woman to a higher level of development, 'mould' woman as a biological type. This evolutionary faith is succinctly evoked when, in conversation with the disguised Prince, Ida gestures toward a rock formation in which a fossil is conveniently exposed: 'As these rude bones to us, are we to her/That will be'.[21] Similarly hopeful alignments of social and evolutionary development will of course become increasingly common during the century. But this scheme of progress deeply unsettles the Prince:

> 'Dare we dream of that,' [he] asked,
> 'Which wrought us, as the workman and his work,
> Which practice betters?'
>
> (IV, 280–2)

Ostensibly, the Prince objects to Ida's blasphemy: dare one substitute for the conception of an omniscient and omnipotent Creator the image of a far-seeing but limited workman whose products improve with practice?[22] But the theological objection envelopes a more inchoate fear, as is hinted by the ease with which the Prince's convoluted syntax can be truncated: 'Dare we dream of that?' The 'dream' which captivates Ida terrifies the Prince because he sees in the exposed bones an image of himself – more precisely, of the sense of self that from his very infancy has been largely founded upon his 'dream' of eventual marriage to Ida.[23] The context calls attention to one facet of the appeal of that recurrent motif of Tennysonian narratives, a marriage envisioned or contracted in childhood. In *The Princess* as in *Maud*, the device urges us to see a woman's repudiation of a man's desire not merely as a momentary rebuke, but as a blow at the very foundations of male selfhood. The notorious 'weird seizures' added to the poem with the third edition enforce a similar design.

They underscore the extent to which the Prince's identity rests on his dream of Ida, and thus the precariousness of that identity, which threatens to dissolve when Ida fails to accommodate the dream. Hence it is that when the Prince is gravely wounded in battle, Cyril's furious denunciation holds responsible, not the hostile army, but Ida's indifference:

> Orbed in your isolation; he is dead,
> Or all as dead . . .

> (VI, 152–4)

Ida's mere remoteness, like that of Nature in *In Memoriam*, has been transformed into a murderous agency.

With this emphasis on the precariousness of male selfhood, the enigmas of evolution merge with the bafflements of romantic desire. When the Prince asks, 'Dare we dream of that?' he poses a theological question that much exercised Tennyson: might mankind turn out to be, like the woolly mammoth, merely a false start, or a species to be superseded in some as yet ungraspable 'progress'?[24] But the question has a more personal bearing: might my own self-conception be nothing more than a fossilized illusion, a dead self? Princess Ida entertains both facets of the question with perfect equanimity. As she describes her dream of woman's future, she dismisses her childhood thoughts of the Prince:

> We touch on our dead self, nor shun to do it,
> Being other – since we learnt our meaning here . . .

> (IV, 205–6)

But the Prince cannot so readily disown his past life, since it is the basis of all the 'meaning' he possesses. His predicament recalls that of the poet at the outset of *In Memoriam*:

> I held it truth, with him who sings
>   To one clear harp in divers tones,
>   That men may rise on stepping-stones
> Of their dead selves to higher things.
>
> But who shall so forecast the years
>   And find in loss a gain to match?
>   Or reach a hand through time to catch
> The far-off interest of tears?

> (I, 1–8)

Ida, like Goethe, is confident that one can discover a genuine progress in a succession of dead selves. But the Prince, like the poet, fears that the dead selves are the records not of self-transcendence, but of mere self-annihilation. One's own history might hold no more coherence than those lawyers of rock that record the destructive power of 'Nature, red in tooth and claw'. And thus Ida, in her remote, passionate devotion to an ideal of perpetual process, seems to the Prince to embody a power as inhuman and destructive as Nature seems to the poet of *In Memoriam*: 'So careful of the type she seems/So careless of the single life'. Nature is virtually and uncannily reconstituted in the figure of the Princess, the woman who rebukes the Prince's desire in her concern for woman as a 'type' – 'her that will be'.

Like Nature, Ida owes her unsettlingly powerful presence in Tennyson's poetry to her refusal to conform to the feminine function of 'caring'. Moreover, *The Princess* suggests that Ida, too, ultimately repudiates not merely 'the single life' but 'the type' itself: the poem's interpretation of her project has a logic precisely congruent with that of sections LV and LVI of *In Memoriam*. While Ida justifies her social goals in evolutionary terms, the male world answers with a biological imperative of its own. In refusing to marry the Prince – or any other man – the Princess emphatically declares that she will have no children. Her refusal of the Prince is thus presented, not merely as a personal rebuke, but as a threat to the very survival of the species. 'No doubt we seem a sort of monster to you', Ida remarks to the Prince (III, 259), thereby inviting precisely the objection of the male world (and of the poem): she is monstrous, profoundly unnatural, in her resistance to the biological continuity sustained by reproduction. Like Nature in *In Memoriam*, she seems to cry, 'I care for nothing, all shall go'. Not only does the poem obliquely hold Ida accountable for the Prince's brush with death, but the male voices of the poem unite to exclaim that her ideal of progress would lead to universal desolation. It is hardly surprising, then, that the Princess's 'iron will' finally begins to melt when she is startled by her own outrush of maternal affection for an abandoned child. And her capitulation is confirmed when the wounded Prince, reduced to the condition of a helpless infant, is brought before her, and she begins to nurse him back to health. The nurturing and erotic instincts that, we are to believe, she has so long, and so 'unnaturally', suppressed, are thus finally released. Ida thereby comes ultimately to 'care for' the Prince in all the manifold senses of that phrase as it appears in *In Memoriam*: she is at once nurse, mother, and lover.[25]

How appropriate, then, that Tennyson should have called the nameless child 'the true heroine of the poem'. The child is without

character, inert, and helpless, but it is the focal point of the feminine
'care' which is the binding force in Tennysonian narratives, both
personal and evolutionary. As such, moreover, the child is also the
most palpable emblem of the biological and social continuity
celebrated in the wake of Ida's capitulation. That continuity is
summed up in its many facets near the close of the poem, in a
passage adapted from a draft of the 'Epilogue' to *In Memoriam*:

> Look up, and let thy nature strike on mine,
> Like yonder morning on the blind half-world.
> Approach and fear not; breathe upon my brows;
> In that fine air I tremble, all the past
> Melts mist-like into this bright hour, and this
> Is morn to more, as the golden Autumn woodland reels
> Athwart the smoke of burning weeds.

> (VII, 330–7)

The two poems thus seem to converge in their resolutions, as the
disruptions of loss are repaired in a renewed continuum of being
that is confirmed by an emblematic marriage. As Hallam's loss is
recuperated through the reconstruction of a teleological order in
nature, so in *The Princess* a frighteningly impersonal scheme of social
evolution is humanized by the domestication of Princess Ida.

Domestication, indeed – for the new social order heralded by the
Prince seems to leave little place for Ida's earlier vision of woman's
future. The 'statelier Eden' the Prince envisions is the paradise of the
Victorian drawing room, a paradise to be won and sustained not by
social reform but by procreation. With his tableau of man and wife
sitting side by side, 'full-summed in all their powers,/Dispensing
harvest, sowing the to-be' (VII, 272–3), the Prince assigns to Ida what
the poem endorses as her true vocation: motherhood, whose 'harvest'
will be children. Of course the two vocations need not be
incompatible, but the poem insinuates a radical disjunction between
them when Cyril locates the 'one pulse that beats true woman' (6:164)
in Ida's maternal susceptibility to the claims of a helpless infant
(whether it be Psyche's child or the Prince himself). Such appeals
neatly reverse Ida's goal: whereas she has urged her sisters to 'lose
the child/And gain the woman', the poem implies that one gains the
woman by finding the child.[26] The implication makes itself felt in
the hint of self-immolation when Ida accepts the male world's
designation: her caring, she admits, is 'that/Which kills me with
myself' (VI, 286–7). Such reversals articulate a doubled logic, which
undercuts the ostensibly progressive sympathies of the poem.
Tennyson clearly wishes to present marriage and social reform as

complementary states, even extensions of one another. Hence, most
obviously, he attempts to disarm and dissociate himself from familiar
conservative views of 'woman's place' by embodying them in the
Prince's reactionary father, who is all patriarchal outrage and bluster:
'Man for the field and woman for the hearth,/Man for the sword
and for the needle she' (V, 437–8). Ultimately, however, it is the voice
of the Prince's father which triumphs. 'The bearing and the
rearing of a child/Is woman's wisdom', he proclaims (V, 455–6) –
which is precisely the conclusion of the poem.[27]

III

It is hardly surprising that Tennyson's poetry should embody a
conservative attitude toward the advancement of women. But my
point is to stress the importance of 'woman' in that conversation – to
argue that the ostensibly progressive ideology of *The Princess* is
dislocated by the immense importance assigned to 'woman's wisdom'
as a force which holds together not only social frameworks but the
very fabric of intellectual and historical coherence. In particular, an
ideal of feminine caring figures in Tennyson's poetry as a binding
force of continuity and conversation in an age which welcomes change
as progress but deeply fears that the continuity of progress might
be punctuated by revolution, whether as social and political
transformation, as displacement of moral and intellectual
frameworks, or even, in nature itself, as extinction.

The crucial role of the feminine as an index of continuity is
confirmed in one further passage of *In Memoriam*, from section CXIV,
which has an important bearing both on *The Princess* and on my topic
as a whole:

> Who loves not Knowledge? Who shall rail
>   Against her beauty? May she mix
>   With men and prosper! Who shall fix
> Her pillars? Let her work prevail.
>
> But on her forehead sits a fire:
>   She sets her forward countenance
>   And leaps into the future chance,
> Submitting all things to desire.
>
> Half-grown as yet, a child, and vain –
>   She cannot fight the fear of death,

> What is she, cut from love and faith
> But some wild Pallas from the brain
>
> Of Demons? Fiery-hot to burst
>   All barriers in her onward race
>   For power. Let her know her place;
> She is the second, not the first.
>
> A higher hand must make her mild,
>   If all be not in vain; and guide
>   Her footsteps, moving side by side
> With wisdom, like the younger child.

(CXIV, 1–20)

Similar injunctions can be found again and again in Victorian schemes of history: let us have progress – social, political, intellectual – but let us be certain that it is progress and not revolution. (Tellingly, the first stanza of this section is taken over verbatim from an 1832 Tennyson hymn to British political continuity, 'Hail Briton'.) As often noted, moreover, Tennyson frequently makes this appeal by way of a traditional distinction between knowledge and wisdom. As in discussions of 'Nature', however, critics have failed to attend to the emphatically feminine embodiment of Tennyson's abstractions, which in this instance have an extraordinarily provocative resonance alongside *The Princess*.[28] The poet's attitude toward Knowledge is precisely that of the Prince towards Princess Ida. 'Let her work prevail': thus much the Prince initially seems to urge, but he recoils from her work when it assumes a militant form that seems to rupture 'the ties of love and faith'. Ultimately he unites with the rest of the male world in concluding that Ida, too, must 'know her place'. As an incarnation of Knowledge, Ida learns that a higher hand must make her mild – the hand, it is implied, that belongs to a husband. In the personification of Knowledge, then, as in his personification of Nature and his depiction of Princess Ida, Tennyson incarnates the violence lurking in a threat to social and historical continuity as a female agent who subverts the maternal norms of Victorian femininity. Mother Nature yields to Nature red in tooth and claw; Pallas Athene to a 'wild Pallas, from the brain of demons'. The contrast between Knowledge and Wisdom neatly embodies the dualism of demon and angel.[29]

Tennyson's feminine personifications thus can be aligned with a phenomenon that Neil Hertz has discerned among Tennyson's French contemporaries, in which male writers appropriate images of woman to embody a hysterical reaction to the threat of political revolution.[30] But I want to conclude by pointing to an unexpectedly similar reliance on the feminine in a work that itself calls for a social and conceptual revolution: John Stuart Mill's *The Subjection of Women* (1869). Mill of course argues that masculine and feminine attributes cannot be viewed as ahistorical essences, since they are so profoundly shaped by social conditions. Hence his admirable impatience with arguments that appeal to 'woman's place', as if that place ratified a timeless biological femininity. And yet, when Mill discusses the contributions women might make to intellectual and social advance, he falls back on an epistemology of gender remarkably like that of Darwin and Tennyson. In chapter 3 of *Subjection*, Mill points out that 'speculative minds' are beset by the dangerous tendency to lose 'the lively perception and ever-present sense of objective fact'. Hence, he continues,

> hardly anything can be of greater value to a man of theory and speculation . . . than to carry on his speculations in the companionship, and under the criticism, of a really superior woman. There is nothing comparable to it for keeping his thoughts within the limits of real things, and the actual facts of nature. A woman seldom runs wild after an abstraction. The habitual direction of her mind to dealing with things as individuals rather than in groups, and (what is closely connected with it) her more lively interest in the present feelings of persons, which makes her consider first of all, in anything that claims to be applied to practice, in what manner persons will be affected by it – these two things make her extremely unlikely to put faith in any speculation which loses sight of individuals, and deals with things as if they existed for the benefit of some imaginary entity . . . not resolvable into the feelings of living beings.[31]

Although the passage obviously pays oblique tribute to Harriet Taylor, Mill couches his praise in provocatively universal terms. Through the equivocality of 'individuals', a term which functions here both as a logical category and as a synonym for 'persons', he assigns to woman a distinctively feminine epistemology. Woman, Mill urges, deals with *things* 'as individuals rather than in groups' – because, it would seem, her domestic role dictates that she attend to *persons* in the same way. Unlike man, she is responsive to (and responsible for) 'the present feelings of persons'.[32] As a consequence, the 'really superior woman' regulates the coherence of, but does not fully participate in, what seems an exclusively masculine mode of speculation. The feminine confines the masculine 'within the limits of real things' and restrains the masculine when it threatens to go astray into 'regions not peopled with real beings'. 'A woman,' in short, 'hardly ever runs wild after an abstraction.' But what better description of the transgression of Princess Ida, or of Knowledge in *In Memoriam*? When these feminine figures pursue their allegiance to an abstract ideal, they deny precisely the regulative, conservative principle inherent in the belief that woman's wisdom resides in a care for 'the feelings of living beings' – or, to adapt Darwin's phrase, for the beings which she *should* tend.

Even as Mill rejects a traditional version of the feminine as a social norm, he recuperates the category as a cognitive ideal. For Mill, as for Tennyson and Darwin, the domestic, maternal ideal continues to codify a mode of acting and knowing that is essentially different from, and subordinate to, male agency, yet which men (and their systems) require and celebrate as a principle that is needed to complement and regulate masculine activity. The feminine ideal is motivated not only as a source of immediate erotic and social gratification, but as a discursive category that underwrites the coherence and stability of the existing cultural order. The motif of the femme fatale embodies a disturbance of this order, an unsettling of the established typologies of masculine and feminine. The motif is thus pathological, not in the narrowly psychological sense urged by Mario Praz in *The Romantic Agony*, but in the more inclusive sense of an intellectual pathology – a disorder in the dominant cultural and discursive systems of the age. Hence the perhaps surprising connection between early Victorian science and a motif commonly associated with the narrowly 'artistic' culture of the fin-de-siècle. When evolutionary speculation unsettles traditional conceptions of nature as a maternal being, it also disturbs Victorian typologies of the feminine; yet the same speculation thereby prompts a new recognition of the significance of the feminine, not only as a biological category but as an organizing principle of Victorian discourse. To be sure, one must study the femme fatale as but one aspect of the extraordinarily complex topic of gender in the nineteenth century.[33] Yet numerous examples of the motif declare an unmistakable affiliation with images of nature derived from British empiricism. After all, what is perhaps the most famous femme fatale in British literature, Walter Pater's Gioconda, appears in an essay on a figure who is both homosexual artist and Faustian scientist – an essay, moreover, which takes as its motto a phrase drawn from Bacon: *Homo minister interpres naturae* – Man the servant and interpreter of nature.

Notes

1. The remark was inserted in the third edition (1861): CHARLES DARWIN, *The Origin of Species: A Variorum Edition*, ed. Morse Peckham (Philadelphia: University of Pennsylvania Press, 1959), p. 165. Further references to the *Origin* will be to the text of the first edition (1859), in the Pelican edition edited by J. R. BURROW (Harmondsworth: Penguin, 1968).

2. For a brief historical survey of the concept of Mother Nature, see CAROLYN MERCHANT, *The Death of Nature: Woman, Ecology, and the Scientific Revolution* (San Francisco: Harper and Row, 1983) pp. 1–41. Merchant locates 'the death of Nature' conceived as a nurturing mother in the seventeenth century, when an organic theory of the earth gave way to a mechanistic model. Yet the appeal within scientific discourse to a maternal nature persists at least into the early Victorian period: see SUSAN GLISERMAN, 'Early Victorian Science Writers and Tennyson's *In Memoriam*: A Study in Cultural Exchange', *Victorian Studies* 18 (1975), 277–308 and 437–460.

3. SIMONE DE BEAVOIR, *The Second Sex*, trans, and ed. H. M. Parshley (Harmondsworth: Penguin, 1973), p. 218.

4. THOMAS CARLYLE, *Past and Present*, ed. Richard D. Altick (New York: New York University Press, 1977), p. 13.

5. 'The angel in the house' was not one half of a simple dualism. In *The Woman Question: Society and Literature in Britain and America, 1837–1883*, 3 vols (New York: Garland, 1983) III, xiv–xv, ELIZABETH HELSINGER, ROBIN LAUTERBACH SHEETS, and WILLIAM VEEDER distinguish at least four 'myths of the feminine: 1) the angel in the house; 2) the angel out of the house (the model of which would become Florence Nightingale); 3) an 'apocalyptic' feminism, which looked to woman's nature for a redemption of the world; 4) the model of complete equality. For my purposes, however, it is important that the second and third models can be seen as in large part a simple extension of the domestic ideal to a wider sphere, within which woman remains distinguished as a nurturing being; the radical model of equality, as the authors point out, played a much smaller role in the debate.

6. The mere fact that it seemed necessary to spell out a position like that of Ellis, as RAY STRACHEY pointed out in *The Cause* (1928), in itself reveals undercurrents of resistance to 'the duty of female submissiveness which before had been entirely taken for granted' (quoted in WENDELL STACY JOHNSON, *Sex and Marriage in Victorian Poetry* [Ithaca: Cornell University Press, 1975], p. 28).

7. The two terms are notoriously elusive, as is the phenomenon they are invoked to describe. Broadly speaking, I use the two terms interchangeably to denote an image of a woman who repudiates the nurturing, maternal qualities of the domestic ideal of femininity ('the angel in the house') and thereby strikes the male observer as enigmatic and profoundly 'unnatural' but also hostile; moreover, her hostility betrays a powerful erotic fascination she exerts on the male observer.

8. As ROBERT YOUNG remarks, 'Even by the loose standards of biological explanation, it is surprising to find such rank anthropomorphism at the heart of the most celebrated unifying theory in biology' (*Darwin's Metaphor: Nature's Place in Victorian Culture* [Cambridge: Cambridge University Press, 1985], p. 93).

9. EDWARD MANIER, *The Young Darwin and His Cultural Circle* (Dordrecht: Reidel,

1978), pp. 150–86. The literature on Darwin's relation to the discourse of natural theology is vast and growing; for a recent development of Manier's views, see JOHN HEALY BROOKE, 'The Relation Between Darwin's Science and His Religion', in JOHN DURANT, ed., *Darwinism and Divinity: Essays on Evolution and Religious Belief* (Oxford: Blackwell, 1985), pp. 40–75.

10. For an anthropological account, see SHERRY B. ORTNER, 'Is Female to Male as Nature Is to Culture?' in MICHELLE Z. ROSALDO, ed., *Woman, Culture, and Society* (Palo Alto: Stanford University Press, 1974), pp. 67–87.

11. In *Darwin's Plots* (London: Ark, 1984), GILLIAN BEER also notes the alignment of man/nature with male/female (pp. 68–74). The typology is more explicitly outlined in *The Descent of Man*: 'Woman seems to differ from man in mental disposition, chiefly in her greater tenderness and less selfishness . . . Woman, owing to her maternal instincts, displays these qualities towards her infants in an eminent degree; therefore it is likely that she would often extend them towards her fellow-creatures. Man is the rival of other men; he delights in competition, and this leads to ambition which passes too easily into selfishness . . . It is generally admitted that with women the powers of intuition, of rapid perception, and perhaps of imitation, are more strongly marked than in man' (2 vols, [London: John Murray, 1871], II, 326). This is a rather different and far more precise image of woman than that which NINA AUERBACH discovers when she claims that Darwin incorporates in his personifications 'his century's "myth" ' of woman as 'mysteriously, boundlessly metamorphic creatures' (*Woman and the Demon* [New York: Columbia, 1982], p. 52).

12. STANLY EDGAR HYMAN, *The Tangled Bank* (New York: Atheneum, 1962), pp. 37–40; WALTER F. CANNON, 'Darwin's Vision in *On the Origin of Species*', in GEORGE LEVINE and WILLIAM MADDEN, eds, *The Art of Victorian Prose* (New York: Oxford University Press, 1968), p. 158.

13. *The Poems of Tennyson*, CHRISTOPHER RICKS, ed. (London: Longman, 1969). References to Tennyson's poems are to this text; line references are given parenthetically.

14. T. S. ELIOT, '*In Memoriam*', *Selected Essays*, (London: Faber, 1976), p. 335.

15. Hence the deep mistrust of newly assertive women in the 1840s, who would soon become branded by a new epithet, 'strong-minded', that came to stereotype the 'unnatural' woman (HELSINGER *et al.*, III, 82–93).

16. TERRY EAGLETON, 'Tennyson: Politics and Sexuality in *The Princess* and *In Memoriam*', in *1848: The Sociology of Literature*, ed. Francis Barker (Essex: University of Essex Press, 1978), p. 105. Eagleton's loosely Lacanian account of gender in the poem might be usefully complemented by GLISERMAN's attention to the contrast in the poem (and in early Victorian science writing) between a nurturing, feminized environment and a more hostile, 'masculine' cosmos ('Early Victorian Science Writers and Tennyson's *In Memoriam*').

17. Although a precise dating of the two poems is not essential to my argument, the material supplied by SUSAN SHATTO and MARION SHAW in their recent edition of *In Memoriam* (Oxford: Clarendon Press, 1982) suggests that composition of *The Princess* and thematically related passages of *In Memoriam* occupied Tennyson almost simultaneously. Hallam Tennyson declared that the passages of *In Memoriam* dealing with evolution were written 'some years before' the publication of Chamber's *Vestiges of Creation*, in 1844, but Shatto and Shaw, on the basis of handwriting and placement in the manuscript, conclude that section LVI was a late addition to the Lincoln manuscript begun

in November of 1842 (p. 218). This surmise (along with my suggestion that the section echoes Carlyle's *Past and Present*, published in 1843) would suggest a composition date very close to, perhaps even within the period of, Tennyson's most sustained work on *The Princess*, from 1845 to 1847.

18. I offer an admittedly schematic reading of *The Princess* in pursuit of a typology of the feminine that cuts across not only traditional genre distinctions, but also conventional boundaries between poetry, science, and social criticism. In concentrating on the ideology of gender, however, I will be slighting much valuable recent commentary that links gender to the peculiar complications of genre within the poem. See especially GERHARD JOSEPH, *Tennysonian Love: The Strange Diagonal* (Minneapolis: University of Minnesota Press, 1969), pp. 75–101; JAMES R. KINCAID, *Tennyson's Major Poems: The Comic and Ironic Pattern* (New Haven: Yale University Press, 1975), pp. 72–7; W. DAVID SHAW, *Tennyson's style* (Ithaca: Cornell University Press, 1976), pp. 114–31; EILEEN TESS JOHNSTON, 'This Were a Medley: Tennyson's *The Princess*', *ELH* 51 (1984), 549–74; DANIEL ALBRIGHT, *Tennyson: The Muses' Tug-of-War* (Charlottesville: University of Virginia Press, 1986), pp. 214–48, HERBERT TUCKER, *Tennyson and the Doom of Romanticism* (Cambridge: Harvard University Press, 1988), pp. 350–75. The critics most attentive to ideology are Eagleton, Tucker, and EVE KOSOFSKY SEDGWICK, *Between Men: English Literature and Male Homosocial Desire* (New York: Columbia University Press, 1985), pp. 118–33. None of these critics, however, has much to say about the prominence of evolutionary science in the poem – a topic still left largely to John Killham's valuable scholarship in *Tennyson's 'The Princess': Portrait of an Age* (London: Athlone Press, 1959).

19. A. DWIGHT CULLER applies 'uniformitarianism' and 'catastrophism' to Tennyson's poetry in a broader sense, as analogues of literary form (*The Poetry of Tennyson* [New Haven: Yale University Press, 1977], pp. 15–16, 151). Thus he sees *In Memoriam* as the culmination of Tennyson's movement from catastrophic (or apocalyptic) to gradualist modes, a movement underscored by Tennyson's avoidance of pastoral elegy.

20. In a very different approach to Tennyson, Albright describes *In Memoriam* as 'a series of jagged, discontinuous, unconnectable moments of pain and revelation' (p. 217) – an apt (if unintended) description, I think, of what Tennyson saw in the evidence of the rocks. Both time scales – of the individual life and of geologic time – shadow the poet's evocation of human history in section LXXVII, 'the songs, and deeds, and lives, that lie/Foreshortened in the tracts of time', where 'tracts' deftly summons up both physical expanses and literary works. All of these passages testify to Tennyson's obsession with 'eternal process', in which, as Tucker points out, it is remarkable 'how little difference it makes what the time scale may happen to be' (p. 21).

21. IV 279–80. In 'The Two Sides of Early Victorian Science and the Unity of *The Princess*', *Victorian Studies* 23 (1980), 369–88, G. GLEN WICKENS rightly emphasizes the symbolic and structural importance of this episode (and its scientific allusions) but contrasts the poem as a whole with *In Memoriam* as 'a more detached examination . . . of the developmental sciences in Victorian culture'. Hence Wickens views evolution as a theme 'played contrapuntally against the main subject', the place of women, whereas I am arguing (to use Wickens's musical terms) that the themes are harmonic.

22. The analogy invokes a teleology much like that at which Darwin glances near the close of *The Origin of Species*, where he urges his readers to 'regard every

complex structure and instinct as the summing up of many contrivances, each useful to the possessor, nearly in the same way as when we look at any great mechanical invention as the summing up of the labour, the experience, the reason, and even the blunders of numerous workmen; (p. 456). Although the trope underscores Darwin's indebtedness to Paley, here (characteristically) teleology is subordinated to an aesthetic apprehension of nature much like that of Ruskin responding to a Gothic cathedral.

23. This continuity offers a rationale for the curious fact, stressed by Sedgwick, that the Prince never seriously considers the Princess's resistance to the enforced marriage (p. 124): it seems that a future without the Princess, a future disjoined from the past, is quite literally unimaginable. As many commentators have noted, Ida's repudiation of the past entails a rejection of Tennysonian elegy, which 'moans about the retrospect' to the neglect of 'that other distance', the future (4:67–8).

24. In 'The Natural Theology of Tennyson's *In Memoriam*', rpt, in JOHN DIXON HUNT, ed., *In Memoriam: A Casebook* (London: Macmillan, 1970), GRAHAM HOUGH aptly cites Tennyson's remark to John Tyndall: 'I should consider that a liberty had been taken with me if I were simply made a means of ushering in something higher than myself' (p. 141).

25. The emphasis the poem places on Ida's role as a surrogate mother to the Prince can be gauged by the unanimity on this point of readings which otherwise differ radically in method and conclusions. See, for example, JOSEPH, p. 98; JOHNSON, p. 131; EAGLETON, p. 101; SEDGWICK, p. 123. The Prince, as Sedgwick notes, thus retains 'the privileged status of a baby . . . along with the implicit empowerment of maleness'.

26. Accounts of the child form a revealing index of critical preoccupations, since the child is so richly overdetermined as a symbol. For importantly different views, see JOHNSTON and ALBRIGHT.

27. Few recent commentators agree with W. STACY JOHNSON, who finds *The Princess* 'a remarkably liberal poem about woman's role in society' (p. 110). But it is curious that many of the most strenuous critics of the poem's ideology look to explain the poem's conclusion by a logic internal to Ida's project. SEDGWICK, for example, finds a 'conceptual flaw' in Ida's authoritarian vision of social change – change 'from the top down' – which she identifies with the complacent view of Sir Walter and the frame narrative. But surely the more apt comparison would be to Carlyle's Abbot Samson – a model of heroism for which, one assumes, Tennyson had a fair amount of respect, and which could be dramatized without such glaring contradictions. Ida's stature as a Carlylean hero suggests that her fate is ultimately responsive specifically to an ideology of gender.

28. GERHARD JOSEPH's 'Tennyson's Concepts of Knowledge, Wisdom, and Pallas Athene', *Modern Philology* 69 (1972), 314–22, is the most extended treatment of the theme; Joseph discusses section CXIV at some length, but makes no reference to gender – and indeed fails to distinguish the 'wild Pallas' from the 'Pallas Athene' hallowed by myth.

29. Ida and her academy are at several points aligned with Pallas Athene, and the Prince's account of her apology (which has the ring of an official confession) echoes the distinction between Knowledge and Wisdom: 'She prayed me not to judge their cause from her/That wronged it, sought far less for truth than power/In Knowledge: something wild within her breast,/A greater than all

knowledge, beat her down' (VII 220–3). CHARLES KINGSLEY's 1850 review of the poem in *Frazer's* offers a final illuminating gloss on Ida's transgression: 'at last, she loses all feminine sensibility . . . and becomes all but a vengeful fury, with all the peculiar faults of woman and none of the peculiar excellencies of man' (cited by HELSINGER, *et al.*, III, 95).

30. NEIL HERTZ, 'Medusa's Head: Male Hysteria under Political Pressure', *Representations* 1 (1983), 27–54.
31. JOHN STUART MILL, *The Subjection of Women*, in *Three Essays* (Oxford: Oxford University Press, 1975), p. 496.
32. Note that in the relation Mill sets forth, feminine apprehension of things as individuals is not determined by social function; it is merely analogous to it, 'closely connected with it'. We are left to believe that a distinctively feminine cognition, like that closely related and distinctively feminine concern for 'the feelings of living beings', has its origin less in society than in some biological essence.
33. A recent, stimulating analysis of the symbolic economy of gender, focusing on the 'artificiality' of its binary logic, can be found in MARY POOVEY, *Uneven Developments: The Ideological Work of Gender in Mid-Victorian England* (Chicago: University of Chicago Press, 1988).

6 Tennyson, 1857–67: Divorce, Democracy and Thermodynamics*

ELAINE JORDAN

Elaine Jordan in the following essay, omitted from her 1988 book *Alfred Tennyson*, uses a variety of textual and visual material produced between 1857 and 1867 to show, like Adams, how discourses of sexuality and fears of revolution are related to discourses derived from the new evolutionary sciences. Like Eagleton, Jordan limits her analysis to a mid-century decade and like Sinfield she seeks to understand these texts as cultural interventions, part of the means by which sense is made of a moment of crisis. She takes the figure of the adulterous wife in three texts – the beginning of Tennyson's *Idylls* entitled 'The False and the True' (1857), Augustus Egg's triptych of paintings which came to be known as 'Past and Present' (exhibited 1858) and Mary Braddon's 1862 sensation novel *Lady Audley's Secret* – and shows the mid-century interconnections between divorce, democracy and thermodynamics and thereby how female adultery comes to be blamed for national evils. In a reading of Tennyson's 'The False and the True' and later *Lucretius* (seen alongside the Reform League demonstrations in Hyde Park in 1866 and the Morant Bay Rebellion in Jamaica of 1865), Jordan argues that both poems present women's desires as poisonous and destructive of male authority.

Ah, Heaven help a strong man's tender weakness for the woman he loves! Heaven pity him when the guilty creature who has deceived him comes with her tears and lamentations to throw herself at his feet in self-abandonment and remorse, torturing him with the sight of her agony, rending *his* heart with her sobs, lacerating *his* breast with her groans, multiplying her own sufferings into a greater anguish for him to bear, multiplying them by twenty-fold, multiplying them in the ratio of a brave man's capacity for endurance. Heaven forgive him if, maddened by that cruel agony, the balance wavers for a moment, and he is ready to forgive *anything*, ready to take this wretched one to the

---

*This chapter was originally a conference paper given at Birkbeck Day School, 1993.

shelter of his breast, and to pardon that which the stern voice
of manly honour urges must not be pardoned. Pity him, pity
him, philosophers who ponder the perplexities of life. The wife's
worst remorse when she stands without the threshold of the
home she may never again enter is not equal to the agony of
the husband who closes the portal on that familiar and entreating
face. The anguish of the mother who may never look again upon
her children is less than the suffering of the father who has to
say to those children, 'My little ones, you are henceforth
motherless'.

> (Mary E. Braddon, *Lady Audley's Secret*, Ch. 31, 1862)

>   . . . terrible! for it seemed
> A void was made in Nature; all her bonds
> Cracked; and I saw the flaring atom-streams
> And torrents of her myriad universe,
> Ruining along the illimitable inane,
> Fly on to clash together again, and make
> Another and another frame of things
> For ever: that was mine, my dream, I knew it – . . .

>   and that hour perhaps
> Is not so far when momentary man
> Shall seem no more a something to himself,
> But he, his hopes and hates, his homes and fanes,
> And even his bones long laid within the grave,
> The very sides of the grave itself shall pass,
> Vanishing, atom and void, atom and void,
> Into the unseen for ever, – till that hour,
> My golden work in which I hold a truth . . .
> Shall stand . . .

> (*Lucretius*, 36–43, 251–9, 263)

In July 1857, the year of divorce reform, the Poet Laureate gave his
wife some lines of poetry on her birthday:

> But hither shall I never come again,
> Never lie by thy side; see thee no more –
> Farewell!

A strange birthday present. However, Emily Tennyson was well
pleased. These were the first lines to be written of 'The Parting of
Arthur and Guinevere', and follow the discovery by the British king
of his wife's adultery with his best and most beloved knight, Lancelot.

I imagine Emily taking the pathos of dear Ally's 'no nay never no more' as an affirmation of their married love, so different from the court cases and the home life of monarchs. The poem was published in 1859 as one of four studies in 'The False and the True', from the Arthurian cycle of legends which Tennyson had been interested in from the 1830s, but put aside to engage with questions of 'the Age', as Victorian reviewers were always telling writers to do. These studies were of two good women, Enid the long-suffering wife and 'Elaine the fair, Elaine the loveable / Elaine the lily maid of Astolat', and two bad women, Vivien and Guinevere. The set exemplifies how idealizations of the good woman generally come at the expense of another sort: to construct an ideal of the good wife it helps to have an idea of the dark unhappy or unfair one, who's no lily.

'The False and the True' marked the beginning of the *Idylls of the King*, completed in 1885. This was his grand national poem, modernizing the legends which Malory in the sixteenth century had used to serve royal propaganda, the 'matter of Britain' which Tennyson no more than Milton or Wordsworth could turn into an epic, but unlike them he did use the material: for a story of degeneration and a very English ethical despair. Like paintings in the Oxford Union and House of Commons and of the Prince Consort, ideas of chivalry were used to project an image of the modern gentleman. Gladstone wrote of 'The False and the True': 'It is national: it is Christian . . . it is human, it is universal'. Though Gladstone was criticized for lacking imperialist enthusiasm, the assumption that English Christian values were universal, built into what it was to be human, was entrenched in his thinking. He also claimed Tennyson as the great poet of woman. But the national mood which Tennyson caught in 'Guinevere' was far from giving women a great or a self-determining role, such as *The Princess* envisioned; rather it made them responsible for failures of the social bonds between men.

'Guinevere' was positively received by some of the most radical liberal minds of the period, for example George Eliot and Arthur Clough, though *he* did comment that 'he should have told her to get up' (Guinevere lies on the floor at Arthur's feet while he delivers his prolonged judgement on her). It's not clear which of them Clough thought was behaving worse, in this respect. Alongside 'Guinevere' I want to invoke an analogous scene in a sensation novel of 1862 (quoted above), but first to describe one of the most famous works exhibited at the Royal Academy, summer 1858. It is actually three paintings, like a sacred triptych. Augustus Egg's nameless work came to be known as 'Past and Present'. We can think of it now as archetypally Victorian, but it was shocking to Victorian sensibilities, and in his lifetime no one bought it. Critics wrote of depths of morbidity, sewers of vice, horrors of the dissecting room, and of course unsuitability for the young female viewer.[1]

Instead of a title Egg offered a fragment of a story: 'August the 4th. Have just heard that B. has been dead more than a fortnight, so his poor children have now lost both parents. I hear *she* was seen on Friday last near the Strand, evidently without a place to lay her head. What a fall hers has been!' The central painting shows the scene of domestic disaster. On the right, the husband holds a letter, which, if you know the code, must reveal the wife's infidelity; he makes a sad gesture of repudiation. At his feet, the fallen body stretches away from him, towards the observer, her clasped, braceletted hands straining for forgiveness. On the left the little daughters build a house of cards on a novel by Balzac. Details – a bitten apple on the floor, paintings of Adam and Eve and shipwreck to left and right on the walls – are loaded to the point of collapse. The central mirror reflects an open door, sign of the command to 'Go!'. To either side of this are, on the left, the daughters five years on, in a bare room, looking yearningly out; on the right, the dying mother, homeless under the arches of the Thames, gazing up at the same moon. The law did not allow adulterous wives access to their children. Egg's triptych can be seen as a protest, though signs of the fall are more clearly readable; it would be interesting to know of anything like a feminist response.

Tennyson's Guinevere poem, completed early 1858, and Egg's central painting, exhibited from May 1858, both focus on the wronged husband's grief. This is repeated in Mary Braddon's 1862 sensation novel, *Lady Audley's Secret*, set in 1858. Again there's the bad wife flinging herself down; unlike the neat hairdo of the bourgeois wife in Egg's painting, Lady Audley's golden hair spreads out all over the place, like Guinevere's. Tennyson complained to Holman Hunt at the hair 'wildly tossed about as if by a tornado' in his illustration of 'The Lady of Shalott' – this recalls his rejection of some of his own earlier work because an artist 'does not overflow illimitably to all extent about a matter', perhaps disciplining a self too abundantly or indefinitely feminine or sexual.[2] Complaint at excess pervades Tennyson's comments on the Pre-Raphaelite art inspired by his early poems, although 'the Tennysonian' is often associated with just these images, of bound/unbound hair and something illimitable, erotic signifiers mixed up with the sacred. Mrs Braddon's staging of the scene, like Tennyson's, is more concerned with what a wife's transgressions mean for the husband and public morality than with the consequences for the wife, which Egg does depict. The daughters are a concern in Egg's triptych; possibilities they suggest are excluded in Tennyson and Braddon's scenes, which throw down a wife beneath a husband and focus conflict between passion and wider social responsibility on the man.

What, in the mid-nineteenth century, motivates these specific repetitions of marital disaster, prone wives and nobly unhappy husbands? An easy answer is the Matrimonial Causes Act, passed just before Tennyson made his birthday offering to his wife. It had been possible though expensive for husbands to divorce wives; the new legislation, argued for from the late eighteenth century, removed control of divorce from Church courts, and made it not only cheaper for all, but easier for women to get a divorce – though a husband's adultery still had to have some 'atrocious' element, like incest, bigamy or repeated infection with venereal disease, to qualify as grounds, while a wife's adultery alone was still sufficient cause. The centrepiece of Tennyson's poem is Arthur's denunciation of Guinevere; he never wrote a comparable denunciation of Lancelot. The ideal Arthur blames his *wife's* infidelity for the destruction of the chivalric ideals of the Round Table, and for every national evil:

> Well is it that no child is born of thee.
> The children born of thee are sword and fire,
> Red ruin, and the breaking up of laws,
> The craft of kindred and the Godless hosts
> Of heathen swarming o'er the Northern Sea.
>
> ('Guinevere', *Idylls of the King*, 421–5)

While a man's 'maiden passion for a maid' is said to be the foundation for all noble thought and activity, Guinevere's example has corrupted the court and the country (457–490). He loves her still, but to condone her adultery would be like failing to check a contagious disease, with which she is identified:

> Yet must I leave thee, woman, to thy shame.
> I hold that man the worst of public foes
> Who either for his own or children's sake,
> To save his blood from scandal, lets the wife
> Whom he knows false, abide and rule the house:
> For being through his cowardice allowed
> Her station, taken everywhere for pure,
> She like a new disease, unknown to men,
> Creeps, no precaution used, among the crowd,
> Makes wicked lightnings of her eyes, and saps
> The fealty of our friends, and stirs the pulse
> With devil's leaps, and poisons half the young.
>
> (505–19)

A woman's sexuality is poison, a disease capable of corrupting social order. In 1857 legislation controlling the sale of poisons had been passed just before the Obscene Publications Act. The association of female sexuality and social degeneration is made also in Tennyson's *Lucretius*, with its visions (53, 156–57) of 'hired animalisms', 'prodigies of myriad nakednesses, / And twisted shapes of lust, unspeakable', tending towards revolt and invasion:

> How should the mind, except it loved them, clasp
> These idols to herself? or do they fly
> Now thinner, and now thicker, like the flakes
> In a fall of snow, and so press in, perforce
> Of multitude, as crowds that in an hour
> Of civic tumult jam the doors, and bear
> The keepers down, and throng, their rags and they
> The basest, far into that council-hall
> Where sit the best and stateliest of the land?
>
> (164–72)

When Tennyson became a lord in the 1880s he voted for the third Reform Act; Gladstone persuaded him it would be safer than refusing pressure for extending the franchise. Like many who had been enthusiastic reformists in the 1830s, Tennyson thought things had gone far enough, that democracy would lead to what we call fascism. In 'Tiresias' (1885) the old seer complains that no one would attend to his prophecy, in fact rather a traditional one:

> My warning that the tyranny of one
> Was prelude to the tyranny of all?
> My counsel that the tyranny of all
> Led backward to the tyranny of one?
>
> (71–5)

Lucretius on civic tumult can be related to skirmishing around Hyde Park in July 1866, after the ban on a demonstration there by the Reform League campaigning for the rights of men *as men*, rather than as owners of property. The official 'force' that produced popular 'violence' was that those who looked like workers were refused entry to the park, while 'the stateliest' were admitted. Cooperation from Reform League leaders was needed to restore order, and this had its effect in the summer of 1867, when the remembered threat of corresponding force from 'respectable' workers and the 'dangerous classes' led to four times as many men getting the vote than had been planned, by a late extension of the franchise to lodgers.[3]

My selection of events and legislation is not arbitrary: all concern a threat or appeal to masculine authority, and connections between them were made in contemporary disputes about the rule of law and the force of change. Paul Gilroy has stressed the significance of 'the cleavage in the Victorian intelligentsia around the response to Governor Eyre's handling of the Morant Bay Rebellion in Jamaica in 1865 . . . an instance of metropolitan, internal conflict that emanates directly from an external colonial experience'.[4] Protest against the bias of magistrates had become a riot after troops shot seven black protesters. Official reprisals with peculiarly sadistic variations lasted more than a month, though meeting with no further resistance: a thousand homes were burnt, hundreds flogged, more than four hundred executed. Dissatisfied with the Commission of Inquiry, a group of liberals in England set up a campaign for the trial of Eyre for murder of a 'mixed race' minister. This group was supported by Huxley, G. H. Lewes, George Eliot. Defenders of Eyre included Tennyson, Ruskin, Dickens. Eyre was not a gentleman on 'outdoor relief' in the colonies, as Bertrand Russell later put it, but wholly dependent on his salary; the case was further complicated by his having been in the 1840s a fervent advocate of the rights of Australian indigenes to defend their land and formerly viable culture against settlers.

Tories and liberals alike made analogies between events in Jamaica and Hyde Park in the 1860s. Actual representations of contesting claims being made over into metaphors for each other suggests the anxiety in these years about deciding the limits of protest and authority, even the possibility of distinguishing legitimate rule from 'illimitable' violence. While franchise for white men was creaking open in England, representative government in Jamaica, dating back to 1660, abolished itself, preferring direct rule to widening political participation.[5] Producing a sense of crisis is of course not exclusive to the period; figurative activity goes on beyond the bounds of poetry, fiction, art. Trying to find a public form, Tennyson took the 'English Idyll' in the 1830s and 1840s as a poetry of celebration and argument, to refine values within an order established by the 1832 Reform Act. The later *Idylls* reek of loss and degeneration, of anxiety national, imperial, and sexual. The simplicities of imperial adventure stories took on the epic role.

Science might seem a more ordered region, given the objective laws that nineteenth-century positivism promised, but here too there was a struggle for authority, between established religion and the scientific professions, and within each. Professional status supported by institutions and funds was particularly important for physics, since this was not research that could be carried on by clerical and gentlemanly amateurs, unlike chemistry, biology, geology. The appeal to the classics in Tennyson's *Lucretius* is only one facet of its nervous energy; contemporary physics is another context. Twentieth-century representations of 'the Victorians' emphasize the reverberations among the gentry and middle classes of evolutionary science, Darwin's *On the Origin of Species* (1859) in particular. These sciences, with palaeontology's reconstruction of extinct forms of life from scattered bones, produced extraordinary changes in the sense of time, which are hauntingly evoked in *In Memoriam* CXXIII. Variations on the rhetorical figure of chiasmus – a balanced crossing from one form to its inversion – mime the abysses of temporality that, rolling and ruling, cancel trees with seas, seas with streets, making something equally insubstantial of the strangely new and the strangely old, and the familiar. Here it is not elemental nature but the city that roars:

> There rolls the deep where grew the tree.
>   O earth, what changes has thou seen!
>   There where the long street roars, hath been
> The stillness of the central sea.
>
> The hills are shadows, and they flow
>   From form to form, and nothing stands;
>   They melt like mist, the solid lands,
> Like clouds they shape themselves and go . . .

Ideas of evolution had been dominant from the eighteenth century, and were compatible with liberal Christianity, which assumed that God's message was adapted to developing understandings; Tennyson's monologues often depend on this 'accommodation'. The new hypothesis in Darwin's work was that evolution worked by *natural* selection. His sense of the need for a proliferation of ingenious forms, if 'selection' without agency were to occur, is one precursor of green modernism – a revaluation of 'myriad excess' which may not be 'illimitable', but contrasts with the *destruction* of values with which his work was associated earlier: we may turn out to need things which don't make sense or fit in with present projects.

Darwin was so careful not to challenge the biblical account of creation that it was possible for contemporaries not to see what he was saying. The devastating idea that whole species had perished was already available in the influential work of the geologist Charles Lyell in the 1830s. Though Lyell was also careful to dodge claims about origins, his work implied that the human could disappear like any other species, and this was a terror and fascination to Tennyson, for whom morality, immortality, his own identity and the possibility of love were all bound up together. That everything known to human intelligence and affection could disappear is at the heart of *In Memoriam*, and of *Lucretius*:

> terrible! for it seemed
> A void was made in Nature; all her bonds
> Cracked; and I saw the flaring atom-streams
> And torrents of her myriad universe,
> Ruining along the illimitable inane,
> Fly on to clash together again, and make
> Another and another frame of things
> For ever: that was mine, my dream, I knew it – . . .
>
>   and that hour perhaps
> Is not so far when momentary man
> Shall seem no more a something to himself,
> But he, his hopes and hates, his homes and fanes,
> And even his bones long laid within the grave,
> The very sides of the grave itself shall pass,
> Vanishing, atom and void, atom and void,
> Into the unseen for ever, – till that hour,
> My golden work in which I told a truth . . .
> Shall stand . . .
>
>   (36–43, 251–59, 263)

There's a tremendous energy in despair in the language, syntax, metre, here, in its acute imagination of impotence, sustaining that 'terrible!' which registers nightmares in an ordinary idiom, something Tennyson could do, part of why he became popular and why we write about his poetry now. It calls on the metaphors of modern fear and wonder which I've recalled more prosaically – 'bonds / Cracked'; rushing and clashing myriads, the 'illimitable' threat; the exposed bones, last trace of the chiming differences of 'hopes', 'homes', 'hates', 'fanes'; a man claiming to be 'something', to have a power to stand, to make something that can hold value, 'golden', reduced beyond the extreme of nothing, and this is what he knows as the condition of his work, thinking it very literally; anyone's grave swinging in the void like a cradle rocked by a murderous mother, as the last hold on things, 'even his bones long laid within the grave, / The very sides of the grave itself' going, an absurd fear, but true, terrible! The ruining – 'Ruining along the illimitable inane' – is done by fluid forces in annihilating motion, burning up energy – ruining what? It should be a transitive verb, but it is intransitive, simply in motion, ruining *along*, there is nothing to ruin, nothing but ruin.

Transitive assault and ruin are forced on us every day, actually or in representation. Yet there is *poetic* energy, an energy of making, so, though I hesitate to say this as I hesitate to say 'gothic' because there are bones and a grave, maybe there is a shamanistic power to rearticulate the bones in this language, which powerfully envisages ruination, faces it, almost makes itself a party to it, at home in dislocated creation. Tennyson's *Lucretius* derived from Lucretius's *De Rerum Naturae*, translated from the Latin by his friend Hugh Munro in 1864. It was also up to the minute. The notorious speech by the physicist John Tyndall in Belfast ten years later quoted the atomistic, materialist ideas of Lucretius; like other scientists he was given to quoting poetry. His speech provoked the most intense debate about science and religion in the nineteenth century: where we think 'Darwin' they were more likely to think 'Tyndall.'

The revolution in physics drew on existing commonplaces, as Darwin had drawn on selective breeding to describe the unmanaged: commonplaces such as Bacon's 'everything changes, nothing perishes'. The 'first' law of thermodynamics defined energy as elemental and distinct from force (an attribute of matter in motion). The lines I've quoted from *Lucretius* could be read as setting energy against force, in contrast to the balanced stillness of *In Memoriam* CXXIII, where the heavy triple stress on 'long street roars' replicates VII's hopeless '[On the] bald street breaks', and the 'central sea' is utterly inert: nothing changes, everything perishes. The popular example of thermodynamics was the steam engine, a system for converting heat into mechanical energy. The 'second' law was that energy in a closed system remains the same, nothing perishes, but the system becomes less efficient, increasingly disorganized, everything changes. Entropy is the measure of this change in everything organized.

These ideas were linked to social thinking, in a universalizing vision of history. Lord Kelvin, credited with the first law of thermodynamics in 1852 and with 'throwing the universe into the ash-heap', supported his argument with statistics and Biblical prophecy: he thought the earth was younger than Darwin said, but that it was passing from molten origins to an icy end, the 'heat death of the universe'. As Greg Myers puts it, prophets have predicted the end of the world, Kelvin gave the formula for its final temperature. Other physicists were less enthusiastic for apocalypse, stressing the limits of knowledge: maybe God had ensured that the system was not entirely closed. Popularizers explained thermodynamics by economic metaphors, linking social science to positivist laws: 'The sun . . . is in the position of a man whose expenditure exceeds his income. He is living upon his capital, and is destined to share the fate of all who act in a similar manner.' 'The tendency of heat is towards equalization: heat is *par excellence* the communist of our universe, and it will no doubt ultimately bring the present system to an end.'[6]

Scientific law and social degeneration became analogies for each other. Lynda Nead's study of mid-nineteenth-century art invokes an atmosphere of 'moral panic', linking divorce liberalization with the Indian Mutiny and fears about health in the armed services, which led to the passage of the Contagious Diseases Acts in 1864, 1866, 1869. Surveillance of soldiers was not increased, but a female found 'unprotected' at times and places not obviously respectable could be arrested as a prostitute, forcibly examined for venereal disease, and committed for treatment. Campaigners for the repeal of these acts colluded with repressive authorities, insisting on a restraint thought more natural to women. At the same time Robert Buchanan was denouncing the Pre-Raphaelites and Swinburne, 'The Fleshly School' in painting and poetry; and Eliza Lynn Linton, a career journalist, produced her equally famous article against the bold and showy 'Girl of the Period'. These excitements are satirized in an 1865 cartoon reproduced by Lynda Nead: a fashionably dressed woman is approached by a man who offers her a tract. She replies 'I am not a social evil, I am only waiting for a bus'. Pious or a punter, he's pestering her. Reading Tennyson's 'Guinevere' or *Lucretius*, it's hard to imagine a woman waiting for a bus. These medievalizing, classicizing poems make a local panic into something timeless.

Lady Audley in Mary Braddon's 1862 best-seller is described as 'a worthy model for a pre-Raphaelite pencil': 'no-one but a pre-Raphaelite' could have painted the portrait with its mass of golden hair, no one else

> would have exaggerated every attribute of that delicate face as to give a lurid brightness to the blonde complexion, and a strange, sinister light to the deep blue eyes. No-one but a pre-Raphaelite could have given to that pretty pouting mouth the hard and almost wicked look it had in the portrait . . . it was as if you had burned strange-coloured fires before my lady's face . . . it seemed as if the painter had copied mediaeval monstrosities until his brain had grown bewildered, for my lady, in his portrait of her, had the aspect of a beautiful fiend.
>
> (*Lady Audley's Secret*, Ch. 8)

The excessive pencil depicts a truth – Lucy Audley, a ray of sunshine in her aging husband's life, is a bigamist. When her first husband turns up as a house guest, she pushes him down the well; later she sets fire to the house where witnesses and the young man on the track of her secret are sleeping. Finally, to save the family honour, she is confined to a mental asylum overseas, though the doctor does not diagnose her insane; the novel's reader-appeal seems to endorse this evasion of the law in the service of an elite. Elaine Showalter argued that Braddon is 'subversive' from a feminist point of view, in that it is not the child of the streets or an alien femme fatale who threatens domestic sanctity, but the sweet angel herself, in her dissatisfied dependence, unenfranchized, enclosed. However, Braddon seems equally to sustain identification with male authority, and fears of such a woman. Maybe the ambiguity of Lady Audley fascinated readers hovering between proper horror and sympathy. Braddon allows her an extraordinary honesty, for all her secrecy, in the scene of Sir Michael's proposal. He wants her to marry him for love: 'You ask too much of me! . . . I *cannot* be disinterested; I cannot be blind to the advantages of such a marriage . . . I do not love anyone in the world.' Tennyson's Guinevere is unlike Lucy in that she did have a 'maiden passion', the same one as the pure Elaine and Arthur, Lancelot. Self-confined for safety in a religious house, she becomes its head, renowned for sanctity, and finally acknowledges her husband as her true love, untrue to her first love in this.[7] You could say that in the end she's allowed to have it all, adulterous passion, ultimate marital loyalty, and a life of virtuous power, but the big scene is Arthur's condemnation.

Sensation novels of the 1860s drew on the material and the popularity of proliferating publications with mass appeal, some of which were suppressed. Tennyson, like other Victorians, was an avid reader of murder reports and sensation novels: it was said of Mrs Braddon that she made 'the literature of the Kitchen the favourite reading of the Drawing Room'. Not only the poor child loose on the midnight streets but the angel of the hearth became a dangerous character. As for the gentleman, figures for prostitution indicate that his sexuality was not confined within marriage. In any period there is a web of symbolic cross-reference, in which one set of events may become a metaphor for another – actuality is underlaid and overlaid by fantasy. My quartet of images of sexual disorder, female and manly, mocks barriers between the kitchen and the study. In Egg's painting the wife's body cuts across the confines of the drawing room; the door opens only onto the dereliction indicated by the paintings which hem in the central scene. Connections could be traced between these confinements and the opening and slamming of the domestic door in Ibsen's *The Doll's House* (1879) which reverberated beyond that drama's provincial origin. Does the invisible and silent wife in Tennyson's 'Lucretius' signify anything different?

Tennyson's Lucretius models himself on his idea of what the Gods are like: remote from human life, not passionate as myths said. For Tennyson's Cambridge contemporaries, Arthur Hallam and Charles Kingsley, God did not intervene by miracles or in response to prayers but worked by general laws set in motion at the creation of the world.

Lucretius as a classical thinker would not, however, have accepted the Christian story that something could be created out of nothing, or come to a final end: a closed system requiring apocalypse. Tennyson is clearly fascinated with Lucretius's vision of atoms continually re-forming in a void – this may have something to do with his image of poetry as shot-silk, dependent on interpretation – and he represents it powerfully, but still thinks of it in terms of a ruinous apocalypse. He confines Lucretius's monologue within a narrative frame drawn from a legend recorded by a church father: that Lucretius killed himself after his disappointed wife had given him a love potion which provoked sensual visions. This legend served to discredit Lucretius's materialist philosophy, also suggesting that it is women's desires which destroy great minds and male authority.

Certainly this mad monologue associates female powers – Nature, Helen of Troy, Venus – with an endless round of reproduction and destruction, very like the actual mortality rates, and the prolific breeding associated with the irresponsible classes, against which the middling and aspiring wanted protection. Lucretius, who would be cool, thinks that Venus – the 'all-generating powers and genial heat / Of Nature' (97–8) – is punishing him for neglecting her worship, with dreams which include a startling image of Helen's breasts. Their beauty makes a threatening sword 'sink down shamed', while a fire shoots from them, scorching Lucretius as it had Troy, in a surreal inversion of phallic power (60–6):

> And therefore now
> Let her, that is the womb and tomb of all,
> Great Nature, take, and forcing far apart
> These blind beginnings that have made me man,
> Dash them anew together at her will
> Through all her cycles . . .

> (242–7)

Tennyson, unlike Darwin, was terrified by visions of a world teeming with new births: who wouldn't be while so many die in poverty and technologically assisted wars which we can only not call stupid because we know the interests they serve? Lucretius's last words to his wife, his offstage audience, tell her not to care (2–9). His dreams of destructive lust can be read not only as the *motive* for transcendence, but also as the *result* of his cool visions; the result also of the invisibility to him of his wife. She is not the object of his fantasies, just their refuse.

In the last of his dramatic monologues, Tennyson revised the myth of Demeter and Persephone, with Demeter as fertile Earth Mother, the other-than-divine heat of Nature, while her daughter becomes, through her sojourn in hell, symbolic of a religion of love and care replacing that of law and force. Each is a heterosexual or androgynous image: the phallic Venus Generatrix represented in Demeter is veiled, for example, in Spenser's *The Faerie Queene* because the symbolic body is not that of a naked woman alone, but the mystery of heterosexual reproduction; Persephone is Christ, the violated Son and Bride, open to more than one kind of life and claim. In Tennyson's version the mother and daughter dominate these mysteries. Egg's triptych might also suggest a mother-daughter bond trashed by the law of the father. These versions of power and victimization are not necessarily liberating; but they help to suggest that what Tennyson represents in 'Lucretius' is a masculinity which in erecting a fearful dignity projects onto female figures and 'red ruin' what it wants to disavow, and control.

Notes

This essay fills the place of a chapter, 'The Morbid, the Manly and the Classical', omitted from my 1988 book on Tennyson. It would have come between *Maud* and *Idylls of the King* and discussed how Tennyson turned away in his middle years from unconventional explorations of sexual love and difference, and feminist demands, to more anxiously conservative attitudes. It would have considered *Lucretius*, experiments with classical metres and dialect poems, and the ornate-but-simple tale of a fishing community, 'Enoch Arden' – all concerned with nation and manhood. Had he called the *Enoch Arden* volume 'Idylls of the Hearth', a title favoured by Emily Tennyson, it would have underlined his claim on the less-than-epic idyll as his chosen form, emphasizing continuity between the 'English Idylls' and *Idylls of the King*. Since (maybe) Enoch is able to enjoy the hearth no more than the exotic island, the volume takes its title from this manly hero, self-sacrificed to the idyll from which he is excluded.

1. T. J. EDELSTEIN, 'Augustus Egg's Triptych', *Burlington Magazine*, 125, (April 1983), pp. 292–10. He notes that the framing of the drawing room by the two other scenes prevents the triptych being read in sequence as a moralizing narrative: the middle-class home is surrounded, even supported, by these other spaces.

2. For 'illimitably' see ELAINE JORDAN, *Alfred Tennyson*, Cambridge: Cambridge University Press, 1988, p. 33. For Hunt, see R. B. MARTIN, *Tennyson: The Unquiet Heart*, Oxford: Clarendon Press, 1983, pp. 414–15.
3. ROYDEN HARRISON, 'The 10th April of Spencer Walpole', *International Review of Social History*, VII (1962), 351–99.
4. PAUL GILROY, *The Black Atlantic: Modernity and Double Consciousness*, London: Verso, 1993, p. 11.
5. I am indebted to CATHERINE HALL for this amazing news, from her unpublished paper 'The White Brotherhood of Britain in the Mid-Nineteenth Century'.
6. GREG MYERS, 'Nineteenth-Century Popularizations of Science and the Rhetoric of Social Prophecy', *Victorian Studies*, 29 (1985), 36–66, and 54 and 57 respectively.
7. A. S. BYATT's 'The Conjugial Angel' in *Angels and Insects* recalls this obsession with fidelity to first love; Elizabeth Barrett Browning was one who found it hard to forgive Emily Tennyson's marriage.

Further reading

BEER, GILLIAN, *Darwin's Plots*, Routledge, 1983.
LORIMER, D. A., *Colour, Class and the Victorians*, Leicester, 1978 (Chapter 9 on Eyre).
NEAD, LYNDA, *Myths of Sexuality*, Blackwell, 1988.
POOVEY, MARY, *Uneven Developments*, University of Chicago Press, 1988 (Chapter 3 on divorce).
SHOWALTER, ELAINE, 'Family Secrets and Domestic Subversion', in *The Victorian Family*, ed. A. S. Wohl, Croom Helm, 1978, pp. 101–16.
SPRINGHALL, JOHN, 'A Life Story for the People', *Victorian Studies* 33 (Winter 1990), 223–46.
VICINUS, MARTHA, ed., *Suffer and Be Still*, Indiana University Press, 1972.
WILLIAMS, RAYMOND, *Keywords*, London, 1976, pp. 82–7.

7 Nation, Class and Gender: Tennyson's *Maud* and War*

JOSEPH BRISTOW

Joseph Bristow's essay takes as its subject the Crimean War and examines the 'textual and cultural contradictions' that place pressures on notions of Victorian manhood and poethood within Tennyson's Crimean War poem, *Maud*. In an age when the expression of emotion in poetry was becoming feminized, tensions arose between being a man and being a poet. Bristow argues that *Maud* presents a case for women as emotional healers of men and seeks to prove that poetry enables full expression of the maddening emotions which constitute proper masculinity. For Bristow the text represents a conservative masculinism, but simultaneously betrays the values it seeks to endorse by revealing the cracks in that ideology and by enacting a conflict between different models of masculinity: effeminate radicals and manly conservatives. Finally the poem resolves the contradictions it sets up by suggesting that men must go mad in order to prove that they are men. Such a reading aims to begin to put together the cultural history of Victorian masculinities in relation to class and political identity.

'And ah for a man to arise in me, / That the man I am may cease to be!' (I, 396–397),[1] declares the maddened hero of Alfred Tennyson's *Maud*, a poem voicing a particular set of mid-Victorian anxieties about competing versions of masculinity in the testing climate of the Crimean War (1854–56). This essay examines the textual and cultural contradictions that place extraordinary pressures on ideas about Victorian manhood and, almost as importantly, poethood in a poem strategically placed to speak on behalf of the nation at a key turning point in nineteenth-century British history. *Maud* was Tennyson's second major poem as Poet Laureate. A public servant of high standing, he laboured under an obligation to give voice to the nation's truest feelings. But, as his poem all too clearly registers, there is an enduring conflict between emotion and gender in poetry at this time that *Maud* makes extraordinary manoeuvres to reconcile.

Reprinted from *Genders* 9 (Autumn 1990), pp. 93–111.

The question of male identity in Victorian poetry has generated much recent debate and has revealed a number of tensions between the roles of man and poet, indicating that these identities were becoming increasingly discrete. Carol Christ usefully draws attention to Alfred Austin's caustic retrospect on Tennyson's career, first published in *Temple Bar* in 1869.[2] In his acerbic but acute essay, Austin (a future Laureate himself) railed against Tennyson's weakening infatuation with 'woman, woman, woman', an obsession, he thought, that was so great it rendered the poet's works sentimentally feminine.[3] By 1869, when Austin was writing his vituperative accounts of 'The Poetry of the Period', the heroic male models figured in Thomas Carlyle's *vates*, promulgated by Carlyle in his lectures on hero-worship published in 1840, were far less stable than they had been at the start of Tennyson's career. Besides, the spontaneous overflow of conspicuously male genius from the earlier Romantic period – which Tennyson's 1832 and 1842 volumes insistently interrogated with particular regard to female creativity (notably, 'The Lady of Shalott') – had reconfigured itself in two controversial formations: Tennyson's seemingly perverse, feminine poetics is one; the Pre-Raphaelites' pornographic erotics is another (the controversies around Dante Gabriel Rossetti and Algernon Charles Swinburne are the key points of reference here). Both formations pointed to disturbances within and about male desire in poetry, a site discursively marked out for the direct expression of feeling. An aesthetics based on humanistic assumptions about sincerity and emotional truth certainly dominated the critical theorization of poetry at mid-century. It was, indeed, the problem of directly expressing emotion in poetry that was seen to be more and more at odds with Victorian masculinities.

Austin's irritation with the effeminizing incursion of 'woman' into Tennyson's writing is a symptom of another area of discomfort with gender and poetry at this time. In many respects, Austin's pointed remarks are a defensive reaction against the emergence of the now widely published 'poetress', not just in the figures of Elizabeth Barrett Browning and Christina Rossetti (both well established in the public mind by the mid-1860s – even if Rossetti's first volume went out on sale a year after Barrett Browning's death), but also in works of equally popular women poets, such as Adelaide Anne Procter, reputedly Queen Victoria's 'favourite poet'[4] and to whose writing on the Crimean War this essay finally returns. At roughly the same time, the best-known Victorian anthologist of poetry, Francis Turner Palgrave, was emphasizing that the inadequacies of women's poetry stemmed from a 'deficiency in comprehending poetry as an art'.[5] His long two-part essay on 'Women and the Fine Arts' opens up further instabilities about the gendering of mid-Victorian poetry, as well as artistic practices in general. Repeating a key verb on successive occasions, Palgrave remarks that women poets fail to 'grasp' the idea they are depicting. Infirm in constitution, women can only represent the affective qualities attached to the noble subjects of poetry. And to substantiate his argument he makes the following comparison, interestingly with the very man Austin has vilified for being too feminine: 'Such a feeling as Tennyson's "Behind the veil" [*In Memoriam* (LV1, 28)] is alien to them' (215). (Unsurprisingly, few women feature in *The Golden Treasury of English Poetry* [1861].) It was not just lack of education that made women poets 'deficient', according to Palgrave, but something else – as yet unknown – about their 'internal conditions' (127). Tennyson, a man, could be appropriated to demonstrate that he had more feeling than even those affective beings, women.

By the 1860s, then, Tennyson could stand both as a *model* for poetic strength and sensitivity of mind (a truly masculine identity) *and* as a man *effeminized* in his vocation. And the variance of these mid-Victorian criticisms was, of course, enabled by the undecided struggling articulation of the male voice in Tennyson's writing. The considerable emotional reach of his work – fervidly patriotic, on the one hand; lyrically sensuous, indeed sensual, on the other – could simultaneously touch on things truly masculine and yet worryingly feminine, depending on his reader's expectations of what a man who was also a poet could and should produce. Christ is undoubtedly correct when she observes that both the work of Robert Browning and that of Tennyson 'shows an anxiety, typical of the century, about which gender possesses the power of authorship' (399), and she closes her essay with a statement that provides a helpful starting point for analyzing the maddened man in *Maud*: 'Fearful of the feminization of culture, the poet of the period strove to make the female subject bear his name' (400).

Maud – as the eponymous subject whose name literally means war or battle – has, in the main, two purposes in mind: first, to demonstrate how woman can salve the emotional suffering of men; and second, how a 'monodrama' (as the poem is subtitled), dedicated in a woman's warring name, can, paradoxically, prove that poetry, as a genre, is ideally suited to men. Poetry is ideally male because it gives full rein to the febrile and maddening emotions that constitute proper masculinity. As a representative document of the conservative masculinism of its age, *Maud* is closely aligned with the Ruskinian conception of the angel-wife to be found, notoriously, in 'Of Queens' Gardens' (in *Sesames and Lilies* [1865]). But *Maud*, as a 'monodrama' rather than an essay, gives a unique inflection to this prevailing ideology of gender. In fact, as its complex narrative unfolds, this remarkable poem betrays the precariousness of the noble masculinity it attempts to vindicate. Pushed to the limits of its astonishing logic, *Maud* finally stakes a claim that the finest men are those who must justify their place in the world through acts of not only physical and but also psychical violence – to the degree that men must go mad in order to prove they are *men*. Why should this be? The answer lies in the discriminations Tennyson makes between antagonistic types of Victorian manhood, ones which were very much at the centre of a political war of words during the crisis of the Crimean War.

Effeminate radicals versus manly conservatives

'Is it peace or war' (I, 27, 47), demands Tennyson's tormented speaker. But in this, the earliest section of the poem, it is not the Crimean War he is ranting about. The 'war' in question here concerns Britain's appalling domestic degeneration since the ravages of the 'Hungry Forties'. In the increasing squalor of urban areas, detailed in the opening lines of the poem, 'the poor are hovelled and hustled together, each sex, like swine' (I, 34). And in the relationships worked out in this clause, the carefully marked term of gender ('each sex') prominently intersects with that of class ('the poor'). This may seem to be a minor feature, but it makes a highly significant point: class, importantly, is gendered; and in this poem class and gender cut through and against each other in a way they could not have done in earlier decades. Metaphorically speaking, these terrible conditions – that make men *and* women into nothing less than pigs – constitute a state of 'Civil war' (I, 27). This 'war' is a conflict between 'Mammon' (Carlyle's grotesque god of industrial capitalism) and the painfully and unequally divided upper, middle, and working classes. Capitalism, in other words, is ruinously set against the nation.

In these dire circumstances the speaker tells of his own disinheritance, which has been the result of a 'vast speculation' that 'failed' (I, 9) – conjecturally, the 'railway mania' of 1847[6] – and which drove his father to the brutal, blood-gorged suicide that cleaves open the poem's furiously jolting first lines. Throughout, money, commerce, and industry are associated with self-destruction, which is destined to bring about the total collapse of Britain. In the speaker's eyes, this 'Civil war' is an unjust and unnatural form of combat because the country is not fighting a true enemy but itself instead. This undesirable type of 'war' erodes the idea of patriotic nationhood, which it is the project of *Maud* to champion. The only strategy available to counter the machinations of capital is by pitching the military events in the Crimea against them. Put simply, a war abroad should rightly make for peace at home. And this view was, for its time, a widespread one. Patriotism always served conservatives with a just cause to minimize class (and related) differences in the name of uniting the nation under one banner.

War, then, is a confusing, because rhetorically deployed, term in *Maud*. War refers, all at once, to the poem's eponym, to the economic disarray in a time of so-called peace, and, of course, to the Crimea itself. In terms of class politics, the poem seeks to assert the proper value of war as the focus of a broader strategy on behalf of the landed classes to restore Britain to its age-old feudal order. The nationalism derived from the opportune Crimean War (ostensibly against Russia's violence against the Turks) has, in fact, another motive: to combat the dissolute scenes of suffering among the unsanitary conditions of poor city dwellers. Although like many writers of the 1850s – such as Carlyle and Charles Kingsley, both of whose works echo in the poem[7] – Tennyson's protagonist registers the cruelties of class distinctions in a time of accelerated industrialization, he is unlike most of them in mourning the dislodgement of the aristocracy and wealthier gentry from this recently disrupted social system. With a striking vengeance, the monodramatic hero wishes to resurrect an idyllic picture of an era when, implicitly, serfs are once again enfeoffed to their paternalistic landed masters. His was a conservative vision of Victorian Britain celebrated by the likes of Benjamin Disraeli's 'Young England' coterie somewhat earlier in the century:

> it lightened my despair
> When I thought that a war would arise in defence of the right,
> Than an iron tyranny now should bend or cease,
> The glory of manhood stand on his ancient height,
> Nor Britain's one sole God be the millionaire:
> No more shall commerce be all in all, and Peace
> Pipe on her pastoral hillock a languid note,
> And watch her harvest ripen, her herd increase.
>
> (III, 28–25)

War is the stage on which the aristocracy may emblematize the pageantry of its ancestral birthrights. It is where they can make a valiant display of patriotism when fighting the Russian Bear. And, finally, warmongering is a practice which enables Tennyson's hero to convince the world that the defence of the nation depends on the passionate responsiveness of those men who immediately express their outrage for queen and country.

Both the ideological manoeuvres and rhetorical outcries of *Maud* owe much to Carlyle, who proposed that 'an aristocracy of talent', rather than the aristocracy as it stood, should run the country. Like the venerated Victorian sage, Tennyson's speaker casts blame for the 'vitriol madness' (1, 37) on the 'ledger' (1, 35) or profit. Time and again, 'commerce' is denounced. The controversial third and final section of the poem (which, in the light of several hostile reviews, Tennyson saw fit to emend for a second printing) counts among the earliest written parts of the poem 'when the cannon was heard booming from the battleships in the Solent'.[8] Robert C. Schweik demonstrates that what have always been seen as the aggressively patriot elements of *Maud* clearly correspond with one of two articles in *Blackwood's* magazine on the question of 'Peace and War'.[9] Not only are specific details of peacetime corruption – from the adulteration of foodstuffs to the supposedly self-interested strategems of the Quaker Peace Societies – evident in both 'Peace and War' and Tennyson's poem, they also share a defiantly aristocratic polemic.[10] The article from this Tory journal is structured in the form of a Socratic dialogue between Tlepolemus (the warmonger) and Iranaeus (the voice of peace). Like Tennyson's hero, Tlepolemus is committed to the belief that war accomplishes national unity: 'War . . . makes us feel we are countrymen, brothers, friends, and neighbours, all of us (not Quakers only), while peace sets us all together by the ears like hounds in an ill-regulated kennel' (595). There is an explicit reason for the association of peace here with social degradation: the Quaker pressure groups who travelled the country campaigning against the unnecessary expense of the Crimean War. Repeatedly, Tennyson's speaker duplicates Tlepolemus's condemnation of the self-seeking commercialism of the Quaker Peace Societies and allied promoters of peace hailing from that base of Victorian economic theory, the Manchester School (namely, Richard Cobden and John Bright).

In *Maud*, particularly when juxtaposed to the debates in *Blackwood's*, it is clear to see why the Manchester School theorists are considered completely alien to all that conservative manhood stands for. For a start, they count among the wealthiest members of the rising bourgeoisie. Maud's future husband, whom the protagonist rivals in her affections, is a ridiculed 'new-made lord, whose splendour plucks / The slavish hat from the villager's head' (I, 332–333). Moreover, the speaker vociferously censures the means through which such 'new-made' money has been earned:

[the fiancé's] old grandfather has lately died,
Gone to a blacker pit, for whom
Grimy nakedness dragging his trucks
And laying his trams in a poisoned gloom
Wrought, till he crept from a gutted mine
Master of half a servile shire.
And left his coal all turned into gold
To a grandson, first of a noble line,
Rich in the grace all women desire,
Strong in the power that all men adore.

(I, 334–43)

This newfangled, ironically 'noble' line has only recently risen from
dark and unnatural depths – from the ignorance of the pit. Likewise,
it is merely a mine-worker whose hard labour at the coalface has, just
as unnaturally, subverted the aristocracy's life of rightful leisure.
Capitalism and its bourgeois proponents, therefore, have achieved an
improper line of inheritance between forefathers and sons whereby
the latter wrongly reap their benefits from the sufferings of the former.
What is worse, this apparently anomalous line of kinship has given
birth to a man whose good looks emulate those prized by his betters.
The 'new-made lord' causes the greatest indignation of all because
he is a perfect simulacrum of what the old order commanded as its
greatest virtue: true masculinity. The landed classes may not have
had to work in the past but they were, all in all, *men*. But this factitious
lord has managed to win the favours of an aristocratic maiden,
Maud, as well as those of her treacherous brother. Tennyson's hero,
then, has to negotiate a new configuration of rival masculinities in
this muddled and madness-inducing scenario of 'peace and war'.

Tennyson's emotional hero begrudges the *nouveaux riches* for their
misuse of money. He questions the credibility of these new upstarts:
'Who but a fool would have faith in a tradesman's ware or his word'
(I, 26). Similarly attributing trade with dishonourable behaviour,
Tlepolemus indicts Iraeneus: 'You pay your bills at Christmas; you
are chary of your signature – in fact, never use it except when it is
really necessary' (595). Elsewhere in *Blackwood's* there is more
propaganda that condemns the Manchester School, amplifying the
bigotry against the peacemakers. Promoters of *laissez-faire* – notably
Cobden – are convicted of selfishly attending to economic objectives
while ignoring the moral justice of the Crimean War. When the
Crimean War erupted, with Britain and France going to the aid of
Turkey to protect sovereign states from Russian expansionism, the
free-traders argued that a war would only create additional hardship
among the poor since the price of bread would rise. They claimed

that Britain was dependent on imports of Russian grain and that war would inevitably curtail these supplies. (*Blackwood's* was eager to refute this argument [9].) In the brief historical outline given here, the respective apologists for peace and war were espoused to blatantly opposed sets of concerns. On the one hand, the landed classes fostered their case for freedom and honour under the banner of nationalism – war sought to keep the notion of nation intact. On the other, industrialists and traders expressed the economic dangers of war because of the likely interference with the international circulation of capital. Where, then, does Maud, who names and, in a sense, provides the rationale for this poem, fit into this world of money-making pacifists and soldierly gentlemen?

From the outset, Maud's position within this sexual, political, and economic field of conflict is one of vulnerability. Continually at the mercy of these competing classes of men, Maud's voice is never heard speaking out at any point in the poem. She is always spoken for. Capitalist enterprise dangerously encroaches on her ancestral home: 'The old dark place will be gilt by the touch of a millionaire: / I have heard, I know not whence, of the singular beauty of Maud' (I, 65–6). Abruptly yoked together, these lines bring disparate elements into a revealing conjunction. The superficial glitter of capital rivals Maud's noble feminine beauty. Soon that strange hybrid, her 'dandy-despot' (I, 231) brother, will seduce her into marrying the young member of Parliament, the 'new-made lord' – and the economic power of both of them will annihilate her. Maud certainly should not belong to this class-conflictual universe. Instead, she represents the spirit of bygone days, ones constantly invoked not only in *Blackwood's* 'Peace and War' dialogues but also in the iconography of several illustrations in *Punch*. As Marion Shaw probingly observes: 'Maud must die to save herself from – death. The poem warns of this; within the terms of its self-hatred, no matter how the nature of woman is questioned, and her complicity as scapegoat or redeemer courted the answer to the problem of living is death'.[11] In fact, after her demise, Maud's ghost enters the eerie second part of the poem where the hero makes a statement that could well account for her presence – or lack of it – throughout the whole narrative: 'She comes from the another stiller world of the dead' (II, 308). Whenever glimpsed, Maud appears insubstantial, a shadow or a fleeting image, and when meditated upon, she turns out to be a contradictory source of despair and desire.

Fragmented parts of the hero's identity are repeatedly projected and displaced onto Maud, and so she becomes a representation of a fracture that exists in his psyche. Elevated as the ultimate object of veneration within the chivalric code, Maud is the silent guarantor of her suitor's love for battle. On many occasions, she stands not unlike the national emblem of her country – Britannia the armorially clad figure haunting the pages of *Punch* in 1854. Such images clearly demonstrate the power of Britannia's image in mid-Victorian Britain. In one illustration, Britannia kneels as a crusading woman-warrior symbolically laying the just sword of war before the altar of God. In another picture, she represents an image reminiscent of Christ – suffering little children unto her welcoming embrace – but offering the generous wisdom and guidance of a caring mother. She is both the spirit of war and the heal to its wounds. Britannia came pressingly to *Punch*'s propagandist mind in a culture presided over by laudatory images of Queen Victoria. (It was in this climate that another icon of noble, soldierlike femininity could thrive – that of Florence Nightingale.[12])

Britannia, Nightingale, Victoria – like all these saving female graces, Maud is a true patriot and lends lyrical charm to war in the most natural of surroundings. Here, Tennyson's man gathers up his heroic resolve in response to the inspiring tones of Maud's battle song:

A voice by the cedar tree
In the meadow under the Hall!
She is singing an air that is known to me,
A passionate ballad gallant and gay,
A martial song like a trumpet's call!
Singing alone in the morning of life and of May,
Singing of men that in battle array,
Ready in heart and ready in hand,
March with banner and bugle and fife
To the death, for their native land.
Maud with her exquisite face,
And wild voice pealing up to the sunny sky,
And feet like sunny gems on an English green,
Maud in the light of her youth and her grace,
Singing of death, and Honour that cannot die.

(I 162–77)

Maud's femininity, however, is curiously divided against the patriotism she so sweetly sings of. In one respect, her song supports male codes of honour and the lives of proper, valiant men. These were men from the landed classes who maintained a tenacious foothold in the armed forces. But in another sense, like Britannia the woman-warrior, she represents the living continuity of the nation for which noble *death* is necessary. Men die so that she – both the nation and prized femininity – may live. But, then again, she – Maud – can only subsist by being converted into something higher than life: a dead, and thus spiritual, ideal. Her role, therefore, is twofold. On the one hand subservient to male power, she remains, on the other, the very ideal they are fighting for. She is the source of a myth of feminine power that serves to regulate the place of woman within patriarchal law. Like most myths, this one is at its most incontestably alive when it appeals to something that can only be controlled when it is deceased.

The multiple sensuous love lyrics of *Maud* immortalize this mythical portrait of her. But the fact that Maud can only exist permanently as a national icon at the moment she is dead takes the logic of its frenzied 'monodrama' to breaking point. In several places, the incompatible claims of the bourgeois 'peace' and aristocratic 'war' make their respective bids for her affections. At times, when still courting her favours, the speaker finds it difficult to decide whether Maud is truly a noble lady or a woman who has lamentably prostituted herself to the formidable lure of middle-class economism. The virgin/whore dichotomy – tediously intersecting through so much Victorian writing – often emerges in the narrative:

> Ah, well, well, well, I *may* be beguiled
> By some coquettish deceit.
> Yet, if she were not a cheat,
> If Maud were all that she seemed,
> And her smile had all that I dreamed,
> Then the world were not so bitter
> But a smile could make it sweet.
>
> (I, 278–84)

(These lines recur, in slightly different order, at I, 215 and 224–8, insisting upon their significance.) For some time, the hero cannot tell whether she genuinely loves him and will fulfill the marital precontract, according to the measures taken by their fathers when Maud and the hero were born. Alternatively, he is unsure whether she places her affections with – as she is reported as naming her fiancé – the 'rough but kind' (I, 753, 762, 766) new lord. Early on, Maud's femininity represents a puzzle, a potential deception: She is 'faultily faultless' and 'splendidly null' (I, 82), extravagantly imaged in jewels and yet as cold and sharp as chiselled stone. (She is even imagined as a potential Cleopatra [I, 215] – seductive and orientally treacherous at once.) And yet these extremes of difference are central to her attraction and the sexual power she commands. Eventually, Tennyson's protagonist is driven to duel with Maud's brother to prove his honour and devotion to her.

Even if it kills off Maud's brother, the duel achieves little other

than more pain. Yet that seems to be the desired effect. Duelling is
certainly a necessary ceremony, as one of the most vociferous
influences on Tennyson's poem states. In 'Two Hundred and Fifty
Years Ago', published in 1850, Carlyle wrote fervidly of those days
before capitalism when duelling guaranteed a sense of firm
(aggressively masculine) identity:

> A background of wrath, which can be stirred-up to the murderous
> infernal pitch, does lie in every man, in every creature; this is a
> fact which cannot be contradicted; – which indeed is but another
> phasis of the more general fact, that every one of us is a *Self*,
> that every one of us call himself *I*. How can you be a *Self*, and
> not have tendencies to self-defence! This background of wrath,
> – which surely ought to blaze-out as seldom as possible, and then
> as nobly as possible, – may be defined as no other than the general
> radical fire, in its least-elaborated shape, whereof Life is
> composed. Its least elaborated shape, this flash of accursed
> murderous rage; – as the glance of mother's love, and all
> intermediate warmths and energies and genialities, are the same
> element *better* elaborated. Certainly the elaboration is an immense
> matter, – indeed, is the whole matter! But the figure, moreover,
> under which your infernal element itself shall make its
> appearance, nobly or else ignobly, is very significant. From
> Indian Tomahawks, from Irish-Shillelahs, from Arkansas Bowie-
> knives, up to a deliberate Norse *Holmgang*, to any civilized
> Wager of Battle, the distance is great.[13]

Carlyle's argument overruns its rational limits when making its case
for locating the self in just wrathfulness, since such anger can
mistakenly appear ignobly barbaric – hardly gentlemanly. But that is
its point. Here it is the *feeling* of anger sufficiently aroused to an
'infernal pitch' that is claimed to be fundamental to human life. In a
vocabulary made up of elemental alchemy, apposite to the cultural
values of two hundred and fifty years ago, Carlyle's essay insists that
the stuff of life can only be expressed when its fire is ignited and
driven toward self-defence and, presumably, murder.

For Tennyson's hero, the duel precipitates a further stage in the
drama, leading him toward a stage where he can re-establish who
he is. Murder here certainly contributes to the meaning – the
knowability – of his life. In Part II, having killed the brother, the
madness bursting in upon the opening lines of the poem reaches its
true potential. His intervening period in the Breton mental asylum
is one of terrible distress and delusion where imaginary horses'
hooves trample his disturbed soul. This sustained meditation on the

horrors of war is the product of the horrors of 'peace'. His recovery plunges him into a correct, just, and spiritually uplifting form of combat where the mixed-up values of 'peace and war' can, as much as possible, be magically resolved. In Part III, sound in mind and body, he decides to fight it out against the Russians. To die for one's country – this particular slogan takes on profound dimensions in *Maud* since these words imply that the country can only exist through death. It is only through the immortal icon of Maud – nation, nobility, and nurture in one – that madness can be exorcized and manhood sanely asserted. And yet, to reiterate, in order to live, this ideology must commit itself to the compulsive repetition of armed combat in the name of a woman who has died.

Victorian poets and Victorian war

The Crimean War gave rise to an extraordinary amount of heroic poetry written by men during its brief and despairing course. The journal that most inclusively reviewed poetry at this time, the *Athenaeum*, turned its readers' attentions to a host of minor volumes, many of them focusing on the battle of Inkermann.[14] *Punch* referred to such verses as 'the nuisances which always attend great exploits'.[15] It seemed that any man, anywhere, could become a poet in this epoch of war. Better-known poets also produced collections about events in the Crimea. Among these were Tennyson's friends from the days of the Cambridge Apostles, Henry and Franklin Lushington. But not all of them, like these brothers, were Tories. The Chartist poet, Ernest Jones, published *The Emperor's Vigil and the Waves of War* in 1856, articulating a staunchly republican patriotism. Likewise, Gerald Massey – another self-educated writer who, in the 1840s, stood at the forefront of Chartist poetry – produced his rather lurid *War Waits* in 1855. Moreover, a poet who had attracted much controversial attention, with considerable implications for *Maud*, was Sydney Dobell, energetically completing two collections – *Sonnets of the War* (1855) and *England in Time of War* (1856). Dobell was recognized for his outlandish, 'Spasmodic' writing. At this point, it is worth returning to the question of how and why poetry could function as a discourse for patriotic feeling on such a remarkable scale among different classes of men with distinct political affiliations.

This question has, of course, one obvious answer. Poetry was closely associated with the voice of the nation. Poetry – via rhythm and rhyme – could lend urgency as well as dignity to the battle cries leading the British army forward: 'Will the bloody day of Alma be the bloodiest to be won? / Will the mighty fortress crumble before the battering gun?' wrote Franklin Lushington, typically, in his poem upon that military fiasco.[16] But this question of masculinity in mid-century poetry is complicated by the increasing identification of the poet with femininity, particularly feebleness of mind. In fact, there was – as has been mentioned earlier – a link being forged between poetry, madness, and female weakness in the 1850s that would cause retrospective embarrassment, for example, to Matthew Arnold, who agonized over the inclusion and then rejection of his poem of classical suicide, 'Empedocles on Etna' (1852), which his famous 'Preface' of 1853 details. The connections between Dobell's 'Spasmodic' work and that of the working-class poet Alexander Smith, author of *A Life-Drama* (1852), with *Maud* have long been recognized.[17] *Maud*, in its style as well as theme, was very much a poem of the mid-1850s.

Tennyson seized upon the opportunities raised by this discordant, unstable moment when political questions seemed in as much upheaval as poetic ones. (They were, of course, entwined.) It was, in any case, his job as Laureate to be responsive to the shifts and changes of his era. And that engagement with being emotionally attuned to the vicissitudes of the age affects his hero's every action. It would be fair to generalize that Tennyson's whole canon tries to make sense of history not through rational argument but by means of intuition which necessarily involves confusion and, at its most hard-pressed, irascibility, even insanity. *Maud* enacts how proper feelings are always prompt, and indignant, reactions. Such strong feelings are opposed to the radical rationalism of the abominated Manchester School. Although calumniated here as 'feminine', this expanding empire of bourgeois men has a rational strength that sends the speaker completely mad – but only momentarily. In an unadulterated world of unrestrained feeling lay the freedom to love, to desire, even to go mad, and what is more important, to go mad on one's own terms, not those of the pacifists, who have plunged the nation with their economic theories into 'Civil war'. Poetry, then, could give a particular kind of upper-class masculinity the permission to gain its potency when the hero is deranged.

One section from Part I demonstrates exactly what is at stake in this world of divided masculinities, of those men who have the controlling power to think, and those who explode with emotion – like the wrathful men whose infernal desires consume Carlyle's prose:

> The man of science is fonder of glory, and vain,
> An eye well-practised in nature, a spirit bounded and poor;
> The passionate heart of the poet is whirled into folly and vice.

> I would not marvel at either, but keep a temperate brain;
> For not to desire or admire, if a man could learn it, were more
> Than to walk all day like the sultan of old in a garden of spice.
>
> (I, 138–43)

These lines are syntactically organized to lend unequal weight to two
different moral positions about two different kinds of men. On the
one hand, scientists, poets, and sultans share the same basic quality
– a seemingly negative capacity to indulge in feeling. They are 'poor'
and thus at fault. Yet, on the other, to be 'vain', to pursue 'folly and
vice', and 'to admire and desire' are claimed to be inevitable parts
of masculine identity. Cool reason – 'a temperate brain' – cannot be
achieved, even if it may seem to be greater in its ethical stature than
the passionate faults of these men. In a tentative conditional clause,
the speaker suggests he 'would not marvel at either' the scientist
or the poet were if possible to overmaster the 'desire' to 'admire'
them. It is, then, natural to desire and admire the *faults* of such men
since it is their faulted natures that precisely constitute them *as
men*. Therefore, even by acknowledging his moral 'other' – the
emasculated 'temperate brain' of the Manchester School – the
protagonist feels his way toward a faulty, but by virtue of that, true
masculinity in an appropriately haphazard syntax – one
accommodating his equivocations of emotion. Such feeling, then,
may be at fault, but it is none the less the sign of the finest masculinity.

Weak rationality and irrational strength

Maud produces some unexpected conclusions about the right-wing
male mind at mid-century. Tennyson draws together the potentially
emasculated mode of poetry – the 'feminine' world of feeling – with
the spirit of heroic military ambition under the banner of irrational
passion. But it is this illogical weakness which does, in its hellish
fury, make men into the strongest of men. Madness can thus be
accommodated into the ideal of potency. Such a view may appear
somewhat remote from general perceptions about Victorian
masculinity; but this view is a specific outcome of how one
Victorian writer could negotiate a way of legitimating the perceived
contradiction of being both a poet and a proper man. It now leaves
open the question of the function of women in this domain of
feeling. And this observation leads back to Maud, who, living on as
a myth only by dying at mid-point in the poem, is the *reason* for the
madness, pain, and battle that are both suffered and glorified by

the speaker. A woman's name – the name of war itself – provides
the framework, indeed the motive, for this extraordinary 'monodrama', and, as the illustrations from *Punch* demonstrate, woman
was seen to embrace both the military and maternal identities of
Britain itself. Representations of both men and women, therefore,
bore the burden of conflictual qualities within this conservative model
of the gender hierarchy.

This complex – and, in fact, highly contradictory – piece of sexual
ideology gains a clearer focus when the work of a woman poet,
Adelaide Anne Procter, is examined alongside *Maud*. Procter's poetry
is written in a consistently direct style, frequently working with the
forceful juxtapositions achieved by parataxis. The first three stanzas
of 'The Lesson of the War' (1855) provide a representative sample
of Procter's carefully measured clauses where the exceptional
passions aroused by the Crimean War are kept under remarkable
verbal control:

> The feast is spread through England,
>   For rich and poor to-day;
> Greetings and laughter may be there,
>   But thoughts are far away;
> Over the stormy ocean,
>   Over the dreary track,
> Where some are gone, whom England
>   Will never welcome back.
>
> Breathless she waits, and listens
>   For every Eastern breeze
> That bears upon its bloody wings
>   News from beyond the seas.
> The leafless branches stirring
>   Make many a watcher start;
> The distant tramp of steed may send
>   A throb from heart to heart.
>
> The rulers of the nation,
>   The poor ones at their gate,
> With the same eager wonder
>   The same great news await.
> The poor man's stay and comfort,
>   The rich man's joy and pride,
> Upon the bleak Crimean shore
>   Are fighting side by side.

$(1-24)$[18]

141

There are a few useful points to be learned from this calm meditation on the war. Far from invoking a jingoistic rhetoric, Procter depicts a nation waiting for news of victory and yet hearing only of one military disaster after another. And this nation is, of course, female. In this respect, England (rather than the more inclusive 'Britain') may seem passive. Yet this is not the case. England, later in the poem, actively calls upon her 'children' (45) to perform their 'duty' (56) in her name. It is a predictable sentiment. However, its significance derives from the fact that all classes of men are obliged to comply with a female imperative to fight. This female authority is unquestionable. Procter, the woman poet – like England herself – insists:

> Brothers, you are in sorrow,
>   In duty to your land.
> Learn but this noble lesson
>   Ere peace returns again,
> And the life-blood of Old England
>   Will not be shed in vain.
>
> (55–60)

This highly respected 'poetess' is placed in a strategic position to demand military devotion and patriotic unity between the country's rich and poor male citizens. Hers is the stable and assured poetic voice that grants men the permission to place feeling above thought – to recognize that to fight, whatever the consequences, ennobles the spirit. But, as *Maud* discloses, this is a female power that, if it is to be obeyed, must also be mastered by men and thereby subsumed into the stuff of myth. That is the reason why Maud's beauty is multiply 'luminous gemlike, deathlike . . . / Growing and fading and growing' (I, 95–6). The power of woman is certainly generated by the contradictory oscillations of her image in a time of war.

Woman, then, is both rational (a national force) and irrational (domesticated; infirm in mind and soul; best mythologized, like Maud). Adjacently, rationality is effeminate (the Manchester School) as well as feminine (Nightingale, Victoria, Britannia, Maud). This is certainly an intricate, partly muddled network of associations between the meanings of reason, passion, and gender, wherein femininity cannot rest between either forcefulness or feebleness. But one significant point emerges from these discoveries. For Tennyson to be able to rationalize the war as a poet, it is reasonable to say, he would have had to have been a woman. But as a man, he was duty-bound by the national symbolic force of woman to act out a feminine role. An implicitly feminine role involved accepting his duty, *responding* to commands, and, above all, *feeling* that what he was doing was both correct and appreciated. There is, curiously, something very wifely about the passive duty expected of a soldier here, especially one mesmerized by a female icon that is also an embodiment of nationhood.

And yet, to keep this flux of genders in play, only by bearing a comprehensive list of faults – striking weaknesses, including madness – can Tennyson's hero recuperate the fundamental strengths that become a man. In other words, to become appropriately masculine, he has to outwoman conventional expectations of woman. Therefore, to reiterate an earlier point, he can feel more than any woman because he finds justification for going – furiously – mad and then into battle. To put this point another way: a man's madness turns out to be greater than a woman's affective responsiveness. Procter, meanwhile, writes in a rational as well as patriotic style about this military catastrophe. Her culturally attributed weakness as a woman turns out to be an indicator of her poetic strength – and thus, in broader cultural terms, a threat to the male poet's sense of self, since she enshrines an image of woman as the power guiding and saving the nation.

Given these complex coordinates of gender and poetry in the 1850s, it appears that only within the form of a militaristic 'tragic blunder' (as recorded in 'The Charge of the Light Brigade' [1854]) has this version of masculinity the right to an identity. Men, after all, make mistakes. And such mistakes – the defeats at Alma, Sebastopol, Balaklava, all on a massive scale – are what go into making men into *men*. These are blunders, errors, and disasters committed in the name of one's country. And they belong to the inevitable course of a history in which wars always occur and through which men unquestioningly (and irrationally) must risk taking their lives in order to exhibit their supposedly natural masculine strength. It is, then, a man's duty to be angrily passionate in the course of professing either amatory or patriotic love. Without these charged responses – especially to the perceived formidable power of woman – the hero would not in *Maud* be able to feel his true and ultimately outraged masculinity. All in all, the poem's hero has to become more than a woman (maddened) to save himself from becoming less than a man (effeminate). And so, finally, he vindicates his right to be a man on the basis of having *felt*, and thereby secured, his national identity: 'I have felt with my native land, I am one with my kind' (III, 58).

As this analysis of *Maud* should indicate, there is clearly much more work to be undertaken to comprehend the cultural history of Victorian masculinity, particularly to understand how it divides across the classes and works through and between political formations of conservatism and republicanism; it is also important to gain further knowledge of how and why emotionality among and between men was sublimated into forms of nationalistic heroism. Tennyson's poetry stands as a highly important body of cultural material in this respect, since his work betrays an often toughly conservative masculinism that is dependent on a belief in the historical necessity of feeling the world around him. Moreover, his writing bears the overlayered patterns of a residual chivalric heroism and an emergent homoeroticism.[19] To trace the history of Victorian masculinity may well reveal more about the material conditions in which modern hegemonic masculinities, so often based in violence, have emerged during the course of the past hundred and fifty years. Besides, to learn more of the genealogy of military manhood is perhaps to enable late twentieth-century men in the West to find a new vocabulary with which to change the – perhaps not so unusual – fury to be located in Tennyson's poem.

Notes

Thanks to ALAN SINFIELD and JOSEPHINE MCDONAGH for responses.

1. All citations from Tennyson's poetry are taken from *The Poems of Tennyson in Three Volumes, Second Edition, Incorporating the Trinity College Manuscripts*, ed. CHRISTOPHER RICKS, 3 vols (London: Longman, 1987). Equally important is SUSAN SHATTO, *Tennyson's Maud: A Definitive Edition* (London: Athlone Press, 1986). Shatto's edition contains a thorough account of literary and biographical sources, together with a detailed discussion of the poem's stages of composition (1–38). Much of the analysis in the present essay is indebted to LINDA M. SHIRES, '*Maud*, Masculinity, and Poetic Identity', *Criticism*, 29, 3 (1987), 269–90.
2. CAROL CHRIST, 'The Feminine Subject in Victorian Poetry', *ELH*, 54 (1987), 385. (All further references are included in parentheses.)
3. For a representative excerpt from Austin's polemic about Tennyson, see JOSEPH BRISTOW, *The Victorian Poet: Poetics and Persona* (London: Croom Helm, 1987), pp. 117–26. 'All, as I have said, proves the feminine, timorous, narrow, domesticated temper of the times, and explains the feminine, narrow, domesticated, timorous Poetry of the Period' (124). Austin's essays on contemporary poetry from *Temple Bar* are collected as *The Poetry of the Period* (London: Strahan, 1870).
4. Exceptionally little has been written on Procter's remarkable canon of work, which appeared regularly in Dickens's *Household Words*; see MARGARET MASON, 'Queen Victoria's Favourite Poet', *Listener*, 29 April 1965, pp. 636–7. For a sustained Victorian analysis of her poetry, see ' "Legends and Lyrics," and "The Wanderer" ', *North British Review*, 30 (1859), 403–16.
5. FRANCIS TURNER PALGRAVE, 'Women and the Fine Arts', *Macmillan's Magazine*, 12 (1865), 213.

6. ROBERT C. SCHWEIK makes this suggestion in 'The "Peace or War" Passages in Tennyson's "Maud" ', *Notes and Queries*, 205 (1960), 458.

7. For echoes from Carlyle's *Past and Present* (1843), see RICKS, vol. 2, p. 520. Ricks is following the findings of VALERIE PITT, *Tennyson Laureate* (London: Barrie and Rockliff, 1962), p. 175. BERNARD RICHARDS compares chapter 6 of Kingsley's *Alton Locke* (1850) to 1, 39, in *English Verse 1830–1890* (London: Longman, 1980), p. 133.

8. RICKS, vol 2, p. 582.

9. [G. C. SWAYNE], 'Peace and War: A Dialogue', *Blackwood's Edinburgh Magazine*, 76 (1854), 589–98. (All further references are included in parentheses.) The parallels between this dialogue and *Maud* are obvious: 'I believe this war will show him [the czar] to be a victim of a gigantic system of thieving and adulteration, not of tea and sugar, like ours, but of fortifications, army-lists, and munitions of war . . . What is our daily life but a struggle and a combat against swindling and deception of every kind, and a very unequal struggle on the part of the consumer? The seller wages a war of selfishness against the buyer. The necessaries of life are not exempted, or one might avoid some unpleasantness by avoiding luxuries. Not only your wine merchant drugs your port, but your grocer sands your sugar; your milk comes from Chalk Farm, your baker puts alum in your bread, and shortens your life by shortening the measure of its staff, so that you are almost inclined to wish him the fate of the Pharaohs' (592, 596). For further information, see RICKS, ' "Peace and War" and "Maud" ', *Notes and Queries*, 207 (1962), 230. The relation between *Maud* and the periodical propaganda of the time is explored by JAMES R. BENNETT 'The Historical Abuse of Literature: *Maud: A Monodrama* and the Crimean War', *English Studies*, 62 (1981), 34–45, and CHRIS R VANDEN BOSSCHE, 'Realism versus Romance: The War of Cultural Codes in Tennyson's *Maud*', *Victorian Poetry*, 24, 1 (1986), 69–81. It is important to note that *Blackwood's* reviewed *Maud* unfavourably a year after the appearance of 'Peace and War', see [W. E. AYTOUN], 'Maud, by Alfred Tennyson', *Blackwood's*, 78 (1855), 311–21.

10. 'The largeness of imports, compared with those of previous years, was assumed as satisfactory evidence that we had entered into that state of dependence, and that, like the son of Jacob, we were now compelled to traverse distances for our corn. By the occupation of the Danubian provinces, the Czar would gain possession of the keys of a vast and prolific granary, which in the course of war would of course remain absolutely shut' ([W. E. AYTOUN], 'The War and the Ministry', *Blackwood's* 76 [1854], 602).

11. MARION SHAW, *Alfred Lord Tennyson*, Feminist Readings (Hemel Hempstead: Harvester-Wheatsheaf, 1988), p. 135.

12. Although MARY POOVEY does not make this explicit association with Britannia, her analysis of Nightingale's complex cultural symbolism points to the astonishing pressures on gender relations focused in and around the Crimean War. '[The widely-published adoring poetry] depicting Nightingale as a goddess addressed the anxieties that were raised by a woman's assuming even temporary superiority over an infantalized male patient, for in construing her power as magic or even divine, it removed this woman not only from her mortality, but also from competition with medical men. Representing Nightingale as a queen also addressed fears about female power, for Queen Victoria herself was compared less frequently to a patriarchal commander

than to a loving mother. Comparisons to the housewifely monarch served another function as well: as Nightingale's likeness to the queen was played out, royalty became the site at which problems of class difference could be introduced so as to be dismissed' (*Uneven Developments: The Ideological Work of Gender in Mid-Victorian England*, Women in Culture and Society [Chicago: University of Chicago Press, 1988], p. 171).

13. THOMAS CARLYLE, 'Two Hundred and Fifty Years Ago', *Critical and Miscellaneous Essays in Five Volumes* (London: Chapman and Hall, 1850; repr. 1896), vol. 4, pp. 384–5.

14. 'The War', *Athenaeum* 1423 (1855), 138–9.

15. 'The War Poets', *Punch* 28 (1855), 17.

16. FRANKLIN LUSHINGTON, 'Alma' (37–8), in HENRY LUSHINGTON, *La Nation Boutiquiére and Other Poems Chiefly Political* and Franklin Lushington, *Points of War* (Cambridge: Macmillan, 1855), p. 86. This slim volume bears very close resemblances to the language and sentiments of *Maud*: 'Let at least one more generation of Englishmen speak the language and do the deeds of their fathers. Do not let us, because war is disagreeable and rough, and other roads are smoother to travel, say "there is no adequate cause for all this fighting: the time is not so much out of joint after all." The time is out of joint, as few times have been: and it may be "cursed spite, that ever we were born to set it right" – but that cannot be undone now: here we are. For the moment, dearly as we love him, let Hamlet stand aside: he has but too much to say in Germany: we want Fortinbras just now' (xxv). (Tennyson, coincidentally, refers to *Maud*'s affinities to *Hamlet* [Ricks, p. 515].) Henry Lushington's title poem expresses disgust at how Britain's reputation has sunk, in the eyes of France, into a 'nation of shopkeepers'; 'La Nation Boutiquiére' has a significant bearing on Part I of *Maud*. My thanks to DEREK SHARROCK for this reference.

17. See JOSEPH J. COLLINS, 'Tennyson and the Spasmodics', *Victorian Newsletter*, 43 (1973), 24–8.

18. ADELAIDE ANNE PROCTER, *Legends and Lyrics and Other Poems*, Everyman's Library (London: Dent, n.d.). 'The Lesson of the War' was first published in Charles Dickens's *Household Words* on 3 February 1855 and collected in *Legends and Lyrics* (London, 1858).

19. Since the time of its publication, Tennyson's poetry has been subject to controversial discussions of its emboldened chivalry and its modern homoeroticism. On the latter aspect, the following remarks from a review of *In Memoriam* are well known and worth citing here: 'Very sweet and plaintive these verses are; but who would not give them a feminine application? Shakespeare may be considered the founder of this [homoerotic] style in English. In classical and Oriental poetry it is unpleasantly familiar. His mysterious sonnets present the startling peculiarity of transferring every epithet of womanly endearment to a masculine friend, – his master-mistress, as he calls by a compound epithet, harsh as it is disagreeable. We should never expect to hear a young lawyer calling a member of the same in his "rose," except in the Middle Temple of Ispahan, with Hafiz for a laureate' ('The Poetry of Sorrow', *Times*, 28 November 1851, reprinted in JOHN DIXON HUNT, ed., *Tennyson: In Memoriam: A Casebook* [London: Macmillan, 1970], p. 104). The major study of Tennyson and mid-Victorian 'feminism' (and the word is used advisedly) JOHN KILLHAM, *Tennyson's 'The Princess': Reflections of an Age* (London: Athlone Press, 1958). *Maud* has conventionally been read as an

expression of Tennyson's own feelings at being jilted by his beloved, Rosa Baring: see RALPH W. RADER, *Tennyson's Maud: The Biographical Genesis* (Berkeley: University of California Press, 1963). Among the most significant writings on Tennyson's sexual politics, particularly on the (ef)feminization of the male hero, are EVE KOSOFSKY SEDGWICK, *Between Men: English Literature and Male Homosocial Desire* (New York: Columbia University Press, 1985), pp. 118–33; ELLIOTT L. GILBERT, 'The Female King: Tennyson's Arthurian Apocalypse', *PMLA*, 98 (1983), 863–78; ALAN SINFIELD, *Alfred Tennyson*, Rereading Literature (Oxford: Basil Blackwell, 1986); SANDRA M. GILBERT and SUSAN GUBAR, *No Man's Land: The Place of the Woman Writer in the Twentieth Century,* vol. 1, *The War of the Words* (New Haven: Yale University Press, 1988), pp. 5–16; and CHRISTOPHER CRAFT, ' "Descend and Touch and Enter": Tennyson's Strange Manner of Address', *Genders*, 1 (1988), 83–101.

8 The Ideological Moment of Tennyson's 'Ulysses'*

MATTHEW ROWLINSON

Matthew Rowlinson's 1992 essay uses reception theory to examine a poem which did not enter into the canon of literature until some time after its date of publication (1830s) as it came to be seen as a vehicle for the propagation of imperialist ideas in a late-Victorian drive to establish the English language as a world language. Its popularity, then, is due to historical developments that considerably *postdate* its writing and publication: the construction of an imperial ideology. Rowlinson draws on a range of critical reading strategies including reception theory, Marxist literary theory and formalist close reading in his investigation of the ways in which this poem has entered and been processed by the canon. He argues with reference to Louis Althusser's essay 'Ideology and Ideological State Apparatuses' that the 'time of textuality' of this text is not the moment of its production – 1833 – but instead the point at which 'Ulysses' and the discourse of a colonialist pedagogy (late nineteenth, early twentieth century) intersect.

They use me as a lesson-book at schools, and they will call me 'that horrible Tennyson'.[1]

I would like to begin with a problem of reception, which I can most clearly illustrate with an autobiographical episode. Some years ago, my parents – who were British emigrants – sent me to a boys' boarding school in Ottawa, Canada. More recently, I was interested to discover an international survey of private education which concluded that English Canadian private schools had more completely than any others transplanted the ethos, structures, and ideology of their British public school models.[2] This was certainly true of the school I attended, where not only the regiment – which included cricket, prefects, canings, housemaster, and a militant low-church Anglicanism – but also many of the teachers (we called them masters) were of British origin.

---

*Reprinted from *Victorian Poetry* **30**, 3–4 (1992), pp. 265–76.

I mention all this to sketch a context for the particular feature of the school that I want to recall. In the chapel, along with the Boy Scout banner – which I believe had some connection with Baden-Powell himself – and along with a regimental ensign of the Queen's Own Rifles, there was a stained glass window which bore the representation of a scroll. And on the scroll were the words 'Made weak by time and fate, but strong in will / To strive, to seek, to find, and not to yield'.

These lines, the last two lines of Tennyson's 'Ulysses', seemed to me then, as now, in some ways odd ones to find in that context. So I want here to open the question: what are the connections between Tennyson's poem and an ideology of colonialism? Or indeed, between Tennyson's poem and a colonialist pedagogy; for 'Ulysses' appeared not only on the window of my school's chapel, but on its syllabus, as it still does on the syllabi of schools throughout the English-speaking world – which is to say, in England itself and in its present and former colonies. In fact, there is a strong correlation between the teachings of 'Ulysses' and an institutional need to uphold, if not necessarily the prestige of England, then that of English literature. For there is evidence to suggest that 'Ulysses' acquired its current prominent place in Tennyson's canon quite belatedly and as a result of the institution of English literature as a pedagogical discipline – a historical event which has among its causes the late-Victorian drive to establish English as a world language.[3] Among the largely favourable reviews of the 1842 *Poems* in which 'Ulysses' first appeared, there are few that single the poem out for attention.[4] Two exceptions to this general rule suggest what we may call the latent engagement in the poem with imperialist themes; one is the review by John Sterling, who admires the poem, but complains that it fails to take up the topic of European expansionism: 'We know not why . . . a modern English poet should write of Ulysses rather than of the great voyagers of the modern world, Columbus, Gama, or even Drake'.[5] The other is interesting by reason of its context – it appears in the *Foreign and Colonial Quarterly Review*, a periodical whose distribution was mostly in the colonies. This review complains of other critics' neglect of 'Ulysses', and reprints it entire.[6]

One way of charting the reception of 'Ulysses' is to examine the history of its republication in anthologies. Such an examination shows that it was not ordinarily among those poems of Tennyson selected for anthologies aimed at the general public, while the anthologists of the late nineteenth and earlier twentieth century who produced the early classroom texts in the field of Victorian poetry seem almost invariably to have reprinted it. Thus it does not appear in *Beeton's Great Book of Poetry* (1870); Palgrave's second series of *The Golden*

Treasury (1897); in either Arthur Quiller-Crouch's *Oxford Book of English Verse, 1250–1900* (1900) or his *Oxford Book of Victorian Verse* (1912); or in Ernest Rhys's *The New Golden Treasury* (1914 – published by Everyman and consisting of poems that did not appear in Palgrave). Among American anthologies, it did not appear in William Cullen Bryant's *Library of Poetry and Song* (1871); however, in an exception that proves the rule, it was selected by Emerson for his *Parnassus* (1876), where it appears in a section of 'intellectual' poems. In anthologies whose stated purpose is to teach rather than to give pleasure, however, 'Ulysses' is uniformly present. Thus, it appears in the first edition of T. H. Ward's *The English Poets* to include Victorian authors (1894 – Ward's anthology is notable for having an introduction by Matthew Arnold, which he published separately as 'The Study of Poetry'); in Curtis Hidden Page's *British Poets of the Nineteenth Century* (1904), which was produced in the United States as a college text; and in H. F. Lowry and Willard Thorp's *Oxford Anthology of Poetry* (1935), also produced as a text for the classroom and notable for its contrast with Quiller-Couch's *Oxford Book of English Verse*, still in print at the same period.[7]

On this evidence, it seems reasonable to conclude that the current high visibility of 'Ulysses' in the canon of Tennyson's poetry was the result of historical developments that considerably postdate its writing and publication. These distinct but related developments are, first, the establishment of English poetry as a subject of formal instruction, and second, the elaboration of a notion of English culture as a system of values – with poetry very near its centre – which could be reproduced in societies outside England itself. My concern in this essay is with the amenability of 'Ulysses' to the second of these projects – but it is worth remembering, as we turn to Tennyson's text, that this amenability only becomes widely visible, and indeed might be said only to become historical, with the deployment of the text in the classroom.

Since Tennyson's Ulysses expresses nothing but disdain for his own home country, it seems odd to claim that the poem is a particularly appropriate text for the task of articulating and maintaining the relation between English settler-states and England itself. Nonetheless, I would like to employ my impressions about the uses to which this text continues to be put as a brief to ask whether Tennyson's Ulysses, in spite of this apparent disdain, and in spite of the Homeric prophecy that he would set out on his final journey carrying only an oar, might nonetheless be smuggling out of Ithaca some concealed ideological baggage for distribution abroad.

We can locate one form of such baggage in Ulysses's account of his relations with his subjects. When he complains of having to administer the law to a savage race, and installs Telemachus in his place 'to make mild / A rugged people, and through soft degrees / Subdue them to the useful and the good' (36–8), he seems to be imagining between himself and his subjects not just differences of class, but, bizarrely, cultural and even racial differences. He sounds, in fact, like a colonial administrator turning over the reins to a successor just before stepping on the boat to go home.

But, of course, Ulysses in Ithaca already is at home, even though the lines I have just quoted make him seem somewhat confused on this point. And, in fact, his eagerness to leave his wife and family and quit his job to sail west suggests another colonial stereotype altogether – say, that of the retired adventurer, chafing at the domestic routine, and planning one last voyage to escape it. The conflict of these two topoi – if that is not too dignified a word – opens a problematic that critics have often noticed in 'Ulysses' – namely that he does not seem to know where he is. Inside, outside, by his hearth, on the beach, in private, in public – at different times his discourse apparently demands all of these contexts. I would want to broaden this problematic to include the general questions of where Ulysses thinks Ithaca is: is it a home – a centre, to use the word he uses – from which he proposes to journey outward toward the margin 'that fades for ever and for ever' when he moves? Or is Ithaca itself somehow already marginal, or savage?[8]

I shall want to return to this problematic later on. But I do not think we can deduce from its operation in the poem any clear position with respect to an identifiable imperialist or colonialist ideology. In this regard, of course, 'Ulysses' stands in sharp contrast to much of Tennyson's later writing, in which he is frequently a more or less crude apologist for an imperialist policy. Among many examples, I will cite the epilogue to the *Idylls of the King*, entitled 'To the Queen', which Tennyson wrote in 1872 and published in 1873. There Tennyson rebukes the argument that Britain should give up its military presence in Canada because it is too costly: 'Is this the tone of empire?' he grumbles, and goes on to assert that loyalty to the Crown is necessarily also loyalty to the colonies and to the idea of colonialism:

> The loyal to their crown
> Are loyal to their own far sons, who love
> Our ocean-empire with her boundless homes
> For ever-broadening England, and her throne
> In our vast Orient, and one isle, one isle,

> That knows not her own greatness: if she knows
> And dreads it we are fallen.
>
> ('To the Queen', 27–33)

The position that Tennyson is attacking here – that colonies of British settlers cost more than they are worth – was one that from Adam Smith through Jeremy Bentham down to Richard Cobden and Goldwin Smith had become virtually a tenet of British liberal orthodoxy. The remarkable thing is that until about the period at which Tennyson wrote – say until the 1860s or 1870s – there was very little in the way of an articulate defence of the empire against this orthodoxy. The letter in which the Whig Prime Minister, Melbourne, asked Lord Durham to go to Canada and investigate the causes of the twin uprisings there in 1837 is symptomatic: 'The final separation of these colonies,' he wrote, 'might possibly not be of material detriment to the interests of the mother country, but it is clear that it would be a serious blow to the honour of Great Britain, and certainly would be fatal to the character and existence of the Administration under which it took place'.[9] I think we may take Melbourne's concerns to be listed in ascending order of importance.

Indeed, in the Britain of the 1830s the concepts of empire, or of imperialism as such, had yet to find verbal form. According to Richard Koebner and Helmut Den Schmidt, in its most prevalent usage before mid-century, the phrase 'British Empire' referred in England to the British Isles only. This is the sense in which the term appears in Carlyle's 'Chartism', and in the title of J. R. McCulloch's *Statistical Account of the British Empire*, both published in 1837.[10] The term 'imperialism' moreover, is not recorded as appearing in English at all until 1851 – and at that date it was coined as part of a critical account of Louis Napoleon (*Imperialism*, p. 10). Koebner and Schmidt do not find any use of the term to designate British policy until in 1868 the *Spectator* wrote that imperialism 'in its best sense' might denote 'a binding duty to perform highly irksome or offensive tasks' – launching us, strikingly late, into the age of the White Man's Burden (pp. 24–5).

Nonetheless, when Tennyson wrote in 1872 of an English people whose 'boundless homes' extended around the world, he was articulating a notion that had rapidly become commonplace. In 1869 Charles Dilke had published *Greater Britain*, a book of his travels in 'English-speaking or in English-governed lands' around the world.[11] This survey proposed a unified view of world affairs as determined by the conflicts of 'the English people' with 'the cheaper races' (Dilke, p. 545). Dilke's racist analysis of the expansion of 'Saxondom' had the advantage of enabling him to ignore the nationalist economic policy of the government of a newly confederated Canada, to say nothing of the American Revolution. His title became a catchphrase of British political discussion for the next thirty years, and his book established a vogue for studies of the expansion of English power as a single global phenomenon. Thus Sir John Seeley's *The Expansion of England* (1883) traces the growth of the Empire as the dominant force in English history since the beginning of the eighteenth century, and calls for its reconstitution as a federation – which, if it could not include the United States, was to be modelled on it, having representative institutions and a federal government located in London.[12] Tennyson admired this book so much that he sent a copy to Gladstone, whose response is a model of tactful demurral (*Memoir*, 2:301).

But in 1933, the year in which Tennyson wrote 'Ulysses' it is hard to find a language in which what we now understand as British imperialism could be discussed as a single phenomenon. At that date, for instance, Australia was still in one settlement a penal colony, in others the enterprise of private trading companies; India too was still formally under the administration of the East India Company and not that of the Crown, while Upper and Lower Canada and the West Indies were Crown colonies. The second half of the nineteenth century saw the construction of an imperialist ideology on the foundation of newly evolved notions of race and culture that would make it possible to represent these diverse institutional phenomena as parts of a single national drama. In 1833 this construction did not exist. So if we ask in what sense 'Ulysses' is an imperialist text, we are asking about the prehistory, or preconditions, of a fully articulated discourse of imperialism.[13]

Our argument thus far has led us to a paradox. I have described Tennyson's 'Ulysses' as a part of the prehistory of a certain ideological construction. I have also spoken of this text as implicated in a colonialist pedagogy that is in its essence nostalgic. 'Ulysses' is a text that dates from before it was possible to speak of a British imperialism, and yet seems peculiarly to speak to and about the twilight of that imperialism.

We perhaps should not be too surprised at this paradox in the reception of Tennyson's poem. For it oddly recapitulates a trope that is central both to Tennyson's poetics – in 'Ulysses' and its pendent poem 'Tithonus' as well as elsewhere – and to his politics. That trope may be described as the metonymic interchange of beginnings and endings, of early and late. It is the figure of hesper/phosphor, the double star that Tennyson invokes in Section CXXI of *In Memoriam*, and of the mixing of East and West in Section XCV.

Before discussing this figure in 'Ulysses', we may return to the epilogue to the *Idylls of the King* for an instance in which it appears with a specifically political force. That poem ends with a list of the fears of those who note dangers to Britain, and then with the claim that 'if our ... Republic's crowning common-sense ... not fail – their fears / Are morning shadows huger than the shapes / That cast them, not those gloomier which forego / The darkness of that battle in the West, / Where all of high and holy dies away' (To the Queen', 60–6). In the context of the solar myth that structures the *Idylls*, this passage is asserting that the signs which seem to be indices of approaching evening may in fact be indices of morning and of brightening day. But I want to stress the 'may' in this formulation. Tennyson's assertion is conditional – 'if' our republic's common sense does not fail, 'then' the shapes will mean morning rather than evening. By this conditional construction, the meaning of the signs Tennyson has enumerated – in short, the meaning of his own text – is indefinitely suspended or deferred.

The political force of this deferral is suggested by a passage earlier in the poem, in which Tennyson refers to Britain as an 'isle, / That knows not her own greatness: if she knows / And dreads it we are fallen' (31–3). This assertion, made in 1872, in a poem addressed to a queen who notoriously did know her own greatness, is in more than one way an odd one. I want to notice only its implications about its own status and mode of signification. These lines at once posit that Britain is great, and at the same time assert that the nation does not know its greatness. They posit a fact while asserting that it is unknown and hoping that it remains so. This text thus assumes an absolute split between the time of the literary signifier and the time of a historically effective knowledge. The category of knowledge here, as at the end of the poem, is deferred by relegation to a conditional clause.

In this text, then, the situation of the poem that is interchangeably either early or late is homologous with an assumption that the literary signifier exists in a different order of time from the knowledge that it signifies. I shall soon want to expand on this assumption and its politics; but first, I would like to return to 'Ulysses'.

The interchange of early and late is without doubt the organizing trope of this poem. Here again, the allusions to the solar trajectory will help us sketch a reading. The poem is set at evening, and in the evening of Ulysses's life, but marks the beginning, not the end of Ulysses's journey into the west. Here is Ulysses addressing his mariners in the poem's closing verse paragraph: 'you and I are old; / Old age hath yet his honour and his toil; ... / The long day wanes: the slow moon climbs: the deep / Moans round with many voices. Come, my friends, / 'Tis not too late to seek a newer world'

('Ulysses', 49–57). Who is old here? Ulysses and the mariners, or the world in which he speaks, which he imagines as being at least old enough to need a 'newer' replacement. Furthermore, Ulysses's wish to seek a 'newer world' returns us to the question we posed earlier about the place from which he speaks. The term echoes the phrase that became commonplace for the Americas during the Renaissance – the New World. By using it, does this text identify Ulysses's quest with the Renaissance's westward expansion of European power, or with some further quest, possibly allegorical, of which the historical exploration of the New World would only be a prefiguration? To put it simply, does the Ulysses who sets out to seek a 'newer' world thereby situate himself in an old world or a new world?

The solar figures in the epilogue to the *Idylls* and in 'Ulysses' provide examples of their crossings-over between the categories of early and late, and of marginal and central. These figures may not only afford one set of examples among others, since metaphors derived from the sun's trajectory – heliotropes – recur to structure such crossings throughout Tennyson's poetry, and throughout the discourse of English imperialism. The sun, like Tennyson's Ulysses, is driven westward, to evening and to a continually receding margin. Yet it operates nonetheless as an inescapable figure for beginnings, as at once the origin and the centre of things.[14]

A general thematics of the heliotrope is too much for us to undertake here. But versions of the crossings with which it is associated, in 'Ulysses' and elsewhere, necessarily came to structure the field of British imperialism as its ideology developed in the course of the nineteenth century. An empire conceived as a 'Greater Britain' needed to articulate colonial or colonized subjects both as 'new' English people – new at once in the sense of being new-minted, without the antecedents of British history, and in the sense of representing a new kind of Englishness – and also, so as to preserve the prestige of the parent culture, as belated and behind-the-times provincials.[15] Further, in the case of settler states, it articulated colonial subjects who identified nostalgically with the culture of the imperial centre, and at the same time – and equally nostalgically – with the marginalized indigenous cultures which they had themselves replaced.[16] The production of such subjects became the task of a colonialist pedagogy.

To suppose that 'Ulysses' did not in some way contribute to this task would be naïve. But to theorize how and why it did so – or does so – remains somewhat vexing. It would be equally naïve to envision a response to the poem involving an unmediated readerly identification with Ulysses and with his drive to the margin. While the poem works to make its readers share Ulysses's desire to embark on a journey of exploration, it also, as Goldwin Smith saw in 1855,[17] imparts a sense of limitation that Ulysses himself does not possess, and suggests that such journeys are after all no longer possible. And, of course, if we are concerned with historicizing the production of Tennyson's poem, we have already seen that the ideological constructions which I have claimed that it supports had not yet come into being when he wrote it in 1833.

I will simplify my formulation from above – 'Ulysses' seems to come before an ideological construction for which it nonetheless makes people nostalgic. We could, I suppose, consider this problematic as posing a historical question, to be answered by demonstrating either that Tennyson's text does not authorize a construction which was imposed upon it by a belated misreading, or that Tennyson's text not only authorized the reading we have been working out, but that it somehow brought into being the construction in which we have implicated it. The first of these positions seems to impute too little authority to the text, the second perhaps too much. If what we have said so far, makes possible any advance on such formations, it is because we have seen that the historical problematic of the appearance of the text as at once early and belated with respect to the ideology of imperialism recapitulates the structure of the text itself.

In fact, at least for Tennyson, this problematic characterizes textuality as such. Recall the epilogue to the *Idylls*, where the text situates itself indeterminately before or after the phenomenon it describes. To try to understand what we might make of this peculiar textual moment that never quite coincides with any historical moment, I want to turn, briefly and in conclusion, to some remarks of Louis Althusser in his essay 'Ideology and Ideological State Apparatuses'. Here Althusser adopts and extends Marx's proposition that ideology has no history, to argue that ideology is eternal in the same sense that the Freudian unconscious is eternal. Now, for Althusser, the general function of ideology – as distinct from the specific functions of distinct ideologies – is to constitute the subject by an operation which he calls '*interpellation* or hailing, and which can be imagined along the lines of the most commonplace everyday police (or other) hailing: "Hey, you there!" '.[18] A paradigmatic form of *interpellation*, therefore, would be naming – 'hey, Jack!' – and indeed, Althusser goes on to discuss this topic:

> As ideology is eternal, I must . . . say: ideology has always-already interpellated individuals as subjects, which amounts to making it clear that . . . *individuals are always-already subjects* . . . This proposition might seem paradoxical.
> That an individual is always-already a subject, even before he

is born, is nevertheless the plain reality, accessible to everyone, and not a paradox at all. Freud shows that individuals are always 'abstract' with respect to the subjects they always-already are, simply by noting the ritual that surrounds the expectation of 'birth', that 'happy event'. Everyone knows how much and in what way a child is expected . . . It is certain in advance that it will bear its Father's Name. Before its birth, the child is therefore always-already a subject, appointed as a subject in and by the specific familial configuration in which it is 'expected' once it has been conceived.

(pp. 175–6)

I am not here concerned with the Freudian and Lacanian ordering of Althusser's argument; what I want to hang on to is his use of the name as a paradigm for the devices by which the individual is constituted as a subject in a discourse – ideology – whose time is not the historical time in which the subject is born and dies.

'I am become a name', says Ulysses (11); and, of course, he is right. If he were not, the poem Tennyson wrote for him would be simply unintelligible. The coherence and recognizability of this Ulysses as the subject of the discourse Tennyson assigns to him depends upon the movement of his name in the contexts of other discourses – the poems of Homer and Dante will suffice to mention here. The time in which these different texts construct one another's meanings is evidently not the historical moment in which any of them is produced. Nor is it any historical moment whatsoever – for instance, that of a particular reading, which, even as it finds something 'new' in the texts, will find that it was always already there. This is another meaning of the crossings of new and old in 'Ulysses'.

One point of this concluding excursion is to suggest that the time I have been discussing, the effective time of textuality as such, is the time of the crossing between Tennyson's text and the discourse of a colonialist pedagogy. The moments of such a time are always constituted after the fact, as an interpretative act, and thus do not correspond to any moment of lived experience whatsoever. And the other point is to insist, as against some critiques of formalism and hermeneutics, on the ideological nature of the sorts of crossing I have tried here to describe, and indeed, on their constitutive force for the ideological as such.

Notes

An earlier version of this paper was presented to a session on Victorian imperialism at the NEMLA convention of April 1988. I am indebted for contributions and suggestions to JEFFREY NUNOKAWA, the organizer of the session, to the other participants, and to CARLA FRECCERO.

1. HALLAM TENNYSON, *Alfred Lord Tennyson: A Memoir* (London, 1897), 1:16.
2. C. PODMORE, 'Private Schools – An International Comparison', *Canadian and International Education*, 6, 2 (1977), 8–33.
3. The fullest available case study of the historical relation between the teaching of English literature and the ideological work of imperialism is GAURI VISWANATHAN, *Masks of Conquest: Literary Study and British Rule in India* (New York, 1989). CHRIS BALDICK, *The Social Mission of English Criticism 1848–1932* (Oxford, 1983), pp. 70–2, has a useful account of how the examinations for the East India Company encouraged the development of literary study within England.
4. Neither does 'Ulysses' appear to have attracted the attention of reviewers in the United States. JOHN OLIN EIDSON comments on its neglect in US reviews of the 1842 volumes and also asserts that it was 'almost ignored' by early anthologizers of Tennyson in this country (*Tennyson in America: His Reputation and Influence from 1827 to 1858* [Athens, GA, 1943], pp. 96, 101).
5. In the *Quarterly Review*, September 1842, rpt. in *Tennyson: The Critical Heritage*, ed. JOHN JUMP (London, 1967), p. 120.
6. See EDGAR F. SHANNON, JR., *Tennyson and the Reviewers: A Study of His Literary Reputation and of the Influence of the Critics upon his Poetry* (Cambridge MA, 1952), p. 82.
7. *Beeton's Great Book of Poetry: From Caedmon and King Alfred's Boethius to Browning and Tennyson . . .* ed. S. O. BEETON (London, 1870); *The Golden Treasury* (second series), ed. F. T. PALGRAVE (London, 1897); *The Oxford Book of English Verse, 1250–1900*, ed. ARTHUR QUILLER-COUCH (Oxford, 1908); *The Oxford Book of Victorian Verse*, ed. ARTHUR QUILLER-COUCH (Oxford, 1912); *The New Golden Treasury of Songs and Lyrics*, ed. ERNEST RHYS (London, 1914); *A Library of Poetry and Song: Being Choice Selections from the Best Poets*, ed. WILLIAM CULLEN BRYANT (New York, 1871); *Parnassus*, ed. RALPH WALDO EMERSON (Boston, 1876); *The English Poets*, ed. T. H. WARD (New York, 1984); *British Poets of the Nineteenth Century*, ed. CURTIS HIDDEN PAGE (New York, 1914); *An Oxford Anthology of English Poetry*, ed. H. F. LOWRY and WILLARD THORP (New York, 1935). The dates given in parentheses in my text refer to the first editions of these texts, which I have not in every case been able to consult.
8. For an illuminating analysis of the margin/centre opposition in Tennyson's poetry of the 1830s, see ALAN SINFIELD, *Alfred Tennyson* (Oxford, 1986), pp. 39–56. Sinfield argues that the poems' drive to the margin is, among other things, an always self-defeating attempt to escape the imperial values of the centre.
9. Quoted in EDWARD GRIERSON, *The Death of Imperial Britain: The British Commonwealth and Empire 1775–1969* (New York, 1969), p. 62.
10. RICHARD KOEBNER and HELMUT DEN SCHMIDT, *Imperialism: The Story and Significance of a Political Word, 1840–1960* (London, 1964), p. 45; hereafter cited as *Imperialism*. Koebner and Schmidt's argument is certainly overstated;

Tennyson himself uses 'empire' in its more extended sense in 'Hail, Briton!', which Christopher Ricks judges to date from 1830–31. He does so, however, in attacking 'a power, that knows not check, / To spread and float an ermined pall / Of Empire, from the ruined wall / Of royal Delhi to Quebec' (9–12). The passage suggests that Tennyson expected the term in this larger sense to carry a strong negative charge.

11. CHARLES WENTWORTH DILKE, *Greater Britain: A Record of Travel in English-Speaking Countries during 1866 and 1867* (New York, 1869), 1:ix.

12. SIR J. R. SEELEY, *The Expansion of England: Two Courses of Lectures* (London, 1921). Other entries in this discussion include J. A. FROUDE, *Oceana, or England and Her Colonies* (London, 1886), and DILKE's later *Problems of Greater Britain* (London, 1890).

13. PATRICK BRANTLINGER's suggestion that the discourse of imperialism was produced as a defensive strategy is to the point: 'Early Victorians did not call themselves imperialists or bang the drum for territorial expansion – they traversed the world as advocates for free trade, commerce and Christianity, and the benefits of being British. Only later, as doubts multiplied, would imperialism develop into a self-conscious ideology' (*Rule of Darkness: British Literature and Imperialism, 1830–1914* [Ithaca, 1988], p. 44). Certainly the discourse of Victorian imperialism is from its inception a retrospective one, frequently marked by the nostalgia for an unmediated encounter with the exotic that CHRIS BONGIE analyses in his 'Exotic Nostalgia: Conrad and the New Imperialism', in *Macropolitics of Nineteenth-Century Literature: Nationalism, Exoticism, Imperialism*, ed. JONATHAN ARAC and HARRIET RITVO (Philadelphia, 1991), pp. 268–85. This feature of imperialist discourse is anticipated by Tennyson's 'Ulysses'.

But we should not proceed from this premise to the view that the conquests to which the Victorian imperialists were heirs were pursued unselfconsciously, or that the Empire was acquired 'in a fit of absence of mind' as Sir John Seeley famously put it (p. 10). On the contrary, these conquests were in every era the expression in practice of clearly articulated economic and social theory. From the sixteenth to the mid-eighteenth centuries, the theory was that of mercantilism, which dictated a policy of expansion outside Europe as a means of supplying raw materials to support England in its competition with the other European powers. From the latter part of the eighteenth century until the mid-nineteenth, the economic theory was that of free trade, which frequently went hand in hand with the anti-slavery movement and with Christian missionary work. Though these policies found support in a pervasive racism that was only less consistently articulated than that of the late nineteenth century, that fact ought not to obscure the role of economic theory – operating as a vehicle for class interests – in determining the course of empire.

14. For an analysis of the rhetorical function of the heliotrope in 'Ulysses' and 'Tithonus', see chaps 3 and 4 of my *Tennyson's Fixations: Psychoanalysis and the Topics of the Early Poetry* (University of Virginia Press, 1994).

15. Two quotations will suggest the kinds of temporal crossings in which the discourse of colonialism can become involved. First from J. A. FROUDE, who advocates a colonial policy as a solution to the urbanization and overcrowding that in his view disfigure Victorian England: 'I have travelled through lands . . . where I never met a hungry man or saw a discontented face – where,

in the softest and sweetest air, and in an unexhausted soil, the fable of Midas is reversed, food does not turn to gold, but the gold with which the earth is teeming converts itself to farms and vineyards, into flocks and herds, into crops of wild luxuriance, into cities whose recent origin is concealed and compensated by trees and flowers – where children grow who seem once more to understand what was meant by "merry England" ' (pp. 16–17). And the second from CHARLES DILKE: 'While Quebec is still from many points of view, as it always was, a part of the old world, in Ontario we reach one of those young offshoots of Great Britain which are recognized in Australia and New Zealand, in Natal, and in the Eastern Province of the Cape . . . Just as in Syria, in Central Asia, or in Baluchistan, the traveller feels as though he were among people who lived a thousand years ago – in Ontario, as in Australia, he is in the midst of a population who seem to be living half a century later than his own time' (p. 42).

16. For a discussion of this structure in the context of the Philippines, see RENATO ROSALDO, 'Imperialist Nostalgia', *Representations*, 26 (Spring 1989), 107–122. Since my essay began in a personal mode, I will say that this observation has been shaped by the institution where I currently teach. Dartmouth College was founded in New England in the eighteenth century with the announced purpose of providing Christian education to the indigenous population. Nevertheless, it rapidly evolved into a college whose students were almost exclusively of European descent. It retained the trace of its original purpose, however, by adopting as a 'mascot' or totem the caricatured figure of a Native American. In spite of the efforts of successive college administrations, and of repeated protests by the Native students Dartmouth now recruits, this local cult still persists.

17. See his discussion of 'Ulysses' in 'The War Passages in "Maud" ', rpt. in JUMP, p. 188.

18. LOUIS ALTHUSSER, *Lenin and Philosophy and Other Essays*, trans. BEN BREWSTER (New York), 1971), p. 174.

9 Patriarchy, Dead Men and Tennyson's *Idylls of the King**

LINDA SHIRES

Shires's piece shows a movement away from concepts of patriarchy described as a monolithic entity within contemporary gender studies. She draws particularly on the work of gay theorists to explore the 'oscillations' of gender and models of masculinity in the nineteenth century by an examination of the various stages of the lengthy production of Tennyson's *Idylls of the King*. Taking the figure of the lifeless (dead or dying) male body in this poem, Shires argues that early in his writing Tennyson supports a myth of the paternal manly male but by the end of his career he presents such manliness as a role men play and begins to play with homosocial and asexual models of masculinity. Her goal, she says, is to show how his poems 'participate in the Victorian invention of, exposure of, and death of the figure of the patriarch'. For Shires patriarchy is in the process of constant change and Tennyson's poetry provides a unique glimpse into the processes of such change. For Shires, like Armstrong, Tennyson's revisions show us a poet working away from conservative positions towards a more radical critique of dominant values. This Tennyson comes to 'recognize' the dangers of certain kinds of models of masculinity and a world grounded in rigid gender difference.

This essay takes as a premise that, in spite of remarkable theoretical advances in the past twenty years, traditional American gender studies have, more often than not, straitjacketed the literary text, closing down its most radical meanings.[1] Too often, we continue to rely on terms such as patriarchy without documenting its workings. Likewise, we too often rely on a heterosexual model without carefully investigating competing gender ideologies in a text.[2] Even gay and lesbian studies, which have offered some brilliant analyses of individual works and careers, often return to heterosexual models without subverting their claims to naturalness. Some of the freshest work to date has been done by gender critics, gay and straight, on

*Reprinted from *Victorian Poetry* **30**, 3–4 (1992), pp. 401–19

the provocative texts of the 1890s, but the task, as I see it, for Victorianists of the 1990s committed to gender analysis lies in building on such valuable contributions and in extending our study backwards to the early and mid-Victorian period.

The construction of masculinities, as found in *Idylls of the King* (hereafter *Idylls*), provides a radically different reading of Victorian patriarchy than that still widely accepted. Although a heterosexual model based in patriarchy frames the *Idylls* (Victoria/Albert; Guinevere/Arthur), I am interested in the ways in which Tennyson simultaneously collapses and retains a patriarchal order. The poem replaces gender with desire by proposing and yet undermining the brotherhood as a transgressive alternative. On one hand, Tennyson would give Victorian England a mythical patriarchy which allows male homoerotics; on the other hand, he realizes the impossibility of such a wish because of the variousness of masculinities and the importance of the female.

To interpret gender relations in the *Idylls*, we must understand nineteenth-century oscillations of types of masculinity as well as Tennyson's own varying constructions of gender in a career marked by continuous oscillations of his own. Even the *Idylls*, as a series written, reordered, and revised over many years, can hardly be talked about as a single document. Still, a focal point that remains relatively constant is provided by Tennyson's persistent fascination with the lifeless male body.[3]

While *In Memoriam* (1850) usually acts as the prime example for discussion of this spur to Tennyson's creativity, the dead, emasculated, or weakened male body proves central to much of his greatest work. At certain moments in his career, the deaths or progressive weakenings of both real and imagined men award Tennyson his authorial raison d'être. At those moments, his career intersects crucially with issues of major importance to his times: patriarchy, gender, belief, national authority. Such intersections provide the substance for this argument.

Arthur Henry Hallam died in 1833, and Tennyson's first epical treatment of Malory's materials came in 1833–34 under the shock of Hallam's death, when he explored the death of another Arthur in 'Morte d'Arthur'. As we know from Tennyson's subsequent additions and alterations, the issues in the poem were not easily articulated or put to rest. Having written a frame poem, 'The Epic', in 1837–38, seemingly to excuse the topic for an equivocal audience, Tennyson demurred from including it in his trial publication of 1842. Nearly thirty years later, though, the 'Morte d'Arthur' still retained an urgency for him when he incorporated it with revisions into *The Passing of Arthur* (1870).

162

During the fifty-six years between Hallam's death and publication of the poem about his own death, 'Crossing the Bar' (1889), Tennyson was to find the weak or dead male a compelling image and theme. It appears, for instance, in 'Tithonus' (first as 'Tithon' in 1833) with the withering male who so yearns for death, in *The Princess* (1848) with the epileptic seizures and war wounds suffered by Prince Hilarion, and in *Maud* (1855) with the corpse of the father lying in a bloodied hollow and the hysterical male son/speaker. In each case as the male assumes different (and overlapping) social roles of lover, prince, father, or son, his weakness garners somewhat different meanings. However, the poems I wish to discuss here, 'Ode on the Death of the Duke of Wellington' (1852), 'Morte d'Arthur' (1842), *The Holy Grail* (1870), and *Balin and Balan* (1885), present Tennyson's varying views about the myth of patriarchy. If, when he becomes Laureate, he supports a myth of the paternal, manly male, by the end of his career, he has become much more unsure about the value of such a standard. In addition, each poem, with a progressive overtness, acknowledges patriarchal masculinity as being little more than a role men play. Concurrently, these poems importantly demonstrate that Tennyson never restricts himself to one model of desire, the heterosexual, but inevitably plays with models we would call homosocial and asexual at the same time, without awarding his allegiance to any. Throughout this analysis, my goal is not to pass judgement on Tennyson's sexual politics or to retrieve him for feminist analysis, but to demonstrate how his poems participate in the Victorian invention of, exposure of, and death of the figure of the patriarch. From such an analysis, I hope that we can gain a fresh understanding of the Victorian 'patriarchy', which, while obviously at work in the material effects of institutions and practices, including literature, is shown to be in constant flux as an ideal.

In the 1830s and 1840s, the myth of a strong, paternal masculinity in England, the patriarch, coheres. Meanwhile, another, the Regency dandy and aristocrat of 1811–20, proceeds to dissolve. The Victorian patriarch emerges at this time due to a complicated set of cultural forces: economic, political, and social. The 1830s and 1840s, inaugurated by the death of George IV and accession of William IV and marked by the accession of Victoria in 1837, foreground issues of royal authority, succession, and gender. Important events, of course, such as the Reform Bill of 1832, increasing opportunities for women, the Evangelical revival, workers' revolts, wider public education, and the rise of professionalism continued to change old institutions and hierarchies, already altered under the pressures of a developing capitalism.[4] The cultural need for a virile, wise, dependable father figure is undoubtedly fuelled by the continued fear of revolution, and by the presence of two ineffective kings, and, in 1837, a young woman, Victoria, on the throne. In part, the Victorians invent a patriarch to run the country on behalf of the young Victoria.

Perhaps most important, and related to Victoria's position, an uneasiness about and even fear of female power goes hand in hand with the widely articulated system of sexual difference stressing separate spheres for men and women. Although other kinds of primary documents might be referred to, the great quantity alone of advice manuals to mothers and medical texts of this period testify to women's enhanced status in their increasingly recognized roles as the producers and central guides of the children of England. As Leonore Davidoff and Catherine Hall have documented, women are likewise gaining important if limited influence in the public sphere.[5] Some women are moved to question why, however, in a society governed by a queen, their legal rights are so severely restricted.

Patriarchal masculinity responds, then, to the fact of increased female power in both domestic and public enterprises. The male fear of the feminine is not restricted to one kind of femininity or to one role a woman may play in society (i.e. wife, mother, daughter, worker, sister, aunt, intellectual). If male fear is that of dependence, it gets displaced in various ways and played out differently in different contexts. Nor does this fear stereotype women in one way. However, there is a persistent cultural tendency to fashion the female as maenadic and to desire to regulate this energy. And as Catherine Gallagher has persuasively shown, the maenadic female is usually the mirrored reverse of the angelic mother or wife.[6]

Yet the need for a patriarchal masculinity also responds to men's perceptions about the feminine within themselves. The Victorian rejection of the feminine is also a rejection of a type of excess, as figured, for instance, in the dandy, an excess which will not serve male self-representation during a period of new conservatism. In a confusion over where strength and weakness lie, men fear female strength, denigrate it, and view the feminine in themselves as a sign of weakness.

The history of one part of nineteenth-century gender ideology, that is the history of masculinity as it depends on its relations with femininity, is a history of oscillation. As nineteenth-century gender definitions alter between the 1800s and the 1890s, we can retrospectively see generations of men moving back and forth between poles of what patriarchs would define as manliness and effeminacy. Meanwhile, individual men move along a spectrum between roles based on Oedipal identification (internalization of the father's authority, identification with parent of the same sex, love for

opposite sex) and roles based on varying degrees of gender
transgression (by transgression I refer to the desire to occupy the
subject position of the opposite sex, i.e. disavowal of the positions
offered in the reputedly normal Oedipal scenario). To be human, as
D. N. Rodowick argues, is to be a fragmented subject 'of shifting
and uncertain sexual identity'.[7] While the Oedipal scenario supports
mid-century sexual hierarchy and division of separate spheres,
therefore, it does not supply us with the only prevalent cultural
'types' of masculinity. Not only are there various patriarchies, but
the patriarch is not the only available role for men. Any overview
of the period will indicate perpetual oscillation among types of
masculinities, with attributes of the types altering their meanings
during the era depending entirely on class, racial, national, and
ethnic struggles, and, of course, gender struggles themselves.

'Ode on the Death of the Duke of Wellington', while marking a
turning point in Tennyson's representations of men, also yields
insight into the mid-century politics of masculinity which Tennyson
continued to investigate in his career. In 1852 Tennyson, now Poet
Laureate, ordered that 10,000 copies of his 'Ode on the Death of the
Duke of Wellington' be printed and sold for two shillings to
the funeral crowd outside St Paul's Cathedral.[8] Celebrating two
boyhood heroes, Arthur Wellesley, Duke of Wellington, and Horatio,
Lord Nelson, Tennyson links masculinity with patriotic fervour. In so
doing, he supports a traditional view of separate spheres (the male
belongs in the public realm) and a traditional view of masculinity
(the manly male does his civic duty by defending his homeland).
The connection of war, manliness, and nationalism was established
early for Tennyson, as it was for many boys and girls growing up in
the 1820s who read eagerly of the resounding success of the battle of
Trafalgar and of the eventual defeat of Napoleon.[9] England's youth,
including future writers such as Charlotte Brontë and Tennyson,
worshipped those heroes who had maintained England's might and
had put an end to twenty years of European war. And it was with a
rekindled youthful enthusiasm that Tennyson, at the age of forty-
three, undertook the 'Ode'. He was neither prompted strenuously by
friends nor commissioned by the queen to write such a poem (see
Martin, p. 368). Rather, Tennyson felt that it was his duty to write the
poem, explaining to his aunt Russell in a phrasing reminiscent of
Horatio Nelson's address to his men, 'I wrote it because it was
expected of me to write'.[10] Indeed, we might dub the poem itself an
Ode to Duty. For it celebrates national duty, manly duty, and poetic
duty through Wellington's – and Nelson's – 'great example' of
leadership (20). Offering a model of masculine heroism, the Ode also
confirms Tennyson's sense of himself as Laureate.

The 'Ode' appears to present us solely with the mid-century myth of a homogenous and monolithic masculinity and patriarchy, embodied alike in the two greatest military heroes of England to date, the Iron Duke, Wellington, and his ostensible equal, the naval hero Lord Nelson. To follow Wellington's example is to 'keep the soldier firm, the statesman pure' (220–2). The Ode attests that, in the common mind as well as in the annals of England, the two men represent a standard for heroic masculinity.

On the one hand, then, the poem proposes a sameness between the two men based on their manliness in life. Yet one may also read the burial near each other in St Paul's crypt as a homosocial mating of two types of masculinity in death. The poem documents the dead Nelson's reception of the dead male body of Arthur Wellington. To Nelson's inquiry 'Who is he that cometh . . . breaking on my rest?' (80–2) the narrator replies 'To thee the greatest soldier comes . . . and worthy to be laid by thee' (88–94). The mating of two types of masculinity unites the feminized 'tender and true' (134) Nelson, ruler of the watery realms, now confined in the private sphere of his coffin, with the manly, rough 'statesman-warrior, moderate, resolute' (25) Wellington, foremost captain of the land, who is being honoured in the public spaces of London. A feminine Horatio receives a masculine Arthur.

In mourning the death of Wellington, Tennyson performs a fascinating gesture with the invocation of Nelson. For he weds two heroes whose personal lives and whose war experiences differ importantly. Nelson may be associated in the public mind with heroic masculinity, but his personal life is one fraught with sexual scandal, and he enters Trafalgar already symbolically emasculated by his battle wounds. Tennyson incorporates, in other words, a feminized male into a poem serving masculine ideals. As a result of this literary wedding, Tennyson (re)masculinizes the feminine, but also multiplies the masculine. Tennyson's 'Ode' thus demonstrates the constructedness and malleability of the cultural category 'masculine'. Singling out a feminized male such as Nelson, who bears very different associations in the public mind than does Wellington, Tennyson presses him into the service of a glorified masculinity – thus remasculinizing him. In this poem and at this point in his career, Tennyson wants to make the feminine male masculine. On the other hand, by incorporating Nelson into the poem at all, he suggests that Wellington's masculinity is not the only kind of masculinity. In terms of Victorian standards, one might say Tennyson qualifies Wellington's type of masculinity, without decreasing his importance as military and moral patriarch.

Tennyson's 1852 poem offers residual, dominant, and emergent gender ideologies.[11] Tennyson's wedding of the feminized Nelson and the masculine Wellington into this mid-century myth of masculine sameness demonstrates overtly, I believe, the cultural necessity of controlling the feminine. In this sense the poem supports the myth of the patriarch codified in the 1830s and 1840s. The myth of a coherent and homogenous masculinity, however, is also merely a memory. Both men are dead. And Tennyson's reinvoking of the myth is itself largely nostalgic. The poem, an elegy for a type of masculinity Tennyson wishes to retain, also shows us that already by the 1850s, the myth of the virile, natural man – leader, war hero, captain, statesman, patriarch, and tool of God (all invoked in the 'Ode') – is open to question and to revision. 'Ode on the Death of the Duke of Wellington' boldly illustrates the Victorian's need for the collapse as well as for the survival of Victorian patriarchy. At the same time, the presence of a feminized male in a celebration of heroism previews cultural fascination with different types of masculinity. Feminized males have always interested Tennyson as author, but he takes up an increasingly emerging cultural imperative with his continuing treatment of King Arthur as both masculine and feminine. 'Ode on the Death of the Duke of Wellington', then, magnificently illustrates the very instability of the gender ideals it endorses.

From the first moments of epical treatment in 'Morte d'Arthur' (1842), *Idylls*, like the Ode of 1852, concerns masculine authority and the death of the male. In retrospect, that Tennyson should start his conception of Arthurian materials with the death of the hero is highly significant. As Gerhard Joseph has argued: 'The death of Arthur constituted the key to the king's entire life'.[12] Tennyson's imaginative choice to start with the death scene is consistent with his pattern of writing poems from the end first, backwards as it were. It also illustrates Tennyson's unusually strong interest in liminal times and terminal situations.[13] From the very beginning, Tennyson shows the failure of Arthur's fantasy to build a patriarchy on a homogenous male order. Likewise, Tennyson's own investment in retaining Arthur and Excalibur, expressed through the character of Bedivere, is doomed.

Like Tennyson's depiction of the death of Wellington, the death of Arthur involves the reception of a male body by a feminine principle. Here, instead of a feminized male, such as Horatio, being troubled during his eternal sleep, the three queens present at Arthur's birth receive him in death. However, whereas the 'Ode on the Death of the Duke of Wellington' honours the respectful, public burial of a real English hero, 'Morte d'Arthur' uses a mythic figure to dramatize a crisis of Victorian masculine authority. It establishes for the Victorians that they have monarchical, literary, and ethical traditions, but it isolates a narrative moment when the stability of those traditions is shaken. This drama, played out between Bedivere and the dying Arthur, pits literal patriarchal authority in the object of Excalibur against the assurance of symbolic authority with Arthur's fame in future generations. More accurately, the struggle lies within Bedivere himself who must come to terms with the fact that a literal patriarchal authority is bound to fail.

Arthur, on the other hand, knows that he can live on as a myth in the minds of subsequent generations only if he gives up Excalibur, his brand. Cultural transmission, in other words, requires the loss of literal symbols of authority. In this case, the sword Excalibur represents both masculine and narrative authority, controls which Arthur knows he must forego and which Bedivere must give up too. As his death wish, Arthur requires Bedivere, his last knight, to hurl Excalibur into the lake. If the now dependent Arthur will die into the future, Bedivere must not cling to the past in order to preserve it and must not misinterpret the sword by overvaluing it. He must obey the King's demand.

Yet the dull and self-interested Bedivere finds it difficult to follow orders, assuming incorrectly that masculine authority derives from clinging to its material representative. That Bedivere tries three times to cast away the sword, thinking about it in different terms each time, clarifies for us that the brand itself is but an empty signifier; it is what one makes of it. Like the parentage of Arthur, debated in *The Coming of Arthur*, Excalibur means what one interprets it to mean. Bedivere's first attempt to hurl it away proves unsuccessful because he is so dazzled by the 'diamond sparks, / Myriads of topaz-lights, and jacinth-work / Of subtlest jewellery' (Morte d'Arthur', 56–8), that he becomes troubled about casting off this beautiful object. He conceals the sword in the marge. On his second attempt, 'clouded with his own conceit' (110), Bedivere considers such a glorious object necessary to prove the story of Arthur in aftertimes. Only when Arthur shames Bedivere in gender terms for being dazzled by the seductiveness of the jewels 'like a girl' (127) and threatens to kill him, does Bedivere hurl the sword into the lake. At that moment, the sword is taken by a female, maternal 'arm / Clothed in white samite, mystic, wonderful' (159). As Bedivere bears the dying Arthur to the lakeside, the king is received by the three queens and veiled forms in a barge, itself feminine. She moves away like some 'full-breasted / Swan' singing a wild song before her death (266). At that moment the poem, too, casts away the threatening invasion of girlish vulnerability to re-establish a masculine authority of epic proportions. Concurrent with the removal of the male hero into the realm of the feminine and maternal, the poem asserts a definition of manliness as the letting go of literal objects of masculine authority.

Like its epic forerunner, 'Morte d'Arthur', *Idylls* questions where masculine authority comes from, who may use it, and to what personal and cultural ends. As part of the gender plot of the series, constructed and revised over a period of fifty years (1835–85), the poem complicates the cultural myth of patriarchy.[14] In spite of the lengthy time period involved in composition and arrangement, both the general movement of the finished poem and the complicated order of published parts indicate Tennyson's abiding concern with a fragile and disempowered masculinity. He locates castrated, immobile, or dead men at the crucial moments of beginning, middle, and end.[15]

Having buried the feminine in his 'Ode' to masculinity and ferried the masculine to its feminine source in his elegy for King Arthur, Tennyson was ready to turn in *Enid*, the first poem of the 1859 *Idylls*, to the power of women and the emasculation of man. The publication history of *Idylls* as a whole emphasizes a sustained and increasing confrontation with female power and male powerlessness. The 1859 version of four 'female' idylls, *Enid, Vivien, Elaine*, and *Guinevere*, introduces the key women of the series. The addition of four idylls in 1870 and two in 1872 significantly increases the role of an androgynous Arthur, while also dividing the *Enid* Idyll into two separate poems. The 1885 addition, *Balin and Balan*, illustrates the schizophrenia of masculinity while dramatically increasing the role of Vivien.

The final version of 1885 sustains Tennyson's initial interest in dead or disempowered males and powerful women. The dedication mourns the dead Prince Albert and celebrates Victoria's rule; *The Coming of Arthur* questions Arthur's authority and lineage for marriage to Guinevere ('A doubtful throne is ice on summer seas' [247]); at the mid-point, Vivien's disempowerment of Merlin prefigures the fall of Camelot ('And in the hollow oak he lay as dead, / And lost to life and use and name and fame' [MV, 967–8]); the series ends with Arthur's death and his reception back to a watery matrix (' "From the great deep to the great deep he goes" ' [PA, 445]; the end frame poem 'To the Queen' celebrates Victoria's conquests and begs her acceptance of the poem.

Arthur represents a mixture of both real and ideal and of male and female. He is historically marked as feminine by his asexuality and his position as a cuckold; he is marked as masculine by his aggression in battle, his subordination of women, and his rule as king. His paradoxical goal is to act as a patriarch in a world in which he also seeks to abolish gender difference. Of all the idylls, *The Holy Grail* (1870) illustrates most clearly the sacrifice of various masculinities that must take place in a world that seeks to abolish gender difference. And it documents the impossibility of such a sacrifice. For with its narrative of visionary successes and failures, *The Holy Grail* offers the prime fantasy behind *Idylls*. Above all, *Idylls* proposes to end sexual difference and heterosexuality but also to collapse all masculinities into one. It would accomplish this end not merely through the establishment of a kingdom based on male bonding, but primarily through elevation of a male she to unite all masculinities into Masculinity, all difference into sameness.

The grail quest duplicates the search for an ideal, which men initially find in Arthur. In this sense, the goal of seeing the grail acts as a magnetizing force for the community. When the king first selects his knights and binds them 'to his own self' (CA, 261), a remarkable reaction flows through the group. As Bellicent tells it to Leodogran, all the knights take on the aspect of Arthur in a moment of binding power: 'I beheld / From eye to eye through all their Order flash / A momentary likeness of the King' (CA, 268–70). In a blending of fantasy and medieval Christianity, 'through the cross / And those around it and the Crucified, / . . . smote' (271–3) three rays which fall on the three queens who will help Arthur in his need. Arthur, then, is associated from the first not only with a special feminine power, but also with the dead Saviour. He gains his power partly from a sanctification seemingly granted by the dead Christ, as if he were a worthy successor.

To view the grail is to fulfil a similarly holy vow, but it also means that man must entirely forsake heterosexual love: 'Then after I was joined with Galahad', says Percivale as he renounces his lady, 'Cared not for her, nor anything upon earth' (HG, 610–11). While heterosexual love is rarely celebrated in the poem, its loss is not encouraged. The reader is supposed to feel concerned about Percivale's decision to forsake one entire realm of experience for another. The proper role of heterosexual men appears to be that of loving their women, but not excessively or blindly. Yet it also appears that such a middle course is really not possible for a man. The knights who must leave the kingdom are too sexually aggressive; those who do not see the grail are overly involved with women; those who are most pure withdraw, as Percivale does, into a monastery.

If the goal of the quest is to unite men, the fact of the quest fractures homogeneity. Arthur, realizing that the quest would end the brotherhood, fails in sufficiently warning his knights of both their potential feminization and the power of female sexuality. To see the grail is to become a male she in the sense of a feminized male, for while separating one from male lust for the feminine, the quest firmly links one to the feminine, since it is stimulated by a woman's vision and a man's identification with her. Percivale's sister, the 'pale nun', first views the grail. 'And this Galahad', recounts Percival, 'when he heard / My sister's vision, filled me with amaze; / His eyes became so like her own, they seemed / Hers, and himself her brother more than I' (HG, 139–42).

Tennyson seems to need to feminize the viewer here to make the viewing act acceptable, even though there is nothing culturally unacceptable in the viewing act itself. In religious terms, one must be in touch with one's soul, which Tennyson repeatedly casts as feminine or androgynous in his poetry. Recognizing Galahad's receptivity to the mystical, the nun wastes no time in a mock marriage ceremony with him. She shears her hair, binds it into a belt and figuratively ties him to her and to her sex: 'I, maiden, round thee, maiden, bind my belt. / Go forth, for thou shalt see what I have seen' (159–60). The viewer of the grail must be feminized in this way, but he must also be purified. Here Tennyson demonstrates once again, as he does in *Maud*, the need for a clear separation between the pure and the polluted and yet the awareness of their inevitable mixing. On the one hand, the sexual male cannot obtain this vision of spirituality, this redemption; he cannot reach or mix with the ideal male. On the other hand, sexuality is rampant in *Idylls*. Like *Maud*, *Idylls* is filled with imagery of the body and of sexuality, but it is socialized away. While in *Maud* it is socialized through the embracing of war, here, as in *In Memoriam*, it is tamed through religious discourse and the mourning of a lost ideal as figured in a dead male.

The grail vision itself is tantalisingly sexual, but with a specific scenario of the light beam as a penetrating male, the cup as a confirmation of death of the male (its job is to hold sacramental wine, symbol of the blood which Christ shed), and the viewer as female. The vision commences with music as of a silver horn and climaxes with the entrance of a silver beam of light (euphemistically dubbed the Holy Thing [124]) into the nun's cell:

> and then
> Streamed through my cell a cold and silver beam,
> And down the long beam stole the Holy Grail,
> Rose-red with beatings in it, as if alive,
> Till all the white walls of my cell were dyed
> With rosy colours leaping on the wall;
> And then the music faded, and the Grail
> Past, and the beam decayed, and from the walls
> The rosy quiverings died into the night.

(115–23)

As it replicates penetration and orgasm, the vision also includes enervation and enfeeblement.

In this fantasy, which irrevocably mixes erotic desire, loss, unattainability, and death, the male cannot retain his male position or it would raise the spectre of male desire for a male body. Nor can he assume the position of a desiring female or it would establish female heterosexual desire. Male bonding will occur by the worshippers' common assumption of a female, asexual position. However, as Arthur intuits, the quest for the grail will undermine the kingdom, since it will serve not to bind men but to divide them. Some men will succeed in the quest, some will half-succeed, some will not succeed at all. Differences will be exposed rather than covered over. The grail quest appears to encode multiple meanings for Tennyson and for the *Idylls* generally. As in *Maud* and *In Memoriam*, the quest for completion in *The Holy Grail* is feminized and the ablest questor is feminized and desexualized, while the goal is masculinized, involving as it does a form of connection (identification, vision, touch) with a dead male body. Though ruled by an asexual Christ-figure in Arthur, Camelot turns out to be a place (or a space) where followers battle with their own bestiality. The knights are in a testing space of sexuality – to eschew violence, to learn gentleness, to strike a balance in love. While the ideal is asexual, then, the site is that of sexuality. The project of Arthur's Round Table is doomed from the start, even for Arthur himself. For the line drawn in the *Idylls* separating physical violence from sexual connection is a very thin one indeed. This poem which would forget the primal scene cannot, in fact, do so. When the pure Arthur fights the Red Knight, he directly partakes of the world of male sexuality as well as the world of male aggression. Signalling his personal debasement, this encounter announces the necessary disintegration of the Round Table in the face of encroaching, worldly realities.

Because of Tennyson's own family background, particularly the influence of his drunken and argumentative father, he finds male models and patriachal authority an especially vexed issue. His overt dislike of the aggressive male is connected (and demonstrated graphically in such poems as 'Locksley Hall' and *Maud*, as I have argued in detail previously) with antagonism towards the bourgeois acquisitive male and the sexually (over)active male. His proposal of the celibate hero, then, whether as Arthur Hallam or as King Arthur, encodes a series of rejections of other masculinities in favour of a masculinity which can flourish in the atmosphere of apostleship and brotherhood.[16] In this light, it is important that the tale of the formation of masculinity in *Idylls*, the story of the innocent Gareth in *Gareth and Lynette*, concerns the break from the mother and the adoption by avuncular father figures, Lancelot and Arthur. Tennyson can not imagine a strong patriarch who is not also a bully, so he enlists avuncular figures. Given Tennyson's preoccupation with brotherhood and avuncular, kindly relations among men, how does his work relate to a coherent Victorian myth of masculinity relying on a homogenous, strong, aggressive patriarchy and a guiding notion of separate spheres?

In replacing a myth of patriarchal masculinity, *Idylls* tries to replace both the aggressive patriarch (such as Mark or the Red Knight or the Arthur of battle) and a false she who wields seductive power (selecting as false she, the sexual female as depicted here in Vivien or Guinevere) with a good she (selecting as good she, the asexual male as depicted here in Arthur, Christ, the balding sage from *Merlin and Vivien*, and those who fully see the grail: Galahad, Bors, and Percivale). However, this last grouping of men as asexual ignores differences among them which are important. In effect, only Arthur is being proposed as the good she. The sage, Galahad, Bors and Percivale are, for various reasons, uninterested in assuming power or just unsuited to run a kingdom. Furthermore, Arthur has to be a eunuch. He has to be castrated because the most perfect woman, according to this fantasy, is the castrated male. The fantasy is thus directly in conflict with the Victorian myth of masculinity where the patriarch is certainly not a castrated male.

Or is he? In fact, *Idylls* achieves a fine balancing act ideologically. It appals the Victorian public by making Malory's manly king too effeminate, thus reinforcing the status quo and separate sphere ideology. At the same time, it questions that ideology. For Tennyson sees that to be a Victorian patriarch is to be a castrated male. And a castrated patriarch in a phallocentric order is a contradictory state of affairs. Yet, the Victorian patriarch 'in reality' was a castrated male yearning to be otherwise. *Idylls*, and *The Holy Grail* in particular, exposes the abiding contradiction at the base of Victorian sexual ideology.

Balin and Balan, added last to the *Idylls*, provides, however, one of the strongest critiques of patriarchy Tennyson would ever write. For here he recognizes that the heterosexual gender codes permeating Camelot remain fixed and dangerous. Selecting the trope of twins as a parody of the larger vision of brotherhood, which the *Idylls* celebrates but also questions, this idyll points to an almost inevitable internal strife at the heart of male kinship and, even more to the point, at the heart of male identity. It exposes the patriarch for what he is and demonstrates the vulnerability of a feminized masculinity which cannot survive in a gender-rigidified world. If *The Holy Grail* attempts to figure a world without sexual difference, *Balin and Balan* charts the cost to masculinity of a world all too inevitably grounded in sexual difference.

The codes of masculinity endorsed by the court of Camelot both run and ruin the kingdom. Yet in Tennyson's telling, these gender codes are also based in the sexual and domestic codes of Victorian England. The specific conditions which occasion Balin's and Balan's murdering of each other at the end of the poem include the worship of the queen as part of a strict code of masculine heroism; the worship of the ideal king and the separation of a pair into an irrational, feminine half who stays home (Balin) and a reasonable, dependable half who journeys forth out of the court (Balan). In one sense the poem is a critique of separate spheres, but in terms of masculinity alone rather than in terms of sexual difference. The physical separation of the two brothers means that the irrational, violent Balin is left without the monitoring of the moderate Balan. In spite of the codes of the kingdom, Balin's 'too fierce manhood' (71) cannot be socialized; it can only be kept at bay before it breaks out again in the wounding or killing of other men. In this respect, it represents both that 'natural force of male sexuality of an explosive nature' which Marion Shaw identifies as an implicit assumption of this textual world and that excessive and angry violence which surfaces in characters such as King Mark.[17]

From my point of view, the interesting aspect of this war between instinct and reason, played out allegorically by the twins Balin and Balan, is the role of the feminine principle and its relationship to masculinity. The feminine appears in various guises in the poem. Guinevere's betrayal of Arthur and Vivien's provocations directly contribute to Balin's loss of faith and thus to the brothers' deaths. However, in *Balin and Balan* the feminine principle is invoked in ways other than by being embodied in the adulterous woman or femme fatale. The idyll opens and closes with references to the procreative feminine. At the two still points of the text, beginning and end, when the characters themselves are still, 'statuelike' (22) and sleeping 'the sleep' (619) of death, the feminine is invoked. In the first instance, they sit near a spring which runs down 'From underneath a plume of lady-fern' (24); at the end, the mother is invoked with 'We two were born together' (617), and their union in her womb is replaced by their union in death. The feminine in both of these instances is connected discursively to nature, to calm, and to procreation. Yet one scene leads to defeat in the figure of the masculine, sport-seeking Arthur and one offers death by a brother's misdirected hand. If these still points of the text feature the maternal, the entire middle features the brothers negotiating a fallen world.

Balin and Balan demonstrates, then, as do the tales of Arthur himself and Gareth, a feminine frame for the 'life' of masculinity.

As part of the fallen world they must travel through, however, Balin and Balan deal with vulnerable men growing weaker. In *Balin and Balan*, the figures of Arthur and Pellam are especially important, for they represent failed patriarchs. Arthur, who is initially willing to let the brothers, his former knights, sit outside Camelot and boast of their prowess, wakes up one morning with the 'light-winged spirit of youth' (19) and arms himself. For no apparent reason other than a desire to prove himself again, he rides forth, inquires who they are, and challenges them to fight. He quickly 'smote the brethren down' (39). This action of Arthur's part seems entirely gratuitous, as if a father, feeling extra strong one day, had to make a point of bullying his wayward sons. He then sends for the brothers, pardons them, and accepts them back into Camelot. If Arthur is usually feminized, here he assumes the role of the militaristic patriarch, 'proven' in the 'Paynim wars' (36). Yet the occasion entirely belies the bravado. That such an occasion can serve to prop Arthur's identity reveals how weak a patriarch he has become.

Pellam proves himself to be the double of Arthur and his court a parody of Camelot. Having witnessed the prospering of Camelot in the name of Christ, Pellam has withdrawn from worldly affairs into holy orders. Formerly a strong rival of Arthur, he is now a rival of a different sort. He rejects his wife, does not care to eat much, allows only the privileged beyond his gates, and spends his time in worship. Surely, he has outArthured Arthur in many respects, and he has just as little control over his real son Garlon as Arthur has over his knights. For Garlon, who now runs the court, has become the raging devil of the woods whom all men fear. He is connected directly, through the image of a hissing swan, to the evil of Vivien, whom he meets secretly in the forest. It is Garlon who upbraids and mocks Balin for his belief in Guinevere. Separated from this faith, Balin flees and becomes violent again. As he flees, he seizes from Pellam's chapel 'The longest lance his eyes had ever seen, / Point-painted red' (405–6), as if to redouble his manly anger. The lance is symbolic not only of the intense male sexual energy driving this idyll, but also of the connections made in the poem among sexual energy, war, and religion. Pellam's failure as a patriarch is directly related to the stealing of his lance. That the lance is now located in a shrine documents that religion is being used to shroud male violence.

For as much as it critiques patriarchy, *Balin and Balan* also explores man's concomitant inability to connect with a nurturant femininity. Although the poem is allegorical, abstract, uneven, and above all, distancing, it very much concerns intimacy. The idyll most obviously about kinship between men, it is propelled by the loss of the feminine. *Balin and Balan* tells the tale of a world populated by hypocritical patriarchs, decked out in the illusions of a powerful masculinity, who have replaced women men feel they must reject.

Tennyson suggests that access to femininity, which might restrain or help rechannel Balin's masculine violence, proves unavailable to him. In other words, he does not need only male reason, represented by his brother Balan, but femaleness (or, in Shaw's terms, 'true [Victorian] womanhood', p. 97). He cannot find the feminine in nature, in a mother, in Guinevere, in Vivien, or in himself. He can recognize in Lancelot what 'the King / So prizes – overprizes – gentleness' (180), but he mistakenly assumes gentleness to be a property available to some, but not to others. The failure of Camelot is very much connected to the division of Balin and Balan. In gender terms, the codes of masculinity and femininity by which men and women live are so fixed that they cannot accommodate alterations. So too, Balan cannot recognize Balin, his culturally feminized other half, unless Balin wields the shield marking his devotion to Guinevere. Balan only seems to know Balin by the signifier of his worship of Guinevere, even though these two men are more familiar than any other two presented in the text.

In this idyll man is doomed to undo himself by an adherence to rigid cultural codes. Although the text argues against wanton expression of an aggressive masculine violence, which it treats as excessive, *Balin and Balan* bemoans the fact that society provides no easy solution to alter a pattern of male irrational violence. The closure, with the brothers Balin and Balan locked in each other's arms as they die, graphically illustrates the sacrifice of any alternative masculinity that must take place in a firmly gendered world functioning on stereotypes and separate spheres. The brothers, whose intimacy from childhood ends in a homosexual death kiss, which parodies a liebestod scene, cannot survive together or apart in a divided world. Both must die in service to a rigid regime of sexual difference which holds out purity as necessary, gentleness as possible, and manliness as asexual. The idyll mourns the absence of a nurturant feminine principle and the waste of a Balin who might have been reclaimed.

In place of the homosocial model of desire and exchange which has been analysed so well by Eve Kosofsky Sedgwick, where two men bond over a female object of exchange, Tennyson offers us a homosocial plot with a male body, a male she as the object.[18] And as the two men who barter, we have Knights and Christ, with Arthur alternating as the mediating figure and as the body itself and with Christ also alternating as the mediating figure and as the body itself.

In this totally male triangle, what we may call the complete homosocial plot, then, the men exchange positions of desire and mediation as they identify and counteridentify with each other and with Christ. Woman is present but only in a femininity internalized by men.

In the homosocial/heterosexual plot, on the other hand, Lancelot bonds with Arthur initially through Guinevere. Yet Arthur's very lack of sexuality and Lancelot's increased sexuality and concomitantly weakened vows to Arthur mean a breakdown of the bonding structure. Lancelot's increasing preference for the she who is Guinevere over the male she who is Arthur undermines the stability of the triangle.

Both triangles of sexual desire, fantasy, and power are at work in *Idylls* at the same time. The fact that they co-exist in the text indicates the impossibility of the primary fantasy. Men may gain a vision of the grail; Arthur's subjects may confirm his authority as king; but it is impossible to sustain a brotherhood, making all masculinities one Masculinity, as a foundation for culture. Arthur's version of patriarchy, the Victorian version of patriarchy, must fail because the very presence of sexual difference militates against its success.

Idylls is typically Tennysonian in its equivocation about final allegiances. The poem expresses nostalgia for a gentlemanly, asexual, feminized king during the reign of a queen, as if to say: if we must have a woman on the throne, we would rather have a male she than a she male. However, the poem also expands the boundaries of the cultural understanding of regal authority, sexuality, brotherhoods, and relations between men and women and men and men. Instead of merely supporting patriarchy, the poem offers a variety of masculinities constructed in terms of relations of power and identifications. Galahad and the young Gareth have power but no sexuality; Arthur and the balding sage are asexual; Mark and the Red Knight are violent, including sexually; Lancelot and Merlin must confront their own sexuality when they would prefer to subdue it; other knights take up positions which combine and mix the previous ones. In this sense *Idylls* doubly questions masculinity. If it proves the myth of the Victorian manly patriarch to be untenable, it also demonstrates that there is no such thing as masculinity but just various forms of masculinities, various forms of identifications and of desires.

Two male figures of the *Idylls* provide keys to the Victorian politics of masculinity and to Tennyson's personal interests, which intersect in this series of poems. The figure of Merlin, shut forever in a hollow oak, symbolically represents the absence yet presence of patriarchy, the hollowed-outedness of such a concept in Victorian culture. Merlin, in his dazzling knowledge, is as powerful as the brand Excalibur, but he too must disappear into a blurry world of half-life. Like patriarchy itself, Merlin is there, but he is not there.

Yet the figure of Balin in *Balin and Balan*, which Tennyson purposely withheld from publication for over a decade, most noticeably represents the gender conflicts within Tennyson himself. As we have seen, Balin is the repository of a 'too fierce manhood' which must be kept at bay or it lashes out and kills or wounds men. Yet he is feminized. It would appear that the issue at stake for Tennyson is the powerful and castrating woman/mother and his own enfeeblement. In the poem the dead male body replaces a dead female body; Balin provides a brilliantly conceived site of displacement. The invention of Balin allows Tennyson, in his displacement of fear, loathing, and anger, a connection of violence with its 'proper' Victorian cultural home: man. Tennyson can also express frustration at a man who should have kept Balin's excesses in check: Balan. Finally, Tennyson can defuse anger and master fear in a homosexual liebestod scene where the simultaneous loving and killing of one's brother becomes the ritual of loving and killing of one's male and female self.

Balan/Balin represents a split in the male self which is unaccommodated by the myth of a patriarch but which also helps constitute Victorian culture. Whether Tennyson's personal fascination with dead male bodies indicates a desire to return to a maternal female body, or whether it indicates a strong resistance to the female which would complicate any desire to return, or whether these are even mutually exclusive impulses, is another story. What remains is some of the most erotic poetry of inconsolable loss in the English language.

Notes

1. For an important history and defence of gender studies, see ELAINE SHOWALTER, 'The Rise of Gender', *Speaking of Gender* (New York, 1989), pp. 1–13. The essays, which cover American and British texts, demonstrate the range of gender criticisms in the 1980s, with the most provocative contributions being those on the 1890s by D. A. MILLER, CHRISTOPHER CRAFT, and EVE KOSOFSKY SEDGWICK. For important instances of British gender criticism, see ALAN SINFIELD, *Alfred Lord Tennyson* (London, 1986); MARION SHAW, *Alfred Lord Tennyson* (Atlantic Highlands, NJ, 1988); and ROWENA CHAPMAN and JONATHAN RUTHERFORD, eds., *Male Order: Unwrapping Masculinity* (London, 1988). For some of the more sophisticated theoretical formulations about gender, see R. W. CONNELL, *Gender and Power: Society, the Person, and Sexual Politics* (Stanford, 1987); JUDITH BUTLER, *Gender Trouble: Feminism and the*

Subversion of Identity (New York, 1990); and ARTHUR BRITTAN, *Masculinity and Power* (London, 1989).

2. For a working definition of patriarchy, see TIM CORRIGAN, BOB CONNELL, and JOHN LEE, 'Hard and Heavy: Toward a New Sociology of Masculinity', *Beyond Patriarchy*, ed. Michael Kaufman (New York, 1987), pp. 139–92. The main principles of patriarchy include male dominance, female subordination, and militarism.

3. In following Tennyson's fascination with the dead male, I do not diminish his attraction in poetry to the dead female body. We need only think of 'The Lady of Shalott' as a forerunner to other important instances. I have taken up the feminine generally in 'Rereading Tennyson's Gender Politics', *Victorian Sages and Cultural Discourse: Renegotiating Gender and Power*, ed. Thaïs E. Morgan (New Brunswick, 1990), pp. 46–65.

4. CHRISTINE KRUEGER's analysis of female evangelical preachers' appropriation and complicated uses of patriarchal authority is useful in demonstrating the accessibility of 'male' power: *The Reader's Repentance: Women Preachers, Women Writers and Nineteenth Century Social Discourse* (Chicago, 1992). This critical examination demonstrates, as does recent work by MARY POOVEY, JUDITH NEWTON, and others, the instability of gender codes in the period.

5. LEONORE DAVIDOFF and CATHERINE HALL, *Family Fortunes: Men and Women of the English Middle Class, 1780–1850* (Chicago, 1987). For recent feminist and materialist scholarship citing Victorian medical texts and advice manuals to mothers, see SALLY SHUTTLEWORTH, 'Demonic Mothers: Ideologies of Bourgeois Motherhood in the Mid-Victorian Era', in *Rewriting the Victorians: Theory, History, and the Politics of Gender*, ed. Linda Shires (New York, 1992), pp. 31–51; MARY POOVEY, *Uneven Developments: The Ideological Work of Gender in Mid-Victorian England* (Chicago, 1988), chap. 2; RANDI DAVENPORT, 'Mid-Victorian Motherhood and the Subject of Empire', Doctral Dissertation, Syracuse University, 1991.

6. CATHERINE GALLAGHER, 'Response' to 'Medusa's Head' in NEIL HERTZ, *The End of the Line: Essays on Psychoanalysis and the Sublime* (New York, 1985).

7. D. N. RODOWICK, *The Difficulty of Difference* (New York, 1991), p. 69. The attention to Sigmund Freud's key essay, 'A Child is Being Beaten', by film critics such as Rodowick attests to the importance of fantasy and gender transgression within patriarchy and deserves further attention. One would surmise that partners would entertain the possibilities of playing double / multiple positions in various kinds of scenarios that are inflected with eroticism and would do so with different levels of awareness at different times (i.e. man as man, man subliminally takes culturally assigned role of woman, man aware that he is a man taking role of a woman, etc.). See also the work of JUDITH BUTLER, as cited, on gender roles as performative.

8. ROBERT MARTIN, *Tennyson: The Unquiet Heart* (Oxford, 1980), p. 368. For the compositional background and critical reception of the work, see EDGAR F. SHANNON, JR., 'The History of a Poem: Tennyson's "Ode on the Death of the Duke of Wellington"', *SB*, 13 (1960), 149–77; and CHRISTOPHER RICKS and EDGAR F SHANNON, JR., A Further History of Tennyson's "Ode on the Death of the Duke of Wellington": The Manuscript at Trinity College and the Galley Proof at Lincoln', *SB*, 32 (1979), 125–57, now available as Appendix A in CHRISTOPHER RICKS, *Tennyson* (Berkeley, 1989), pp. 298–323.

9. See W. D. PADEN *Tennyson in Egypt: A Study of the Imagery in his Earlier Work* (1942; New York, 1971), p. 92, and ARTHUR BRITTAN on masculinity as competitiveness, chap. 4.

10. Alfred Lord Tennyson, Letter to Elizabeth Russell, 16 November 1852, as printed in *The Letters of Alfred Lord Tennyson*, ed. CECIL Y. LANG and EDGAR F. SHANNON, JR. (Cambridge, Massachusetts, 1987), 2:50.

11. For a fuller explanation of various ideologies in the 1840s, see RAYMOND WILLIAMS, 'Forms of English Fiction in 1848', *Literature, Politics, and Theory. Papers from the Essex Conference, 1976–84* (New York, 1986), pp. 1–16.

12. GERHARD JOSEPH, *Tennysonian Love: The Strange Diagonal* (Minneapolis, 1969), p. 146.

13. HERBERT F. TUCKER, *Tennyson and the Doom of Romanticism* (Cambridge MA, 1988), chap. 1.

14. Details on the order of composition and publication of the *Idylls* can be found in RICKS, 3:255–563, in prefatory material and headnotes to each Idyll.

15. I thus disagree with ELLIOT GILBERT's more linear reading of the specific trajectory of Arthur from initial femininity and rejection of patriarchy to assumption of the masculinity necessary to reign, although I find many of his other points fully persuasive. See 'The Female King: Tennyson's Arthurian Apocalypse', *Speaking of Gender*, pp. 163–86.

16. See RICHARD DELLAMORA on Tennyson and apostleship *Masculine Desire: The Sexual Politics of Victorian Aestheticism* (Chapel Hill, 1990), chap. 2.

17. MARION SHAW, p. 54. For another especially sensitive analysis of *Balin and Balan*, see JAMES R. KINCAID, *Tennyson's Major Poems: The Comic and Ironic Patterns* (New Haven, 1975), p. 178. See also J. M. GRAY, *Tennyson's Dopplegänger: Balin and Balan* (Lincoln, 1971) and 'Fact, Form and Fiction in Tennyson's "Balin and Balan" ', *RMS*, 12 (1968), 91–107.

18. EVE KOSOFSKY SEDGWICK's landmark book *Between Men* (New York, 1985) has founded an entire school of gender criticism. However, as has recently been argued by others, such as RICHARD DELLAMORA, the model she offers to explain gender relations does not apply in every instance.

10 Tennyson's *Princess*: One Bride for Seven Brothers*

EVE KOSOFSKY SEDGWICK

If Shires's Tennyson eventually comes to recognize the dangers of certain kinds of models of masculinity, Sedgwick's Tennyson is much more subversive, though unconsciously so. Sedgwick's 1985 book *Between Men: English Literature and Male Homosocial Desire* was received as a landmark in literary studies and has been extremely influential in gender studies since. In her introduction she argues for a careful charting of the ways in which relationships between men are cemented by the traffic in women as exchangeable objects or counters of value and bear a close relation to the structure of class. The crucial point is that 'no element of that pattern can be understood outside of its relation to women and the gender system as a whole'. In her chapter on Tennyson's *The Princess* Sedgwick reveals the complex exchange of women within the poem's formal structures: seven male narrators share the narrator position thereby ensuring that women, words and a collective identification with an aristocratic Prince cement the bonds between them. The poem sets out to embody and hold together the contradictions of male homosocial and heterosexual desire at a given cultural moment.

It has seemed easiest for critical consensus to interest itself in the Gothic on 'private' terms and in mainstream Victorian fictions on 'public' terms; but just as the psychological harrowings of the Gothic are meaningful only as moves in a public discourse of power allocation, so the overtly public, ideological work of writers like Tennyson, Thackeray, and Eliot needs to be explicated in the supposedly intrapsychic terms of desire and phobia to make even its political outlines clear. *The Princess* in particular claims to be a major public statement, in a new form, about the history and meaning of femininity; but male homosocial desire, homophobia, and even the Gothic psychology of the 'uncanny' are ultimately the structuring terms of its politics – and of its generic standing as well.

To generalize: it was the peculiar genius of Tennyson to light on

---

*Reprinted from Eve Kosofsky Sedgwick, *Between Men: English Literature and Male Homosocial Desire* (New York: Columbia University Press, 1985), pp. 118–33

the tired, moderate, unconscious ideologies of his time and class, and by the force of his investment in them, and his gorgeous lyric gift, to make them sound frothing-at-the-mouth mad.

Tennyson applied this genius with a regal impartiality that makes him seem like a Christmas present to the twentieth-century student of ideology, but made him something less reassuring to many of his contemporaries. We have suggested that the whole point of ideology is to negotiate invisibly between contradictory elements in the status quo, concealing the very existence of contradictions in the present by, for instance, recasting them in diachronic terms as a historical narrative of origins. For a writer as fervent, as credulous, and as conflicted as Tennyson to get interested in one of these functional myths was potentially subversive to a degree that, and in a way that, Tennyson himself was the last to perceive. Where he did perceive it, it was most often as a formal struggle with structural or stylistic incoherence in his work. These formal struggles, however, also answered to the enabling incoherences in his society's account of itself.

If *Henry Esmond* is an ahistorical diagram of bourgeois femininity disguised as an account of historical change, *The Princess* is in some respects the opposite. Its myth of the origin of modern female subordination is presented firmly *as* myth, in a deliberately a-chronic space of 'Persian' fairy tale. On the other hand, the relation of the myth to its almost aggressively topical framing narrative is so strongly and variously emphasized that the poem seems to compel the reader to search for ways of reinserting the myth into the history. The mythic narrative is sparked by a young woman's speculation about the male homosocial discourse from which she is excluded:

> – what kind of tales did men tell men,
> She wonder'd, by themselves?[1]

Its substance, as well, is about the enforcement of women's relegation within the framework of male homosocial exchange. Some effects of uncanniness result from this magnetic superposition of related tales – along with more explicable historic and generic torsions.

The 'mythic' central narrative begins with the astonishing vision of a feminist separatist community, and ends with one of the age's definitive articulations of the cult of the angel in the house. The loving construction of a female world, centred on a female university, looking back on a new female history and forward to a newly empowered future; and then the zestful destruction of that world root and branch, the erasure of its learning and ideals and the evisceration of its institutions – both are the achievements of Tennyson's genius for ideological investment. In the fairy-tale feudal setting, there are two kingdoms, a northern and a southern; and the crown prince of the northern kingdom has grown up bound by a childhood proxy-engagement to the princess of the southern kingdom. When the time comes for the marriage, however, no princess is forthcoming. The Prince learns from the southern king that Princess Ida has become a feminist, and with two widows from her court, has talked the king out of a summer palace at the northern frontier of the southern kingdom, where the three women have founded 'an University for maidens'. The Prince and his two friends head north again to the frontier. Learning that only women are allowed in the neighbourhood of the University – 'Let no man enter in on pain of death', the gates say – they sneak in pretending to be women from the north who want to be educated. Once in, they are discovered to be men by various of the inhabitants, but each time promising (falsely) to keep quiet and leave at once, they persuade the women not to betray them to the Princess to be killed. Meanwhile the Prince is smitten with the noble, impassioned Princess, and each of his friends also finds a woman to pursue. Finally one of the friends gets a little drunk and finding that he cannot conceal his contempt for the women any longer, bursts out with an insulting song in front of the Princess – 'Forbear, Sir', the Prince exclaims, and the gaff is blown. In the chaotic aftermath the Princess almost drowns and the Prince saves her life; whereupon she pardons his life but sends him back home.

Meanwhile, however, a military confrontation has been shaping up between the men of the two kingdoms over her father's failure to hand over the young bride as originally bargained for. Our Prince, genuinely impressed by the Princess's pride and dedication, argues at first against the use of violence or compulsion, but soon enough he finds himself with his friends and soldiers entering battle against Princess Ida's brothers and their soldiers. Under threat of a military invasion from the north, and subverted by the dissent and demoralization that the men have caused in the women's community, the Princess herself has had to agree to abide by the outcome of the battle, and to give herself up to the Prince if her brother's side loses. As it happens his side wins, but there is general bloodshed on the frontier; our Prince is given up for dead; but he survives, and he and the other wounded from both sides are taken to be cared for in the University, now turned into a hospital, where the women forget their studies and their feminism and fall wholesale in love with the men to whom they are ministering. The Princess, nursing the Prince back to life from his grievous wounds, begs him to forgive her for her mad destructive vision, and he does. 'My bride', he says, 'My wife, my life –

> 'this proud watchword rest
> Of equal; seeing either sex alone
> Is half itself, and in true marriage lies
> Nor equal nor unequal'
>
> (VII, 282–5)

> 'Yield thyself up: my hopes and thine are one:
> Accomplish thou my manhood and thyself;
> Lay thy sweet hands in mine and trust to me.'
>
> (VII, 343–5)

One important feature of the myth propounded in *The Princess*'s inner narrative is that it traces the origin of nineteenth-century bourgeois gender arrangements directly back to the feudal aristocracy. Even there, however, the angel in the house does not seem to be new; for the Prince describes his ideal of womanhood as coming directly from his own mother, and describes it in terms that any middlebrow Victorian would have recognized:

> one
> Not learned, save in gracious household ways,
> Not perfect, nay, but full of tender wants,
> No Angel, but a dearer being, all dipt
> In Angel instincts, breathing Paradise,
> Interpreter between the Gods and men,
> Who look'd all native to her place, and yet
> On tiptoe seem'd to touch upon a sphere
> Too gross to tread, and all male minds perforce
> Sway'd to her from their orbits as they moved,
> And girdled her with music. Happy he
> With such a mother!
>
> (VII, 298–309)

Toward this destiny (presented as both idealized past and paradisal future) Ida, too, is being propelled. At the same time, it is significant that this nostalgic portrait of the Prince's mother is not arrived at until the last pages of the poem; for the poem until then at least gestures at a critique of the aristocratic feudal family that, if not thorough or consistent, is nevertheless part of its purpose. Although the mother who is its product is a good old angelic mother, the family that has created her is the bad old baronial family:

My mother was as mild as any saint,

But my good father thought a king a king;
He cared not for the affection of the house;
He held his sceptre like a pedant's wand
To lash offence, and with long arms and hands
Reach'd out, and pick'd offenders from the mass
For judgment.

(I, 22–9)

The old king thinks his son is lily-livered as a wooer:

'Tut, you know them not, the girls.

Man is the hunter; woman is his game:
The sleek and shining creatures of the chase,
We hunt them for the beauty of their skins;
They love us for it, and we ride them down.
Wheedling and siding with them! Out! for shame!
Boy, there's no rose that's half so dear to them
As he that does the thing they dare not do,
Breathing and sounding beauteous battle, comes
With the air of the trumpet round him, and leaps in
Among the women, snares them by the score
Flatter'd and fluster'd, wins, tho' dashed with death
He reddens what he kisses: thus I won
Your mother, a good mother, a good wife,
Worth winning.'

(V, 144–60)

The Prince is an authentic liberal. His tactic in response to his father
here is Horner's: he presents Princess Ida's feminism as a mirror-
image extreme of his father's crudely patriarchal style, and himself
as forging a new dialectic between them, arriving at the moderating
terms of a compromise. To Ida,

'Blame not thyself too much,' I said, 'nor blame
Too much the sons of men and barbarous laws'

(VII, 239–40)

As we see when Ida is forced to turn into a version of the Prince's
mother, however, far from forging a new order or a new dialectic
he is merely finding for himself a more advantageous place within
the old one. Finding one, or preserving it: since one way of

185

describing the Prince's erotic strategy is that, Yorick-like, while
maintaining the strict division of power and privilege between male
and female, he favours (and permits to himself) a less exclusive
assignment of 'masculine' and 'feminine' personal traits between
men and women, in order that, as an 'effeminized' man, he may be
permitted to retain the privileged status of baby (*within* a rigidly
divided family) along with the implicit empowerment of maleness.
(The privileged avenue from a baby's need to a woman's sacrifice
is one of the most repetitively enforced convictions in this inner
narrative, and most especially in the lyrics.) In short, the Prince's
strategy for achieving his sexual ends in battle differs from his father's
only in a minor, stylistic detail: he gets what he wants by losing the
battle, not by winning it.

The meaningfulness of the concept of fighting *against* a man *for* the
hand of a woman can barely be made to seem problematical to him,
however. And in general, the Prince's erotic perceptions are entirely
shaped by the structure of the male traffic in women – the use of
women by men as exchangeable objects, as counters of value, for the
primary purpose of cementing relationships with other men. For
instance, it never for one instant occurs to him to take seriously Ida's
argument that an engagement contracted for reasons of state, by her
father, without her consent, when she was eight years old, is not a
reason why the entire course of her life should be oriented around the
desires of a particular man. Similarly, as in Tennyson's own life
the giving of a sister in marriage to cement the love of the brother
for another man is central in this narrative. Although romantic love
is exalted in the Prince's view, as it is not in his father's, nevertheless
its tendency in the mythic narrative must always be to ratify and
enforce the male traffic in women, not to subvert it.

This emphasis on a chivalric code in which women are 'privileged'
as the passive, exalted objects of men's intercourse with men, is part
of the point of drawing a genealogy straight from the Victorian
bourgeois family to the medievalistic courtly tradition. To cast the
narrative in terms of a 'Prince' and a 'Princess' is both a conventional,
transparent fairy-tale device, and a tendentious reading of history. Like
the aristocratic siting of the genealogical narrative in *Henry Esmond*,
it accomplishes several simplifying purposes. First, it permits a view
of the Victorian middle-class family that denies any relation between
its structure and its economic functions. By making the persistence
and decadence of a stylized aristocratic family look like a sufficient
explanation for contemporary middle-class arrangements, it renders
economic need invisible and hides from the middle-class audience
both its historical ties to the working class and also the degree to
which, while nominally the new empowered class or new aristocracy,

most of the middle class itself functions on a wage system for males and a system for domestic servitude for females. Even though the fit between the structure of the ideologically normative family and the needs of capital for certain forms of labour-power is anything but seamless, nevertheless the new middle-class family reflects these imperatives in its structure at least as strongly as it reflects internal contradictions left over from the aristocratic family of feudal times. Thus, the appeal to high chivalry obscures the contemporary situation by glamorizing and in fact dehistoricizing it.

As we will see, though, the mock-heraldry of tracing the bourgeois family back to aristocratic origins in feudal society is not the only ideologically useful way of legitimating it. The *Adam Bede* model, the genealogy through the yeoman and artisan classes, has its uses as well: for instance, instead of excluding work and the facts of economic necessity, it incorporates them centrally, but in a form (individual artisanship evolving into a guildlike system of workshop production) that both affirms some of the features of modern industrial discipline (such as the exclusion of women) and conceals its discontinuity from more individualistic modes of work.

Why then is Tennyson's defence of contemporary social arrangements in *The Princess* cast in the archaizing, aristocratic mold? It is through this question, I think that we can move to a consideration of the fascinating frame narrative of the poem. For the poem takes place in a very particular England of the present (i.e. 1847), an England that, with Tennysonian daring, seems almost to represent a simple projection into the present of the inner narrative's fantasy of a feudal past. Like *Wives and Daughters, The Princess* begins on a great estate, on the day of the year on which it is opened up to the tenantry and neighbourhood:

> Thither flock'd at noon
> His tenants, wife and child, and thither half
> The neighbouring borough with their Institute
> Of which he was the patron. I was there
> From college, visiting the son, . . .
> . . . with others of our set,
> Five others: we were seven at Vivian-place.
>
> (Prologue, 3–9)

As these lines suggest, *The Princess* is unlike *Wives and Daughters* in locating its point of view among those who might be at Vivian-place even on a normal, non-open-house day; it is also different from any Gaskell novel in viewing all the activities of the neighbourhood, *including* the industry-oriented sciences of the Institute, as firmly and intelligibly set within a context of aristocratic patronage. In fact, with a characteristic earnest bravado, Tennyson goes out of his way to underline the apparent incongruity of the juxtaposition of on the one hand ancient privilege and connoisseurship, and on the other hand modern science; like a small-scale exposition of arts and industry, the open grounds of Vivian-place are dotted for the day with 'a little clock-work steamer', 'a dozen angry model [engines] jett[ing] steam', 'a petty railway', a miniature telegraph system where 'flash'd a saucy message to and fro'/ Between the mimic stations', and so forth, displayed along with the permanent family museum of geological specimens, Greek marbles, family armour from Agincourt and Ascalon, and trophies of empire from China, Malaya, and Ireland (Prologue, 73–80, 13–24). The assertion that science, or technology, is the legitimate offspring of patronage and connoisseurship, that all these pursuits are harmonious, disinterested, and nationally unifying, that the raison d'etre of the great landowners is to execute most impartially a national consensus in favour of these obvious desiderata – the frame narrative assumes these propositions with a confidence that is almost assaultive.

Along with the breathtaking ellipsis with which *class* conflict is omitted from Tennyson's England, the aristocratic-oriented view of progress-as-patronage affects the *gender* politics of the poem, as well. The feminism presented in Princess Ida's part of the poem is a recognizable, searching, and, in its own terms, radical feminism. Some of the elements of it that are taught or practiced at the University include separatism, Lesbian love, a re-vision in female-centred terms of Western history, mythology, and art, a critique of Romantic love and the male traffic in women, and a critique of the specular rationalism of Western medical science. How is it possible for this elaborately imagined and riveting edifice to crumble at a mere male touch? What conceptual flaw has been built into it that allows it to hold the imagination so fully on its own terms, and yet to melt so readily into the poem's annihilatingly reactionary conclusion?

I am suggesting, of course, that its weakness is precisely the poem's vision of social change as something that occurs from the top down. For Princess Ida's relation to the University and in fact to the whole progress of feminism in the mythical southern kingdom is only an intensification of Sir Walter's relation to 'progress' among his tenants: she is the founder, the benefactor, the theorist, the historian, and the beau ideal of a movement whose disinterested purpose is to liberate *them*, to educate *them*,

Disyoke their necks from custom, and assert
None lordlier than themselves . . .

(II, 127–8)

Ida's main feeling about actual living women is impatience, a sense
of anger and incredulity that she cannot liberate them and their
perceptions in a single heroic gesture:

> for women, up till this,
> Cramped under worse than South-sea-isle taboo,
> Dwarfs of the gynaeceum, fail so far
> In high desire, they know not, cannot guess
> How much their welfare is a passion to us.
> If we could give them surer, quicker proof –
> Oh if our end were less achievable
> By slow approaches, than by single act
> Of immolation, any phase of death,
> We were as prompt to spring against the pikes,
> Or down the fiery gulf as talk of it,
> To compass our dear sisters' liberties.

(III, 260–71)

In an imaginative world where even a genuinely shared interest can
be embodied and institutionalized only in the form of *noblesse oblige*, it
is not surprising that a merely personal snag, encountered by the
crucial person, succeeds effortlessly in unravelling the entire fabric.
A top-down politics of the privileged, sacrificial, enlightened few
making decisions for the brutalized, unconscious many will necessarily
be an object of manipulation (from inside or outside), of late-blooming
self-interest on the part of the leaders, of anomie and sabotage on the
part of the led. A feminism based on this particular nostalgia will be
without faith or fortitude, a sisterhood waiting to be subverted.

Part of the oddity of Tennyson's poem, however, is that the
ideological structure that permits him in the inner narrative to
tumble the feminist community down like a house of cards, is the
same one whose value and durability for class relations he is blandly
asserting, in the frame narrative. It may be this that caused his
contemporaries to view the poem as a whole with such unease, an
unease which, however, both he and they persisted in describing as
formal or generic.

Tennyson describes the male narrator as being caught between the
different *formal* and *tonal* demands of his male and female listeners:

> And I, betwixt them both, to please them both,
> And yet to give the story as it rose,
> I moved as in a strange diagonal,
> And maybe neither pleased myself nor them.
>
> (Conclusion, 25–9)

Indeed, like the slippages of political argument, the formal and generic slippages between frame and inner narratives are very striking, and do catch up and dramatize the issues of class and gender, as well. For instance, the status of the inner narrative as collective myth, as a necessary ideological invention, is underlined by the indeterminacy about its authorship. During the Vivian-place party, the telling of the story, like a woman, is passed from hand to hand among the young men. The identification is directly made between the collectiveness of the male involvement in women and in storytelling: the idea of storytelling had started with an earlier Christmas reading-party of the seven young men from the University, where, Walter tells his sister Lilia,

> Here is proof that you [women] were miss'd: . . .
>   We [men] did but talk you over, pledge you all
> In wassail . . .
>   – play'd
> Charades and riddles as at Christmas here, . . .
> And often told a tale from mouth to mouth
>
> (Prologue, 175–9)

It is to initiate and place the Vivian-place women in the context of this proceeding that the inner story in *The Princess* is begun. Walter jokes of it as an occasion for making a gift of his sister to his friend –

> 'Take Lilia, then, for heroine' clamour'd he,
>   . . . 'and be you
> The Prince to win her!'
>
> (Prologue, 217–19)

The story is to be a 'Seven-headed monster', of which each male narrator will

>   be hero in his turn!
> Seven and yet one, like shadows in a dream.
>
> (Prologue, 221–2)

As we have seen, the interior of the 'Seven-headed monster' story,

the belly of the beast, is no less structured by the male exchange of
women than the circumstances of its conception had been. But there
is a more unexpected and off-centred, thematic echo between inside
and out, as well. The odd comparison of the male narrative
communion to that of 'shadows in a dream', almost unintelligible
in its immediate context, leaps to salience in relation to one of the
most notoriously puzzling features of the internal narrative. The Prince
inherits from his family, perhaps through a sorcerer's curse, a kind
of intermittent catalepsy,

> weird seizures, Heaven knows what:
> On a sudden in the midst of men and day,
> And while I walk'd and talk'd as heretofore,
> I seem'd to move among a world of ghosts,
> And feel myself the shadow of a dream.
>
> (I, 14–18)

This fugue state is described throughout the poem with the words
'shadow' and 'dream', and most often simply 'shadow of a dream'.

> While I listen'd, came
> On a sudden the weird seizure and the doubt:
> I seem'd to move among a world of ghosts;
> The Princess with her monstrous woman-guard,
> The jest and earnest working side by side,
> The cataract and the tumult and the kings
> Were shadows; and the long fantastic night
> With all its doings had and had not been,
> And all things were and were not.
>
> (IV, 537–45)

The link between the seizures and the 'seven and yet one' narrative
frame does not disappear from the poem: one of the fugue states,
for instance, corresponds to one of the moments when the narrative
voice is being passed from one male to another. Its link to the use
of sisters to cement emotional and property relations between men
also recurs. Psyche, one of the Princess's companions, is the sister
of Florian, a companion of the Prince's whom he considers

> my other heart,
> And almost my half-self, for still we moved
> Together, twinn'd as horse's ear and eye.
>
> (I, 54–6)

Cyril, the Prince's other companion, falls in love with Psyche – and he asks,

> What think you of it, Florian? do I chase
> The substance or the shadow? will it hold?
> I have no sorcerer's malison on me,
> No ghostly hauntings like his Highness. I
> Flatter myself that always everywhere
> I know the substance when I see it. Well,
> Are castles shadows? Three of them? Is she
> The sweet proprietress a shadow? If not,
> Shall those three castles patch my tatter'd coat?
> For dear are those three castles to my wants,
> And dear is sister Psyche to my heart . . .
>
> (II, 386–96)

Real estate can give body and substance to the shadowy bonds – of women, of words, of collective though hierarchical identification with a Prince – that link the interests of men.

I have no programmatic reading to offer of the meaning and placement of the Prince's cataleptic seizures. Surely, however, they are best described as a wearing-thin of the enabling veil of opacity that separates the seven male narrators from the one male speaker. The collective and contradictory eros and need of their investment in him – and through him, in each other – seem to fray away at his own illusion of discrete existence. Is the Prince a single person, or merely an arbitrarily chosen chord from the overarcing, transhistorical, transindividual circuit of male entitlement and exchange? He himself is incapable of knowing.

Dickens' novel is directly relevant here. In *Great Expectations*, Pip is subject to fuguelike states rather like the Prince's. The most notable is the one that occurs during Orlick's murderous attack on him at the lime-kiln:

> He drank again, and became more ferocious. I saw by his tilting of the bottle that there was no great quantity left in it. I distinctly understood that he was working himself up with its contents, to make an end of me. I knew that every drop it held, was a drop of my life. I knew that when I was changed into a part of the vapour that had crept towards me but a little while before, like my own warning ghost, he would . . . make all haste to the town, and be seen slouching about there, drinking at the ale-houses. My rapid mind pursued him to the town, made a picture of the street with him in it, and contrasted its lights and life with

the lonely marsh and the white vapour creeping over it, into
which I should have dissolved.

It was not only that I could have summed up years and years
and years while he said a dozen words, but that what he did
say presented pictures to me, and not mere words. In the excited
and exalted state of my brain, I could not think of a place
without seeing it, or of persons without seeing them. It is
impossible to over-state the vividness of these images, and yet
I was so intent, all the time, upon him himself . . . that I knew of
the slightest action of his fingers.[2]

For Pip, as (I am suggesting) for the Prince in Tennyson's poem,
the psychologically presented fugue state involves, not an author's
overidentification with his character, but a character's momentary
inability to extricate himself from his author. Pip's sudden,
uncharacteristic power of imagination and psychic investiture – as in
his later delirium in which 'I was a brick in the house wall, and yet
entreating to be released from the giddy place where the builders had
set me; . . . I was a steel beam of a vast engine, clashing and whirling
over a gulf, and yet . . . I implored in my own person to have the
engine stopped, and my part in it hammered off' (ch. 57) – is
disturbing *to him*, and resembles nothing so much as Dickens's own
most characteristic powers, as a personality, as a hypnotist, and of
course as a novelist. This abrupt, short-lived, deeply disruptive fusion
of authorial consciousness with a character's consciousness occurs
in both works under three combined pressures. These are: first, a
difficult *generic* schema of male identifications, narrators, personae;
second, a stressed *thematic* foregrounding of the male homosocial
bond; third, undecidable confusions between singular and plural
identity.

We have discussed all three of these elements in *The Princess* and
how they are tied up in the passage 'from mouth to mouth' of the
'Seven-headed monster', which links the generic and the thematic
problems of the poem. In *Great Expectations* the elements are on the
whole kept more separate; only the lime-kiln scene brings them
together so combustibly. Throughout the novel, of course, the
delicately calibrated and varying distance between old Pip and young
Pip has been generically constitutive, but in a way that left the
exuberant voice of 'Dickens', or perhaps of Dickens himself, unusually
occluded. Thematically, this scene is one of several very powerful
ones in this paranoid novel to bring men together under a wildly
exacerbated homosocial bond of rivalry. 'How dared you,' asks
Orlick, 'come between me and a young woman I liked?' Of course,
the degree to which Pip is psychically implicated throughout the

novel in Orlick's violence against women – signally, Mrs Joe – has attracted a great deal of critical attention already. But what we have seen most of is Orlick skulking after *Pip*, Pip hounding *Orlick*.

The confusion of one man and many men, and the problem of the author's status in that confusion – so central in *The Princess* – are oddly displaced and doubled in this scene from *Great Expectations*. On the one hand, the problem is Pip's, when his consciousness suddenly multiplies as Orlick's bottle empties. On the other hand, it is attached to Orlick himself, or his new associates. He brags:

> 'I've took up with new companions, and new masters. Some of 'em writes my letters when I wants 'em wrote – do you mind? – writes my letters, wolf! They writes fifty hands; they're not like sneaking you, as writes but one.'

Orlick especially relishes this last phrase ('them as writes fifty hands,' he repeats, 'that's not like sneaking you as writes but one'). It is not the first thing in the novel that has thematically linked Orlick with the other wicked male characters, such as Compeyson and Drummle: all three are characterized as lurking, skulking, following in the rear of other men, 'coming up behind of a night in that slow amphibious way' (ch. 26).[3] All three also commit violence on women, in complicity with other men.[4] In fact, in piecing together the plot of the novel, it is hard to keep this group of violent, heterosexually possessive men distinct from one another. It is startling, however, to have this many-headed monster of male exchange and violence suddenly lending a wild expressiveness to the previously mute and brutish Orlick. And it is more startling that he expresses his boast in terms (rather like 'doing the police in different voices') that suddenly vault *him* to a place in the novelist-surrogate sweepstakes alongside Pip. The cataclysmic pressure of male homosocial complicity is uncannily supra-individual. At its most stressed moments, it can bridge class at the same time as generic/ontological difference – it can melt into one the forge and the forger, or the man who works with his hands and the man who writes fifty of them.

I have mentioned that the collectiveness of male entitlement is not incompatible with, but in fact inextricable from, its hierarchical structure. This fact, to, has formal as well as political importance in *The Princess*. Even though, among the seven young men, young Walter Vivian is surely the one who is closest to the Prince in power and privilege, it is instead the nameless narrator of the frame narrative – the visiting friend, a young poet – who takes responsibility for having put the Prince's narrative into its final form. Thus some of the political shape of this poem might be attributed to its being an argument on behalf of an aristocratic ideology, aimed at an aristocratic as well as a bourgeois audience, but embodied through a speaker whose relation to patronage is not that of the patron but of the patronized. In addition, the confusion – or division – of genre in *The Princess* has an even more direct and explicit link to the division of gender; for the narrative, feminist content and all, is attributed entirely to the young men, while the ravishing lyrics that intersperse the narrative, often at an odd or even subversive angle to what is manifestly supposed to be going on, are supposed to be entirely the work of women in the group:

> the women sang
> Between the rougher voices of the men,
> Like linnets in the pauses of the wind.
>
> (Prologue, 236–8)

Certainly it is among the ironies of this passionate and confused myth of the sexes, that it has come to be valued and anthologized almost exclusively on the basis of its lyrics, its self-proclaimed 'women's work'. Perhaps in the eyes of those who actually enjoyed hegemonic privilege, a mere poet could in that age *not* be trusted with the job of articulating a justification for them, however ready he felt himself for the task. Perhaps in their view, if not in Tennyson's, poets' work and women's work fell in the same ornamental, angelic, and negligible class.

Tennysons's project, his poet-narrator's project, and the Prince's project, then, are all like Wycherley's and Horner's projects: through an apparent self-renunciation to embody, to hold together, the contradictions of male homosocial and heterosexual desire within a given society, in order to parlay a sublimated *knowledge* into a measure of social *control*. *The Country Wife* is, from the viewpoint of cognitive as well as formal control, an almost perfect play; *The Princess* is, from the viewpoint of any form of control, a disastrous poem. No text does or can wield over the modern, homophobically cloven terrain of male homosocial desire, the extraordinarily concentrated cognitive command of Wycherley's earlier fiction. If nowhere else – if not in thematics, if not in subject matter – then the electrified barrier of homophobia will do its crazing work or genre itself, on the bond between the man who writes the book and the man who officiates in it. 'The lyric leak',[5] Henry James' phrase for the spreading, corruptive stain on novels of authorial desire indulged or denied, is itself an aspect of modern homosexual panic.

Notes

1. ALFRED LORD TENNYSON, *The Princess: A Medley*, in *The poems of Tennyson*, ed. C. RICKS (London: Longman, 1969), p. 749, Prologue 193–4. Further citations will be incorporated in the text and designated by section and line numbers.
2. CHARLES DICKENS, *Great Expectations* ed. ANGUS CALDER (London: Penguin, 1965), pp. 437–8, Ch, 53. Further citations will be incorporated in the text and designated by chapter number.
3. Orlick: Chs 15, 17, 35, 43, 53; Compeyson: Chs 3, 5, 40, 44, 47, 54; Drummle: Chs 25, 26, 38, 43.
4. Orlick: Ch. 15; Compeyson: Chs 22, 42; Drummle: Ch. 59. Drummle's violence against Estella is not originally complicitous with Pip, but does in fact form the ground of her final submission to Pip, and thus augments the collective total of male power: she says 'suffering has been stronger than all other teaching, and has taught me to understand what your heart used to be. I have been bent and broken, but – I hope – into a better shape' (Ch. 59).
5. HENRY JAMES, *Letters to A. C. Benson and August Monod*, ed. E. F. BENSON (London: Elkins, Mathews & Marrott, 1930), p. 40.

11 *In Memoriam* and the Extinction of the Homosexual*

JEFF NUNOKAWA

Jeff Nunokawa's 1991 essay confronts the most vexed issue of Tennyson scholarship: Tennyson's sexuality as it is expressed and constructed in the most tricky of all Tennyson's poems, *In Memoriam*. Nunokawa begins with a critique of Christopher Craft's important 1988 gay reading and proposes that *In Memoriam* presents a *developmental* model of male sexuality whereby homoeroticism is presented as a phase to be grown out of in the individual psychosexual and evolutionary movement towards heterosexual patriarchy. Tennyson alludes to Shakespearean desire in the poem (understood by the Victorians as an allusion to Hellenism) but by using Victorian models of homoeroticism (as a stage on a path towards heterosexuality) converts Shakespeare's claim for the deathlessness of his desire into an announcement of its mortality. Thus the homoerotic disappears within the trajectory of male desire. Nunokawa finishes his essay with a brilliant identification of *contemporary cultural rewriting* of Tennyson's model of the cancelled or extinguished homosexual in the figure of the 'live-fast-die-young gay boys such as Dorian Grey, Montgomery Clift, James Dean, Joe Orton'. For Nunokawa, Tennyson's poem helps explain why the dominant media inaccurately identifies AIDS with, even *as*, the early death of gay men.

> So what do I know about being mature. The only thing mature means to me is *Victor* Mature . . .
>
> Mart Crowley, *The Boys in the Band*

'Descend, and touch, and enter; hear/The wish too strong for words to name' (*In Memoriam*, XCIII, 13–14).[1] It is difficult for a contemporary audience to read these lines, in which Tennyson prays for Hallam's embrace, without thinking that the wish too strong for words to name is the love that dare not speak its name. Tennyson's

---

*Reprinted from *English Literary History* **58** (1991), pp. 427–38.

critics have often resisted such interpretations by reminding us that expressions of devotion must be situated historically. Gordon Haight, for example, argues that 'the Victorians' conception of love between those of the same sex cannot be understood fairly by an age steeped in Freud. Where they saw only pure friendship, the modern reader assumes perversion . . . Even *In Memoriam*, for some, now has a troubling overtone.[2] As Haight's comment suggests, there is often more homophobia than history in the traditional appeal to the differences between Victorian and contemporary discourses of desire. Christopher Ricks, no sympathizer with Hellenistic readings of *In Memoriam*, dismisses the claim that such readings are necessarily anachronistic: 'As so often, the position of the historical purist is itself unhistorical . . . Some Victorians, who found Shakespeare's *Sonnets* troubling, found *In Memoriam* troubling.'[3] *The Times*, for example, condemned *In Memoriam* for its 'tone of amatory tenderness'.[4] Tennyson's own trouble with this tone may be registered in his famous protest that while Hallam lived, he never called him 'dearest'.[5]

But the historical particularity of Tennyson's passion in the troubling passages of *In Memoriam* can be taken up to define, rather than deny, its homosexual character: what construction of the homosexual is registered and reproduced in the parts of *In Memoriam* which Victorians themselves could designate as such?[6] I want to begin with the suppressed phrase which has elicited so much attention from critics interested in denying or affirming the homosexual character of Tennyson's poem. The invitation to matrimony that Tennyson excised from the manuscript version of section XCIII ('Stoop soul and touch me: wed me') has been taken by various readers, including, perhaps, Tennyson himself, as a figure of homosexual desire. But it is the revision rather than the original, or better, the revision's relation to the original which we may more accurately designate as homoerotic: the site of homoerotic desire is constituted as the negation of the heterosexual figure of marriage. To apprehend the homoerotic in *In Memoriam* as that which is defined *against* heterosexuality is to gain a sense of it as part of the nineteenth-century formation of sexual abnormality that Michel Foucault points to, a formation which is constituted by, and in turn constitutes its opposite: sexual normality.[7]

And if, according to a logic that Foucault has made familiar to us, the homosexual in *In Memoriam* is formed by its relation to the heterosexual, the heterosexual is formed by its relation to the homosexual. More specifically, *In Memoriam* proposes a developmental model of male sexuality which establishes the homoerotic as an early phase that enables and defines the heterosexual. 'The wish too strong for words to name' is not a desire for matrimony, but rather a primary stage in the formation of the husband and the father:

> How many a father have I seen,
> A sober man, among his boys,
> Whose youth was full of foolish noise,
> Who wears his manhood hale and green:
>
> And dare we to this fancy give,
> That had the wild oat not been sown,
> That soil, left barren, scarce had grown
> The grain by which a man may live?

(LIII, 1–8)

The 'wild oats' and 'foolish noise' which make up the patriarch's prehistory may be aligned with the boyhood love that Tennyson sets against the marital contract in section LIX of *In Memoriam*. This boyhood love is another version of early passion which makes way for, and a way for, heterosexuality:

> O Sorrow, wilt thou live with me
> No casual mistress, but a wife
>
> . . .
> My centered passion cannot move,
> Nor will it lessen from to-day
> But I'll have leave at times to play
> As with the creature of my love.

(LIX, 1–2, 9–12)

Tennyson's post-Marlovian proposal of marriage is preceded and occasioned by the loss of his earlier pastoral play: his bride is a metonym for the loss of Hallam, and his heterosexual situation is thus defined as the ghost of prior passion; marriage is an elegy for earlier desire.[8]

I will seek shortly to demonstrate more specifically how *In Memoriam* identifies these early regions of passion as homoerotic, but before I do this, I want to recall the historical situation of Tennyson's ordering of male desire. The conception of the homoerotic as an early term in the tutelary itinerary of the bourgeois British male, an itinerary which ultimately installs him in the position of husband and father, is a staple of Victorian and post-Victorian ideology. Certainly the definitive site of this erotic apprenticeship is the English public school where, in the words of

one Etonian, 'It's all right for fellows to mess one another a bit . . .
But when we grow up we put aside childish things, don't we?'[9]

In *Between Men: English Literature and Male Homosocial Desire*, Eve
Kosofsky Sedgwick examines the ideological efficacy for the
Victorian bourgeoisie of this evolutionary model of male desire.
Sedgwick suggests that the social distinctions within the class of
Victorian gentlemen were figured as different developmental stages
within an individual psychic career in order to promote 'the illusion
of equality . . . within the class'.[10] We may begin to sense that
importance of such a softening of social distinctions for Tennyson
in his relation to Arthur Hallam when we recall the difference between
Tennyson's rather vexed and confused class and financial
circumstances, and Hallam's far more secure possession of wealth
and aristocratic position. The difference in their social circumstances,
while perhaps not dramatic to our eyes, was sufficiently significant
that, in the words of Robert Bernard Martin, 'it is surprising that
the most celebrated friendship of the century should ever have begun
at all'.[11]

Sedgwick argues that the Victorian narrative of individual
psychosexual development served as the form in which economic and
social distinctions within the bourgeoisie were made to appear. In
Tennyson's poems, the figure of evolutionary scale not only
promotes a conception of potential equality between terms situated
at different stages of development, but also replaces a model of
social organization where there is no such potential equality between
vertically distinct terms. In other words, in *In Memoriam*, we can
witness the decision to rewrite what the poem first designates as
unchanging social differences as different moments in a narrative of
development, a narrative which includes, as one of its passages, the
exodus of the male subject out of the blighted pastoral regions of
the homoerotic.

Throughout *In Memoriam*, Tennyson pictures the difference between
himself and his dead friend as an insuperable vertical distance:

> Deep folly! yet that this could be –
> That I could wing my will with might
> To leap the grades of life and light,
> And flash at once, my friend, to thee.

> (XLI, 9–12)

In section LX, Tennyson describes this difference in height as a
difference of class; the terms that he employs here to measure the
distance between himself and Hallam describe his sense of loss as a
sense of socioeconomic inferiority:

He past; a soul of nobler tone:
My spirit loved and loves him yet,
Like some poor girl whose heart is set
On one whose rank exceeds her own.

He mixing with his proper sphere,
She finds the baseness of her lot,
Half jealous of she knows not what,
And envying all that meet him there.

The little village looks forlorn;
She sighs amid her narrow days,
Moving about the household ways,
In that dark house where she was born.

The foolish neighbours come and go,
And tease her till the day draws by:
At night she weeps, 'How vain am I!
How should he love a thing so low?'

(LX, 1–16)

In the four sections of *In Memoriam* that follow, Tennyson enlists
various models of organic progression which recast and qualify the
class difference figured here. The distinction between Tennyson and
Hallam becomes, in section LXI, the difference between a
'dwarf'd . . . growth' (7) and the 'perfect flower of human time' (4).
For Tennyson to define himself as a dwarfed growth is, implicitly,
to attribute to himself the unrealized potential for *full* growth. While
the 'soul of nobler tone' is simply inaccessible to what is below and
behind him, the 'perfect flower of human time' figures a completion
of development which the stunted plant could have attained. In
section LXIII, Tennyson collates the distinction between himself and
Hallam with differences between lower and higher species of
animals, and if this seems to substantiate rather than diminish their
separation, we need to remember Tennyson's endorsement of both
phylogenic and ontogenetic versions of evolution. In section CXVIII,
for example, the forlorn desire to 'leap the grades of life' is rewritten
as a prescription for a personal practice of evolutionary process:
'Move upward, working out the beast,/And let the ape and tiger
die' (27–8). And if the figure of lesser development can rise to a
higher stage, according to the evolutionary models that Tennyson
sets forth in sections LXI–LXV, the higher rises by means of the lower.
The inferior term of the developmental hierarchy is cast as the seed
that moves the superior term to 'noble ends' (LXV, 12).

Tennyson thus relieves class differences by replacing the simple social barrier between the 'poor girl' and the 'soul of nobler tone' with a permeable boundary: the 'dwarf'd growth' and the 'perfect flower of human time' are related as figures situated at different stages of the same evolutionary narrative. I want to suggest that the scenario of social ascent that Tennyson sets forth in section LXIV, in which Hallam is pictured not as a noble, but instead as a case study of upward mobility, registers the ideological force of these developmental models. The description of Hallam as 'some divinely gifted man,/Whose life in low estate began . . . who breaks his birth's invidious bar' (1–2, 5) is enacted by means of an implicit analogy to the scenarios of natural evolution that surround it.

Identified with these evolutionary models, the scale from homosexual to heterosexual is defined as another version of the development range that displaces the class differences of section LX. Here is Tennyson addressing Hallam in section LXI:

> If thou cast thine eyes below,
> How dimly character'd and slight,
> How dwarf'd a growth of cold and night,
> How blanch'd with darkness must I grow!
>
> Ye turn thee to the doubtful shore,
> Where thy first form was made a man;
> I loved thee, Spirit, and love, nor can
> The soul of Shakespeare love thee more.
>
> (LXI, 5–12)

When the stunted, shadowed growth locates his devotion to Hallam with Shakespearean love, he identifies his desire with a standard Victorian figure for the male homoerotic. It was the homoerotic reputation of the Sonnets which made some of Tennyson's contemporaries uneasy about his fondness for them. Benjamin Jowett, for example, was relieved by what he regarded as Tennyson's retreat from his devotion to the Sonnets. To do otherwise, Jowett, opined, 'would not have been manly or natural . . . The love of the sonnets which he [Tennyson] so strikingly expressed was a sort of sympathy with Hellenism.'[12] Certainly it was the taint of Hellenism attached to the Sonnets which prompted Henry Hallam to 'wish that Shakespeare had never written them'.[13]

Tennyson begins section LXII by again affiliating his lower species of love for Hallam with Shakespearean devotion:

> Tho' if an eye that's downward cast
> Could make thee somewhat blench or fail,
> Then be my love an idle tale,
> And fading legend of the past.

(LXII, 1–4)

These lines allude to the conclusion of Sonnet 116: 'If this be error and upon me proved,/I never writ, nor no man ever loved' (13–14).[14] We need now to notice what Tennyson does with Sonnet 116, and why he does it. If *In Memoriam* takes up the Victorian conception of the Sonnets as an exemplary figuration of male homoerotic passion, it revises the terms of Shakespearean desire to fit with the modern formation of the homosexual which gained hegemony in the nineteenth century. While Shakespeare's devotion is 'the marriage of true minds' in Sonnet 116, it is defined as that which is *not* marriage in *In Memoriam*. In keeping with the construction of the homoerotic as an early point on the developmental agenda of male desire, a stage which *precedes* and is terminated by matrimony, Tennyson's poem draws marriage away from the form of devotion that Victorians attributed to the Sonnets and situates it at a height where that form has been transcended. Tennyson goes on in section LXII to compare his Shakespearean passion for Hallam with Hallam's own ascent to the higher species of heterosexuality:

> And thou, as one that once declined,
> When he was little more than boy,
> On some unworthy heart with joy,
> But lives to wed an equal mind.

(LXII, 5–8)

Shakespeare measures the permanence of his love in 116:

> Love's not Times fool, though rosy lips and cheeks
> Within his bending sickle's compass come;
> Love alters not with his brief hours and weeks,
> But bears it out even to the edge of doom.

(9–12)

But Tennyson, again subjecting the sonnet to the Victorian conception of the homoerotic as an early stage of male erotic development, declares the impermanence of the devotion that it expresses, casting it as a kind of schoolboy passion which 'wholly dies' (10), or becomes 'matter for a flying smile' (12) when boys put away childish things to become husbands and fathers.

Thus, Tennyson's claim that his passion for Hallam rivals Shakespeare's, works less to aggrandize his own passion than to diminish Shakespeare's. The constitution of the homoerotic in *In Memoriam* is most fully registered in its revision of Sonnet 116, a revision which converts Shakespeare's claim for the deathlessness of his desire into an announcement of its mortality.

I want now to examine a subtler announcement of the failure of Shakespearean devotion in *In Memoriam*. Tennyson alludes in section LXII to Shakespeare's designation of the permanence of his passion as the grounds upon which his writing rests: 'If this be error and upon me proved/I never writ, nor no man ever loved'. While Tennyson's echo of those lines slightly alters Shakespeare's contract ('if an eye that's downward cast/Could make thee somewhat blench or fail,/Then be my love an idle tale,/And fading legend of the past'), I nevertheless want to suggest that the connection that Shakespeare sets forth between the existence of his text and the permanence of his passion remains in place in Tennyson's poem, only now in a negative form. When he recasts the passion of the sonnet as temporary rather than permanent, Tennyson cancels the condition upon which Shakespeare's text depends. And the proof of Shakespeare's error is registered by the figure of Shakespearean devotion in section LXI that I referred to earlier, the figure who is 'dimly character'd and slight'. This fading legend of Shakespearean love is the negative realization of Shakespeare's covenant in Sonnet 116: here, the text disappears since the love that it represents is ephemeral, rather than eternal. The Shakespearean text is dimmed and slighted according to the terms of its own contract and according to the Victorian conception of its content.

The negative version of the Shakespearean contract which inhabits Tennyson's text suggests that 'the wish too strong for words to name', another instance of desire contradistinguished from marriage, might as well be called the wish too *weak* for words to name. In 'the wish too strong for words to name', the consequence of Tennyson's cancellation of Shakespeare's claim for the durability of his love is fully realized. The marriage of true minds is described now as the ephemeral predecessor of marriage, a transitional, transitory, and thus wordless 'wish'. Shakespeare's contract enables us to identify the place in *In Memoriam* where the homoerotic is extinguished, the place where Tennyson's love for Hallam is matured and his Shakespearean devotion expunged. Tennyson's fear that Hallam's death left him a dwarfed growth, permanently arrested at the stage of schoolboy love, is allayed in section LXXXI of the poem, where Death declares that through its intervention, Tennyson's devotion to Hallam was fully ripened:

Could I have said while he was here,
'My love shall now no further range;
There cannot come a mellower change,
For now is love mature in ear.'

Love then had hope of richer store:
What end is here to my complaint?
This haunting whisper makes me faint,
'More years had made me love thee more.'

But Death returns an answer sweet:
'My sudden frost was sudden gain,
And gave all ripeness to the grain,
It might have drawn from after-heat.'

(LXXXI, 1–12)

We may locate the repository of the ripened grain of Tennyson's
matured love when we gather together an allusion that is dispersed
in sections LXXXI and LXXXII, an allusion to Keats's 'When I Have
Fears':

When I have fears that I may cease to be
Before my pen has gleaned my teeming brain,
Before high-piled books, in charactery,
Hold like rich garners the full ripened grain.

$(1–4)^{15}$

Tennyson takes up not only the occasion of Keats's poem (the prospect
of premature death), but also two of its figures – the grain in section
LXXXI, ('My sudden frost was sudden gain/And gave all ripeness to
the grain') and, in LXXXII, the garner that Keats pictures as the
container for that grain:

For this alone on Death I wreak
That wrath that garners in my heart;
He puts out lives so far apart
We cannot hear each other speak.

(LXXXII, 13–16)

By reconstituting the reference to Keats's text in these sections of *In
Memoriam*, we can discern the harvest of Tennyson's matured love
in the rancour of his heart, a rancour whose source is the impotence
of speech.

The dispelling of the homoerotic in these lines becomes visible when the resentment that Tennyson garners in his heart is placed next to the *words* that Keats garners, the 'high-piled books, in charactery', which 'hold like rich garners the full ripened grain'. Tennyson's wrath, which, I have suggested, may be identified with his ripened love, represents two linguistic failures; not only his inability to hear or be heard by Hallam, but also the absence of the words, the 'charactery', that Keats pictures as the ripened harvest that fills the garners. And according to the Shakespearean formula active in Tennyson's poem, a formula which equates the termination of what the Victorians constructed as homoerotic desire with verbal disappearance, this absence tells us that the maturation of Tennyson's love is the conclusion of its homoerotic phase. The ripening of love is built upon the disappearance of prior characters, the proof of Shakespeare's error. This verbal absence appears at the conclusion of a section of *In Memoriam* which includes a survey of the stages of evolutionary progress:

> Eternal process moving on,
> From state to state the spirit walks;
> And these are but the shatter'd stalks,
> Or ruined chrysalis of one.

(LXXXII, 5.8)

The 'wild oat' of section LIII, an early version of male desire whose passing is defined by verbal effacement, may be construed amongst the 'shatter'd stalks' and 'ruined chrysalis' as something else abandoned by that which is ripe. The absence of any reminder of this early desire may be the poem's most eloquent elegy for the homosexual; unlike the grain and the butterfly, matured male love leaves behind no mark, no souvenir of a kind of devotion whose failure can have no trace.[16]

But if the homoerotic disappears within the course of male desire as it is charted by Tennyson, this inexorable early loss is incessantly rewritten in subsequent constructions of the homosexual, rewritten and transliterated. If the homosexual is a stage, fated for extinction in the nineteenth-century conception of the homosexual that *In Memoriam* helps to construct, the doom attached to it is visited upon a population as the category of the homosexual passes from stage to subject in the years that follow Tennyson's elegy.[17] The funeral that Tennyson hosts for his own puerile homoerotic desire in *In Memoriam* has its afterlife in the glamorous rumour of pre-ordained doom that bathes the image of live-fast-die-young gay boys such as Dorian Grey, Montgomery Clift, James Dean, Joe Orton, and, most recently, a French-Canadian airline steward who came to be known as Patient

Zero, the spoiled child in whom the dominant media apprehended the embodiment of the lethal effects of a new virus. The youthful fatality of homosexual desire, the youthful fatality which *is* homosexual desire in Tennyson's poem, prepares the way for the story of the bathhouse boy's frolicsome progress to an inevitable early grave. 'Blanch'd with darkness' still, the figure 'dimly character'd and slight' helps explain why the dominant media inaccurately identifies AIDS with, even *as*, the early death of gay men. The 'dwarf'd' 'growth of cold and night' haunts such representations of the current crisis, the 'dwarf'd' 'growth of cold and night' that defines the homosexual as that which dies young.

Notes

1. *The Poems of Tennyson*, ed. CHRISTOPHER RICKS (London: Longman, 1969). All subsequent citations of *In Memoriam* refer to Ricks's edition.
2. GORDON HAIGHT, *George Eliot: A Biography* (New York: Oxford Univ. Press, 1968), 496.
3. CHRISTOPHER RICKS, *Tennyson* (New York: Macmillan, 1972), 219.
4. Quoted by RICKS, *Tennyson* (note 3), 219.
5. Quoted by VALERIE PITT, *Tennyson Laureate* (London: Barrie and Rockliff, 1962), 117. The point that I am rehearsing here, that the homoeroticism of *In Memoriam* has troubled even its first readers, is made most decisively by CHRISTOPHER CRAFT, in his investigation of the poem's homosexual rhetoric, ' "Descend, and Touch, and Enter": Tennyson's Strange Manner of Address', in *Genders*, 1 (1988), 85–6. See also Craft's analysis of the sometimes complex strategies deployed by generations of Tennyson's readers to evade or contain the homosexual elements of the elegy (86–7). Craft's reading of *In Memoriam*'s 'same gender eroticism' (87) touches my own. See note 8.
6. See, of course, MICHEL FOUCAULT, *The History of Sexuality: Volume 1. An Introduction*, trans. ROBERT HURLEY (New York: Pantheon, 1978) for an account of sexual categories as the product of historically specific discursive practices, rather than timeless essences.
7. See especially part 2 of *The History of Sexuality*, 'The Repressive Hypothesis'.
8. Here is the most significant point of convergence between my reading of *In Memoriam* and Christopher Craft's. Like Craft, I locate the homosexual in Tennyson's poem as a primal moment in a developmental narrative that terminates with a form of heterosexual desire that appears removed from the earlier stage that precedes and enables it. But my sense both of the character of this developmental narrative and of its calibrations – the categories homosexual and heterosexual – differ from Craft's. While Craft emphasizes the status of this narrative as 'a disciplinary trajectory' (95), more or less continuous with the project of sublimation that Havelock Ellis prescribed for same-gender desire, my reading takes up an evolutionary narrative in the poem, which casts the homosexual not as the target of proscription or aversion, but rather as something that a person, or population, naturally, necessarily,

outgrows. Craft's reading, like my own, is inflected by a Foucauldian recognition of the dialectical dependence which marks the relations between the heterosexual and homosexual. Craft reads this dependence as the condition of what he sees as the ambivalent persistence of the homosexual within the very structure of the heterosexual: 'The erotics of such a substitutive structure are irreducibly ambivalent: since the homo is lost or banished only to be rediscovered in and as the hetero (which is itself thus constituted as a memorial of a former undifferentiated sameness) all longing remains longing for the homo even as it submits the mediation of the hetero. Difference itself thus bespeaks a desire for sameness – speaks, like the poet, *in memoriam*' (97–8). My reading, on the other hand, seeks to describe a version of heterosexuality characterized by the radical abandonment of a prior homoeroticism which also supplies the condition of its existence. Craft's conviction that the 'homo' persists in the very structure that displaces it depends on his identification of the homosexual with the general category of sameness, and, correlatively, of the heterosexual with the general category of difference. (This identification is compactly performed in Craft's abbreviation of heterosexual and homosexual in the passage I have just quoted.) My reading of the heterosexual and homosexual in Tennyson's poem seeks to consider a different construction of these terms.

9. Michael Nelson, *Nobs and Snobs* (London: Gordon & Cremonski, 1976), 147, as cited by Eve Kosofsky Sedgwick, *Between Men: English Literature and Male Homosocial Desire* (New York: Columbia Univ. Press, 1985.) In *The Worm in the Bud: The World of Victorian Sexuality* (1969; reprint, Harmondsworth, Middlesex: Penguin Books, 1983), Ronald Pearsall discusses the remarkable extent and intensity of homoerotic activity in the English public schools in the nineteenth century, and the comparatively tolerant or indifferent attitude of school authorities towards even overtly sexual relations amongst students (551–60). (See also Louis Crompton, *Byron and Greek Love: Homophobia in Nineteenth-Century England* [Berkeley: Univ. of California Press, 1985]). While the figuration of male homoerotic activity as schoolboy love, a term in the growth of the patriarch, casts this version of such activity as a part of, rather than apart from heterosexual hegemony, this is, of course, not to suggest that all instances of sexual intercourse between males in Victorian England were tolerated by or instrumental to heterosexual authority. Pearsall quotes William Stead's observation during the Wilde trial about the discrepancy between the prevailing attitude toward fleshy versions of schoolboy love and the fierce prosecution of homosexual behaviour when it took place beyond the bounds of early development: 'Should everyone found guilty of Oscar Wilde's crime be imprisoned, there would be a very surprising emigration from Eton, Harrow, Rugby and Winchester to the jails of Pentonville and Holloway . . . boys are free to pick up tendencies and habits in public schools for which they may be sentenced to hard labour later on' (Pearsall, 555).

10. Sedgwick (note 9), 178. Sedgwick's book first alerted me to the activity during the Victorian period of the notion that homosexuality is 'just a phase'.

11. Robert Bernard Martin, *Tennyson: The Unquiet Heart* (New York: Oxford Univ. Press, 1980), 69.

12. Hallam Lord Tennyson, *Materials for a Life of Alfred Tennyson* (privately printed, no date). Quoted by Ricks (note 3), 215. For a detailed discussion

of the complicated career of 'Hellenism' as a signifier of male homosexuality, see CROMPTON (note 9), especially chapter 2.

13. HENRY HALLAM, *Introduction to the Literature of Europe* (1839), 3:501–4. Quoted by RICKS, *Tennyson*, 215.

14. *The Sonnets, Songs and Poems of Shakespeare*, ed. OSCAR JAMES CAMPBELL (New York: Schocken Books, 1964). All subsequent citations of Sonnet 116 refer to this edition.

15. *The Poems of John Keats*, ed. MIRIAM ALLOT (London: Longman, 1972).

16. The psychosexual itinerary that I have sought to identify in *In Memoriam* is, of course, an exclusively masculine model of improvement. It is in section LX of the poem, where the vertical distance between Hallam and Tennyson is figured as an impermeable boundary, that the difference between lower and higher is the difference between a woman and a man. The replacement of 'some poor girl' in section LX with the figure of Shakespearean desire in the sections that follow reflects a crucial dimension of the strategy that Tennyson enacts in *In Memoriam*; to convert a masculine itinerary of desire into a social programme for upward mobility is to confirm the position of women as a permanent underclass, excluded categorically from the potential for ascent. The embarrassed maiden of section LX serves to remind us of who must be left behind by Tennyson's stairway scenario.

17. On the construction of homosexuality as a subject position, see FOUCAULT (note 6), and JEFFREY WEEKS, *Coming Out: Homosexual Politics in Britain, from the Nineteenth Century to the Present* (London: Quarter Books, 1977). EVE KOSOFSKY SEDGWICK considers how the discourse of evolution that I have sought to isolate in Tennyson's construction of the homosexual informs contemporary homophobic accounts of AIDS. See '*Billy Budd*: After the Homosexual', in *Epistemology of the Closet* (Berkeley: Univ of California Press, 1990), 185–90.

Notes on the authors

JAMES ELI ADAMS is Associate Professor of English and Victorian Studies at Indiana University, and the co-editor of *Victorian Studies*. He is author of *Dandies and Desert Saints: Styles of Victorian Masculinity* (1995) and the editor, with Andrew Miller, of *Victorian Sexualities* (1996).

ISOBEL ARMSTRONG is Professor of English at Birkbeck College, University of London. She is the co-editor of the journal *Women: A Cultural Review* and author of *Major Victorian Poets: Reconsiderations* (1969), *Victorian Scrutinies: Reviews of Poetry, 1830–1870* (1972), *Language as Living Form in Nineteenth-Century Poetry* (1982) and *Victorian Poetry: Poetry, Poetics and Politics* (1993) amongst other works.

JOSEPH BRISTOW is Senior Lecturer in the Department of English and Related Literature at the University of York where he is also affiliated to the Centre for Women's Studies. Among his books are *Robert Browning: New Readings* (1991) and *Effeminate England: Homoerotic Writing after 1885* (1995). He has edited *The Victorian Poet: Poetics and Persona* (1987), *Sexual Sameness: Textual Difference in Lesbian and Gay Writing* (1992), *Activating Theory: Lesbian, Gay, Bisexual Politics* (1993) and *Victorian Women Poets: A New Casebook* (1995).

TERRY EAGLETON is Warton Professor of English at Oxford University. He is the author of *Myths of Power: A Marxist Study of the Brontës* (1975), *Marxism and Literary Criticism* (1976), *Criticism and Ideology: A Study in Marxist Literary Theory* (1976), *Literary Theory: An Introduction* (1983), *The Function of Criticism: From the Spectator to Post-Structuralism* (1984) and *Against the Grain* (1986). His most recent publications include *The Ideology of the Aesthetic* (1990) and *Ideology: An Introduction* (1991).

ELAINE JORDAN is Senior Lecturer in the School of Comparative Studies, University of Essex where she directs the MA in Literature: Women Writing. She is the author of *Alfred Lord Tennyson* (1988) and articles on Angela Carter, Toni Morrison and Christa Wolf.

GERHARD JOSEPH is Professor of English at Lehman College and the Graduate School of the City University of New York. He is the author of *Tennysonian Love: The Strange Diagonal* (1969) and *Tennyson and the Text: The Weaver's Shuttle* (1992) and is presently at work on *The Guilty Art of the Copy*, a study of legitimate and illigitimate 'copying' (copyright, plagiarism, etc) and the fictional transformations of such matters in nineteenth-century English and American literature.

JEFF NUNOKAWA teaches at the Department of English, Princeton University. He has recently published *The Afterlife of Property* (1994).

MATTHEW ROWLINSON is Assistant Professor of English Literature at Dartmouth College, New Hampshire. He is the author of *Tennyson's Fixations: Psychoanalysis and the Topics of the Early Poetry* (1994), and is currently writing a book on the allegorical function of money in literature and theory from Keats to Freud.

LINDA M. SHIRES, Associate Professor of English at Syracuse University, is the author of *British Poetry of the Second World War*, co-editor of *Telling Stories*, and editor of *Rewriting the Victorians: Theory, History and the Politics of Gender* (1992). She has published widely on Victorian fiction and poetry and is currently writing a book tentatively entitled 'Victorian Fame'. Her other essays on Tennyson are '*Maud*, Masculinity and Poetic Identity' and 'Re-reading Tennyson's Gender Politics'.

EVE KOSOFSKY SEDGWICK is Newman Ivey White Professor of English at Duke University and the author of *The Coherence of Gothic Conventions* (1980), *Between Men: English Literature and Male Homosocial Desire* (1985), *Epistemology of the Closet* (1992) and *Tendencies* (1993).

ALAN SINFIELD is Professor in the School of Cultural and Community Studies at the University of Sussex. He is the author of *The Dramatic Monologue* (1977), *Literature in Protestant England* (1983), Alfred Tennyson (1987), and most recently *Faultlines: Cultural Materialism and the Politics of Dissident Reading* (1992) and the editor, with Jonathan Dollimore, of *Political Shakespeare: New Essays in Cultural Materialism* (1985).

Further reading

The following choice of further reading is focused very deliberately on the last twenty years of Tennyson scholarship, two decades which have seen the field grow and change in many challenging ways. I have not attempted to divide the criticism into categories such as feminist, deconstructive, Marxist, socio-historical, psychoanalytical, and so on, because in almost every case the book or article draws on at least two such critical models, so that classification of this kind would be misleading. The titles of each item usually give some indication of the critical methodology used, where it does not I have added brief comments.

Background source materials: biographies, bibliographies, editions, letters, reviews

ARMSTRONG, ISOBEL (ed.), *Victorian Scrutinies: Reviews of Poetry, 1830–1870*, London: Athlone Press, 1972.

BEETZ, KIRK H., *Tennyson: A Bibliography, 1827–1982*, Metchuen, NJ: Scarecrow Press, 1984.

BRISTOW, JOSEPH (ed.), *The Victorian Poet: Poetics and Persona*, World and Word Series, London: Croom Helm, 1987 (an anthology of Victorian essays and reviews on poetry).

HAGEN, JUNE STEFFENSEN, *Tennyson and His Publishers*, London: Macmillan, 1979.

JUMP, JOHN (ed.), *Tennyson: The Critical Heritage*, London: Routledge and Kegan Paul, 1967 (reviews and essays on Tennyson's work from the Victorian period to the present day).

LEVI, PETER, *Tennyson*, London: Macmillan, 1993 (biography).

NICHOLSON, HAROLD, *Tennyson: Aspects of His Life, Character and Poetry*, London: Constable, 1923.

MARTIN, ROBERT BERNARD, *Tennyson: The Unquiet Heart*, Oxford: Oxford University Press, 1980 (biography).

ORMOND, LEONEE, *Alfred Tennyson: A Literary Life*, Macmillan Literary Lives Series, Basingstoke: Macmillan, 1993 (biography).

RICKS, CHRISTOPHER, *Tennyson*, Basingstoke: Macmillan, 1989 (biography).

SHAW, MARION, *An Annotated Critical Bibliography of Alfred, Lord Tennyson*, Harvester Annotated Bibliographies Series, Hemel Hempstead: Harvester Wheatsheaf, 1989.

Tennyson, Alfred Lord, *The Letters of Alfred Lord Tennyson*, eds Cecil Y. Lang and Edgar F. Shannon, 3 vols, Oxford: Clarendon Press, 1982–1990.

—— *The Poems of Tennyson* (incorporating the Trinity College Manuscripts), ed. Christopher Ricks, 3 vols, Harlow: Longman, 1987 (the definitive edition).

Tennyson, Charles and Dyson, Hope (eds), *Dear and Honoured Lady: The Correspondence of Queen Victoria and Alfred Tennyson*, London, 1969.

Tennyson, Hallam, *Alfred Lord Tennyson: A Memoir by His Son*, 2 vols, London: Macmillan, 1897.

Tennyson Research Bulletin, Lincoln: Tennyson Society, 1967–

General studies on Victorian poetry, poetics and aesthetics

Armstrong, Isobel, *Language as Living Form in Nineteenth-Century Poetry*, Brighton: Harvester Press, 1982.

—— (ed.), *Major Victorian Poets: Reconsiderations*, London: Routledge and Kegan Paul, 1969 (a collection of essays on the major Victorian poets).

—— *Victorian Poetry: Poetry, Poetics and Politics*, London and New York: Routledge, 1993 (important new re-reading of Victorian poetry).

Christ, Carol, *The Finer Optic: The Aesthetic of Particularity in Victorian Poetry*, New Haven: Yale University Press, 1975.

—— *Victorian and Modern Poetics*, Chicago and London: Chicago University Press, 1984 (argues for continuity between Victorian and modernist poetics).

Dellamora, R., *Masculine Desire: The Sexual Politics of Victorian Aestheticism*, Chapel Hill: University of North Carolina Press, 1990 (includes essays on Hopkins, Swinburne, Pater as well as Tennyson).

Langbaum, Robert, *The Poetry of Experience*, Harmondsworth: Penguin, 1974.

Books and articles on Tennyson and his writing

Adams, James Eli, 'Harlots and base interpreters: scandal and slander in *Idylls of the King*', *Victorian Poetry*, **30**, 3–4 (Autumn 1992), pp. 421–40.

Albright, D., *Tennyson: The Muses' Tug-of-War*, Charlottesville: University Press of Virginia, 1986.

Armstrong, Isobel, 'The Lady of Shalott: Victorian Mythography and the Politics of Narcissism', in J. B. Bullen (ed.), *The Sun is God: Painting, Literature and Mythology in the Nineteenth Century*, Oxford: Clarendon, 1989, pp. 49–107.

—— 'The Collapse of Subject and Object: *In Memoriam*', in Herbert F. Tucker (ed.), *Critical Essays on Alfred Lord Tennyson*, New York: G. K. Hall and Co., 1993, pp. 136–52.

Brooks, Cleanth, 'The Motivation of Tennyson's Weeper', in *The Well Wrought Urn*, New York: Reynal. 1947 (New Critical Reading).

Byatt, A. S., 'The Lyric Structure of Tennyson's *Maud*', in Isobel Armstrong (ed.), *Major Victorian Poets: Reconsiderations*, London: Routledge and Kegan Paul, 1969, pp. 69–92.

Further reading

CHRIST, CAROL, 'The Feminine Subject in Victorian Poetry', *English Literary History*, **54**, 2 (Summer 1987), pp. 385–401.

COLLINS, PHILIP (ed.), *Tennyson: Seven Essays*, London: Macmillan, 1992.

COLLEY, ANN, *Tennyson and Madness*, Athens, GA: University of Georgia Press, 1983.

—— 'The Quest for the "Nameless" in Tennyson's "The Lady of Shalott" ', *Victorian Poetry*, **23** (1985), pp. 369–78.

CRAFT, CHRISTOPHER, 'Descend and Touch and Enter: Tennyson's Strange Manner of Address', *Genders*, **1** (1988), pp. 83–101.

DALE, PETER ALLEN, ' "Gracious Lies": the Meaning of Metaphor in *In Memoriam*', *Victorian Poetry*, **18** (1980), pp. 147–67.

DAVENPORT, HESTER, 'A Gothic Ruin and a Grecian House: Tennyson's *The Princess* and Mid-Victorian Architecture Theory', *Victorian Studies*, **32**, 2 (Winter 1989), pp. 209–30.

GILBERT, E. L., 'The Female King: Tennyson's Arthurian Apocalypse', in Elaine Showalter (ed.), *Speaking of Gender*, New York and London: Routledge, 1989, pp. 163–186.

GRIFFITHS, ERIC, 'Tennyson's Breath', in Herbert F. Tucker (ed.), *Critical Essays on Alfred Lord Tennyson*, New York: G. K. Hall and Co., 1993, pp. 28–47.

HAIR, DONALD S., *Tennyson's Language*, Toronto: University of Toronto Press, 1991.

—— *Domestic and Heroic in Tennyson's Poetry*, Toronto: University of Toronto Press, 1981.

HALL, DONALD E., 'The Anti-Feminist Ideology of Tennyson's *The Princess*', *Modern Language Studies*, **21**, 4 (1991), pp. 49–62.

HARRIS, DANIEL A., 'Personification in "Tithonus" ', in Herbert F. Tucker (ed.), *Critical Essays on Alfred Lord Tennyson*, New York: G. K. Hall and Co., 1993, pp. 100–24.

HILLIS MILLER, J., 'Temporal Topographies: Tennyson's Tears', *Victorian Poetry*, **30**, 3–4 (Autumn 1992), pp. 277–89.

JOHNSON, ROB, 'Strategies of Containment: Tennyson's *In Memoriam*', in R. Machin and Christopher Norris (eds), *Post-Structuralist Readings of English Poetry*, Cambridge: Cambridge University Press, 1987, pp. 308–31.

JORDAN, ELAINE, *Alfred Tennyson*, Cambridge: Cambridge University Press, 1988.

JOSEPH, GERHARD, *Tennyson and the Text: The Weaver's Shuttle*, Cambridge: Cambridge University Press, 1992.

—— 'Tennyson's Sword: From "Mungo the American" to *Idylls of the King*', in Regina Barreca (ed.), *Sex and Death in Victorian Literature*, Basingstoke: Macmillan, 1990, pp. 60–8.

—— 'The Echo and the Mirror en abyme in Victorian Poetry', *Victorian Poetry*, **11** (1985), pp. 403–12.

KIERNAN, VICTOR, 'Tennyson, King Arthur and Imperialism', in Raphael Samuel and Gareth Stedman Jones (eds), *Culture, Ideology and Politics: Essays for Eric Hobsbawn*, London: Routledge and Kegan Paul, 1983, pp. 126–48.

KILLHAM, JOHN, *Tennyson's 'The Princess': Reflections of An Age*, London: Athlone Press, 1958 (makes important connections between Tennyson's poem and Victorian socio-political issues such as the education of women).

KINCAID, JAMES R. and McMULLEN, BUCK, 'Tennyson, Hallam's Corpse, Milton's Murder and Poetic Exhibitionism', *Nineteenth Century Literature*, **45** (September 1990), pp. 176–205.

KINCAID, JAMES, 'Forgetting to Remember: Tennyson's Happy Losses', *Victorian Poetry*, **30**, 3–4 (Autumn–Winter 1992), pp. 197–209.

KOZICKI, HENRY, *Tennyson and Clio: History in the Major Poems*, Baltimore and London: Johns Hopkins University Press, 1979.

KRAMER, LAWRENCE, 'Victorian Poetry/Oedipal Politics: *In Memoriam* and Other Instances', *Victorian Poetry*, **29** 4 (1991), pp. 351–63.

LINLEY, MARGARET, 'Sexuality and Nationality in Tennyson's *Idylls of the King*', *Victorian Poetry*, **30**, 3–4 (1992), pp. 365–86.

McGUIRE, IAN, 'Epistemology and Empire in *Idylls of the King*', *Victorian Poetry*, **30**, 3–4 (Autumn 1992), pp. 387–400.

MILLETT, KATE, *Sexual Politics*, London: Virago, 1977.

O'NEILL, PATRICIA, 'An Aesthetic of Reception and the Productive Reader of Victorian Poetry: Tennyson's "Lucretius" among Victorian and Contemporary Critics', *Victorian Poetry*, **29**, 4 (Winter 1991), pp. 385–400.

PELTASON, TIMOTHY, 'Supposed Confessions, Uttered Thoughts: The First-Person Singular in Tennyson's Poetry', *Victorian Newsletter*, **64** (1983), pp. 13–18.

—— 'Tennyson's Fables of Emergence', *Bucknell Review*, **29** (1985), pp. 143–70.

—— *Reading 'In Memoriam'*, Princeton, NJ: Princeton University Press, 1985.

PLASA, CARL, ' "Cracked From Side to Side": Sexual Politics in "The Lady of Shalott" ', *Victorian Poetry*, **30**, 3–4 (Autumn 1992), pp. 247–63.

ROWLINSON, MATTHEW, *Tennyson's Fixations: Psychoanalysis and the Topics of the Early Poetry*, Charlottesville: Virginia University Press, 1994.

—— 'The Skipping Muse: Repetition and Difference in Two Early Poems of Tennyson', in Herbert F. Tucker (ed.), *Critical Essays on Alfred Lord Tennyson*, New York: G. K. Hall and Co., 1993, pp. 68–82.

SAVILLE, JULIA, 'The Lady of Shalott: A Lacanian Romance', *Word and Image; A Journal of Verbal/Visual Enquiry*, **8**, 1 (Jan–March 1992), pp. 71–87.

SCHAD, JOHN, 'The Divine Comedy of Language: Tennyson's *In Memoriam*', *Victorian Poetry*, **31**, 2 (Summer 1993), pp. 171–83.

SHAW, MARION, *Alfred Lord Tennyson*, Feminist Rereadings Series, Hemel Hempstead: Harvester Wheatsheaf, 1988.

SHIRES, LINDA M., '*Maud*, Masculinity and Poetic Identity', *Criticism*, **29** (1987), pp. 269–90.

—— 'Patriarchy, Dead Men and Tennyson's *Idylls of the King*', *Victorian Poetry*, **30**, 3–4 (Autumn 1992), pp. 401–19.

—— 'Rereading Tennyson's Gender Politics', in Thais E. Morgan (ed.), *Victorian Sages and Cultural Discourse: Renegotiating Gender and Power*, New Brunswick: Rutgers University Press, 1990, pp. 49–62.

—— 'The Subject of Poetry: Tennyson as Woolf's Victorian Other', *Victorians Institute Journal*, **18** (1990), pp. 17–27.

SHERRY, JAMES J., 'Tennyson and the Paradox of the Sign', *Victorian Poetry*, **17** (1979), pp. 204–16.

SINFIELD, ALAN, *Alfred Tennyson*, Rereading Literature Series, Oxford: Basil Blackwell, 1986.

—— *Dramatic Monologue*, The Critical Idiom Series, London: Methuen, 1977.

—— *Faultlines: Cultural Materialism and the Politics of Dissident Reading*, Oxford: Clarendon Press, 1992 (outlines a cultural materialist agenda).

—— 'Tennyson's Strategies of Presence and the Idea of Literature', in Roland Hagenbuchle and Laura Skandera (eds), *Poetry and Epistemology*, Papers from the International Poetry Symposium, Ragensberg: Puslet, 1986, pp. 382–97.

Further reading

—— 'Tennyson's Use Of Language in *In Memoriam*', in Isobel Armstrong (ed.), *Major Victorian Poets: Reconsiderations*, London: Routledge and Kegan Paul, 1969, pp. 51–68.

—— *The Language of Tennyson's 'In Memoriam'*, Oxford: Blackwell, 1971.

STONE, MARJORIE, 'Genre Subversion and Gender Inversion', *Victorian Poetry*, 25, 2 (1987), pp. 101–27.

TUCKER, HERBERT F. (ed.), *Critical Essays on Alfred Lord Tennyson*, New York: G. K. Hall and Co., 1993 (excellent collection of contemporary critical essays).

—— *Tennyson and the Doom of Romanticism*, Cambridge, MA: Harvard University Press, 1988.

—— '*Maud* and the Doom of Culture', in Herbert F. Tucker (ed.), *Critical Essays on Alfred Lord Tennyson*, New York: G. K. Hall and Co., 1993, pp. 174–94.

WORDSWORTH, ANN, 'An Art that Will not Abandon the Self to Language: Bloom, Tennyson and the Blind World of the Wish', in Robert Young (ed.), *Untying the Text: A Post-Structuralist Reader*, London and Boston: Routledge and Kegan Paul, 1981, pp. 207–22.

216

Index